JOHN EVELYN
AND HIS TIMES

BY THE SAME AUTHOR

The Age of Candlelight
Portraits of Genius
Tchehov, the Man
Henry the Eighth

John Evelyn in 1641.

JOHN EVELYN
AND HIS TIMES

BEATRICE SAUNDERS

PERGAMON PRESS

OXFORD · NEW YORK · TORONTO
SYDNEY · BRAUNSCHWEIG

Pergamon Press Ltd., Headington Hill Hall, Oxford
Pergamon Press Inc., Maxwell House, Fairview Park, Elmsford,
New York 10523
Pergamon of Canada Ltd., 207 Queen's Quay West, Toronto 1
Pergamon Press (Aust.) Pty. Ltd., 19a Boundary Street,
Rushcutters Bay, N.S.W. 2011, Australia
Vieweg & Sohn GmbH, Burgplatz 1, Braunschweig

First edition 1970
Library of Congress Catalog Card No. 70–133398

Printed in Great Britain by A. Wheaton & Co., Exeter

08 007118 X

CONTENTS

INTRODUCTION

JOHN EVELYN, the diarist, has for many years been admired and quoted, but, in my opinion, this amiable, accomplished, and worthy patriot has never been given his due. Nor has he ever been drawn in his proper social setting. His diary is so modest, and such an example of understatement, that it does not fully reveal the remarkable drama of his times. He came to manhood when the struggle between King Charles I and his people was tearing the country apart. The civil war which followed produced the most violent and bitter hatreds, the most tragic devastation, and a complete revolution in government and society. The Commonwealth, with its fanatically austere Puritan regime, produced another dramatic upheaval. Then followed the licentious and corrupt Restoration, equally condemned by all who cared for England and the reputation of her people. The revolution against King James II's tyrannical Roman Catholic policy turned the country topsy turvy once again. And at last came a return to sanity and the comparatively calm reign of William and Mary, in which religious toleration at length became a reality.

Evelyn lived through all these violent storms and stresses, yet never lost his head. Loyalties were transferred, time and again, with heat and bloodshed, but he remained calm and sane through all. He was not indifferent, but he realized, with admirable self-possession, that sanity and cool judgement would be far more effective than fanatical hysteria and volcanic action.

It should be remembered that the world of John Evelyn was very different from our own; we have travelled far in 300 years. Religion, for instance, played an extremely important part in every man's life. Evelyn was a firm Protestant, and we cannot judge him or understand the bitter struggles of his day unless we realize how passionately men felt about

1

religion. The average man—Catholic or Protestant—would have died for his faith, which, indeed, promised him the only hope of salvation. It was the soul that mattered—not the body.

Men at this time were capable of the most pious tenderness and of the utmost cruelty. They could watch an execution with interest, and they could see the awful spectacle of a woman being burnt alive, and go on their way. Such sights were only too familiar. In Evelyn's time, too, the reverence felt for monarchy was almost a religion, and men shuddered at the idea of a traitor. The "divine right of kings" was by most men accepted without question, and it was widely believed that this divine right actually came from God himself. The majority of men knew so little of history that they did not realize that this idea of "divine right" was a deliberate policy imposed on a credulous people in order to support the monarchy. Nor did they realize how many English monarchs had achieved kingship by treachery, by right of conquest, and even by murder.

Evelyn was a scholar, an historian, an expert horticulturist and forester, a connoisseur of pictures, an authority on architecture, painting, engraving, and medals. His diary is a masterpiece in English literature, and his book on trees, *Sylva*, is a work of national importance which gave an enormous stimulus to afforestation in Britain. At the Restoration, considerable concern was felt for the stocks of standing timber, principally oak, suitable for shipbuilding. Many of the Royalists had been bound to fell their trees to pay fines, and the Government had done nothing towards conservation. The fleet had increased from a tonnage of just over 17,000 in the year 1603 to the impressive figure of 57,000 by 1660, and was increasing. Stocks of timber in the country were clearly inadequate to meet the expansion, and in 1662 the situation was put before the Royal Society by Sir Robert Moray. Evelyn wrote a paper on the subject, and from this sprang his book, *Sylva*, that magnificent forestry classic. This was primarily responsible for a concerted effort on the part of the Government and private owners to repair the deprivations that had been inflicted on English forests. Not long after the Napoleonic wars, the older D'Israeli wrote: "Inquire at the Admiralty how the fleets of Nelson have been constructed; they can tell you that it was with the oaks which the genius of Evelyn planted."

Evelyn's time was one of bigotry and narrow-mindedness, yet he was never intolerant towards those whose religious views differed from his own. But perhaps Samuel Pepys, a very shrewd judge of character, has summed up Evelyn fairly. When the two men had known each other for some years, Pepys said of Evelyn that he was "a most excellent humoured man, and very knowing". He referred to him on other occasions as "a worthy good man", "a very ingenious man", and "My good Mr. Evelyn". And, finally, Pepys wrote: "The more I know him, the more I love him." Horace Walpole's opinion is also worth quoting, and he declared that "Evelyn's intelligence and philosophy were inexhaustible".

Evelyn's diary was written, in a very small, close hand, over a period of fifty-six years, and it is not strictly a book of confessions; he rarely attempted to unburden his soul. Everything was set down with reserve, restraint, and an admirable serenity.

Evelyn was acquainted with kings and queens, ambassadors, noblemen, statesmen, bishops, and archbishops, and such men constantly sought his advice. Yet he remained to the end a modest and unassuming country-man. He had no thirst for power, no desire for fame or immortality, but merely a wish to communicate; hence the many books and pamphlets he produced. All are interesting and all faithfully reflect the outlook and manners of his day.

CHAPTER 1

THE SON OF THE SQUIRE

THE beautiful old moated manor-house at Wotton, Surrey, in which John Evelyn was born, was a typical example of the many fine ancestral homes that in the seventeenth century were the pride of rural England. It was situated on part of Leith Hill, and surrounded by widespreading forests and pasturelands. The extensive gardens, designed in the elegant Italian style, and "adorned with fountains and groves", were some of the most beautiful in England. John Evelyn's father, Richard Evelyn, J.P., was the local squire and High Sheriff of the County. He kept a retinue of 116 servants: "every one liveried in green satin doublets." But these picturesque followers were merely typical of the times; hospitality was regarded as a pleasure and a duty, and Richard Evelyn—rich, pious, cultured, and affable—kept open house all the year round.

The well-furnished manor-house was entirely self-supporting, and the squire was modestly proud of his excellent library, his picture gallery, and his handsome furniture and tapestries. In the great hall stood the armour, bright and ready for use, and a large drum stood by the massive front doors, to be used for warning in case of fire or robbery. The family coat-of-arms was displayed on bell towers, mantelpieces, and coaches, and—from old custom—the drawbridge over the moat was raised at sundown with the strictest military punctuality. It was the day of hunting and hawking; the stables, therefore, were filled with sleek, well-fed horses, the kennels with hawks, spaniels, and hounds; and in the vast cellars were the finest wines and barrels of good, home-brewed ale.

The Evelyn family fortunes had been founded on the manufacture of gunpowder, and Richard Evelyn owned considerable estates, but he was

4

no feudal lord, and had consistently declined all honours and titles. Every tenant on the estate knew and admired that strong, fresh-complexioned man with the short, brown beard—a typical English gentleman. "His vision", recorded his son, "was great, and his judgement most acute; of solid discourse, affable, humble and in nothing affected . . . severely discreet, yet liberal upon all just occasions. . . ." He was a firm Protestant, and regarded as extremely dangerous any man who threw doubts on the Protestant religion.

Eleanor Evelyn, his wife, was a delicate, pious woman, ten years younger than her husband, and at the age of twenty-three had already given birth to four children. Her son John was born on the 31st of October, 1620, and, according to custom, the church bells were rung and the poor were given alms.

It was a strange world on which this boy opened his eyes: strange in the tremendous contrasts which existed between riches and poverty, strange in its fiery religious fervour, and strange in its almost fanatical worship of class, wealth, and distinction.

Yet something of the morning of life still lingered in England. And, indeed, how charming was the rural scene. The sleepy hamlets bowered in trees, the sunny, flowery meadows, the flocks of grazing sheep, the beautiful woodland glades, the venerable village churches, the waving cornfields, the labourers in their coloured smocks and straw hats, the elderly peasant women in their black bonnets and scarlet cloaks, the ploughing oxen; all these were purely English. The whirr of the spinning-wheel could be heard in every cottage, and men and women working in the fields sang at their work; it was the universal custom.

Yet there were many dark sides to this seventeenth-century world, and the most fearful of these was an epidemic of the plague, the terrible disease which baffled all remedies. When young John Evelyn was five years old, plague arrived in the village; it had spread from London, where the victims were said to be dying at the rate of 5000 a week. Plague always produced panic and terror, so John and his brothers, George and Richard, were sent, for safety, to live with their maternal grandmother at Lewes in Sussex. Here they attended an excellent school, and as good schools were few and far between, the arrangement was an admirable one.

But their training, regarded by their parents and grandparents as a solemn duty, conformed to a rigid pattern, and strict obedience was expected. They were taught to address their parents as "Sir" and "Madam", and in their letters always to present their "humble duty". They were taught to pray regularly and earnestly for forgiveness, humility, and submission to God's will. Heaven and hell were very real, and hell meant, of course, the medieval version of eternal damnation. Indeed, a picture of the Last Judgement was painted over the chancel of every church. The dead could be seen rushing from their graves, while the good were being received into Paradise on the right hand of Christ, and the evil were being carried off by horrid demons to the lower regions, luridly portrayed with flames and torments. But heaven was the lovely city with "walls of jasper, gates of pearl, and streets of pure gold". There would be "Lord Jesus in the clouds" and seraphims and cherubims with trumpets. There would be holy virgins with their harps, and the Elders with their golden crowns.

At the age of eleven years, following the example of his careful, methodical father, young John Evelyn decided to keep a diary. But the boy called it "A Calendar of Events", and one of the earliest entries was: "23rd of August, 1628 . . . I was . . . wakened in the morning with the news of the Duke of Buckingham being slain." The Duke, the King's favourite, had been stabbed by a man named John Felton, and this was an event which had shaken the whole kingdom, as the Duke was regarded by the majority of people as the tyrant and betrayer of his country, and the cause of all their miseries. The news, in fact, had been received, except in royal circles, with immense relief; David had slain Goliath.

Young John Evelyn was far too young to grasp the implications, but he realized, from the conversation of his elders, that the King and his Parliament were seriously at loggerheads, and, if the storm broke, men prophesied that the whole nation would be engulfed in misery.

Misery, however, though of another kind, arrived all too soon for young John, as in December (1634) his dearly loved young sister died in giving birth to her first child. Such deaths at that time were extremely common owing to lack of medical knowledge. But the tragic consequences of his sister's death were quite unforeseen, as John's mother, inconsolable for the loss of her beloved daughter, sank into a state of melancholy, and by September of the following year had developed "a malignant fever". There was apparently no hope of her recovery, and finally she summoned all her servants to her room, and taking each one by the hand, she calmly said goodbye.

To her husband and children she gave rings for remembrance, and with many tears blessed them tenderly. She then resigned her soul to God: "Into Thy hands, O Lord, I commend my soul. Lord Jesus, receive my spirit. Amen." She died on the 29th of September, and according to the custom of the time she was buried at night; a long, mournful procession carrying torches followed her to the grave, and she was interred beside her beloved daughter and the dead child.

Eleanor Evelyn was only thirty years of age, but she had always been delicate "and of a constitution inclined to a religious melancholy, or pious sadness". No one doubted that she had died of a broken heart, and young John himself believed—as he admitted later—that she had realized her danger, but too late. She had left behind three young sons and a daughter.

Meanwhile, the plague was still prevalent in Surrey, so John and his brothers were sent back to their grandmother. John had been entered for Eton, but he confessed to his father that he dreaded the severe discipline there, so was allowed to remain at his school at Lewes. In May 1637, being seventeen years of age, he went as a Gentlemen Commoner to Balliol College, Oxford. He was as yet immature—as he confessed later —owing to the influence of his "too indulgent grandmother".

The city of Oxford itself, with its ancient walls, towers, and battlements, still wore the very air of medievalism, and the magnificent libraries, as books were scarce, were utterly fascinating to a youth thirsting for knowledge.

And now, as serious students, Evelyn and his brother were given strict advice from their father and grandmother. They were urged to rise early, "fail not" in their prayers, and "keep close" to their studies. They were advised to be frugal and moderate in diet, to entertain "with a cheerful courtesy" and to keep the company of "grave learned men who are of good reputation". They were solemnly warned that "sloth and carelessness are equivalent to all other vices".

Most undergraduates brought their own beds, and were apparently expected to find their own fuel for fires. From parents and guardians came haunches of venison, to be made into pies. Poultry, too, was always acceptable. Fast days were rigorously kept.

Evelyn was by nature shy, sensitive, and reserved, and he chose his friends from amongst the scholarly rather than the aristocratic students.

The chief studies at Oxford were Latin, Greek, and theology, but geometry, natural and moral philosophy and metaphysics were taught; there was a strong belief in astrology and divination. Little encouragement, however, was given to speculative thought, either scientific, philosophical, or theological, for although theological discussions were popular, these were discussions on dogma rather than attempts to reconcile the facts of life and natural science with the Bible. Yet a young man who could hold his own in theological discussions was regarded as a man with a future. Medicine was also studied, though not scientifically, as an art which could "bring to a man much credit from the cures he will be able to effect".

That life for the undergraduates was spartan there can be no doubt, as the chapel bell rang at 5 a.m., followed by matins and a short homily by one of the fellows. Then, after an early breakfast, study started in earnest. There were strict regulations, and students were forbidden to attend public performances of plays or to haunt taverns or shops where tobacco was sold, the penalty for these offences being a public flogging. They were not allowed to play football in the streets, to keep large birds (hawks?), to read "irreligious" books, or to play cards or dice except during the twelve days of Christmas.

But many problems of health beset these young scholars, as the majority suffered from agues, fever, and rheumatism; the conditions of college life were unhealthy; the small, medieval rooms being dark and airless.

There was, of course, a small minority of students who "brought the Colleges into much slander", young men who would "ruffle and roist it out, exceeding in apparel and haunting riotous company . . . which grieveth many not a little". It was chiefly such youths who caused the "town and gown" riots which, when swords were drawn, sometimes led to "bloody mishaps". But as there were no organized games or athletics, there was little outlet for the natural high spirits of young men. Evelyn and his brother George (at Trinity College) did not "ruffle and roist it out, exceeding in apparel", but George certainly bought a white satin doublet and scarlet hose, a splendid outfit which he admitted could rarely be worn at Oxford. "But", he explained to his father, "it will be comely for me to wear in the country."

8

From infancy, the brothers had been affectionately intimate. Both were good-looking, with dark, thoughtful eyes, like their mother, who had been a black-haired beauty; and both attended the dancing and vaulting schools and learnt the rudiments of music. The vacations were spent chiefly at Wotton and Lewes. But in the summer they usually travelled with friends on horseback through England. The curiosity to see their native land was insatiable, and they visited castles, cathedrals, monasteries, churches, country seats, gardens, and palaces. John was passionately interested in architecture.

This habit of touring the country had been popular since the Middle Ages, when most men and women regularly went on pilgrimage to holy shrines, and the custom had persisted. Yet, indeed, in fine weather, what could be more enjoyable? Few countries could boast of such beautiful scenery as England, "the land of fair residences, orchards, gardens, rich pasture, clothed in perpetual green and perennial flowers".* How pleasant it was to ride at night into some old walled town, complete with its ancient battlements, towers, and drawbridges. (The majority of towns were still completely walled in at this time.) And here, at some ancient hostelry, the party would find a warm welcome and good food.

The Evelyns had many friends amongst the country squires, so the party would be heartily welcomed. They would be shown the mansion and all the treasures—the library, the portrait gallery (complete with ancestors), the antique porcelain and ivories. They would walk through the extensive gardens and see the stables, fish-ponds, and orchards. The ladies of the party would then be presented with nosegays. This was the old custom. Wine, too, was usually handed round before leaving.

But on returning to Oxford, studies started again in earnest. Evelyn discovered, however, that the tutor assigned to him "had little time for scholars". But he formed "a valuable and lasting friendship" with a "young man of the Foundation", James Thicknesse, who later became a fellow.

But the burning question at the University, which became ever more controversial, was, how could the quarrel between the King and his people

---

* The son of Sir Thomas Browne declared that rural England could only be compared to "paradise".

be resolved. The political horizon was growing ever darker. Charles had inherited from his father a fanatical belief in the "divine right of kings", and was determined to maintain all the ancient privileges of the Crown. His was a curious character—priggish, melancholy, restless, unsympathetic, humourless, and reserved; he was intellectual but unintelligent. Hesitant and stammering, with his high-pitched voice and pronounced Scots accent, he was an unattractive man. Nobles and courtiers shrank instinctively from those mournful, reproachful eyes and that solemn, unfriendly countenance. No one could deny the perfection of his manners, nor the deep piety, the gentleness, the insensibility to flattery, the genuine sobriety. But he sadly lacked the common touch.

He now apparently believed that his popularity would carry every measure, but the spirit of liberty was abroad, and the leaders of the House of Commons were very different from those men who, a century or two before, had come up to the capital not to debate as legislators but to receive commands as inferiors. They were now men of education and determination, who had the courage to speak their minds. They had no intention of being governed by ancient maxims and precedents established in times of ignorance and slavery. Indeed, they insisted that no precedents could justify fraud, tyranny, and cruelty.

The King, in fact, had discovered that his Parliament was not to be brow-beaten, and he had therefore angrily dissolved it. Then in the year 1627, having recklessly entered into a war with France and Spain, he had illegally levied forced loans, and those who had refused to pay had been thrown into prison and their goods seized. These were acts of gross tyranny, and when in the year 1628 he had been obliged to summon a Parliament, men had wept openly and prophesied the ruin of their country.

Many obsolete laws had also been revived, and the King had exacted enormous fines or "rents" from the occupiers of land within the forest boundaries. The old law of knighthood had been revived, and £100,000 had been raised by fines from those who refused to accept knighthoods. Evelyn's father had refused, firmly and consistently. In order to enforce the King's decrees, the infamous Star Chamber and High Commission created by the Tudors had been remodelled, and these bodies had the power to fine, imprison, and mutilate without constraint.

Tyranny, however, was only one grievance. The greater peril, which seemed imminent, was the return of Popery, a terrifying prospect to all earnest Protestants. For was it possible to forget the reign of Bloody Mary and the dastardly Catholic plots against the lives of Queen Elizabeth and King James I? These were comparatively recent history, and if Popery returned, would not martyrs again burn at the stake? And were men to lose their souls because they had been forced to adopt the wrong faith? Was the hope of heaven, the only sustaining hope in a sinful world, to be snatched away?

The signs of returning Popery were obvious, as the King, after his marriage to the Catholic princess, Henrietta Maria, had ordered many changes in church ritual. He had also insisted on the use of popish copes, and had officially received a Papal Agent. Meanwhile, the clergy who had refused to observe all the new edicts had been deprived of their livings by the High Commission Court, all controversy on the points in dispute, either from the pulpit or the Press, being strictly forbidden.

But the latest and most serious step was that the King and his Minister, in order to enforce their decrees, had decided to create a standing army which would, they believed, break the refractory spirit of the nation. To support this, an iniquitous and illegal tax, "ship-money", had been imposed.

These were the grave matters discussed at the University, and the heated arguments amongst the students sometimes ended in fisticuffs. Was not the King's "divine right" unassailable? And were not those who refused to uphold this right traitors to their country? So argued the Royalists. But other students declared with passionate conviction that tyranny could never in any circumstances be justified. When once the rights and liberties of men were conceded they might never be regained, and the country could sink into slavery. These rights had been gained in the past by the sacrifice of precious blood. Men had gladly died for these rights, and they were the country's heritage, not lightly to be relinquished.

On the whole, however, Oxford leaned strongly to the Royalist side, as many of the colleges owed their existence to royal founders, a fact which seemed to demand an unquestioning allegiance.

The long vacations, in fact, were extremely welcome to John Evelyn and his brothers, and in the fascinating pursuit of travel it was possible to forget for a time the dark threat of war. John spent part of the summer vacation of 1638 with George and Richard in touring the country. They visited Portsmouth, "to survey the fortifications", and then sailed to the Isle of Wight, where they spent some very pleasant days with friends.

Meanwhile, men and women of all classes—lawyers, farmers, scholars, some of the best in England—were emigrating to America, as it was believed that the Law Courts were soon to be deprived of all authority, even in questions of civil right between man and man.* Emigration, however, was being prohibited, as eight ships lying in the Thames ready to sail had been detained by Order of Council.

Yet what now appeared to be the grossest folly was the King's determination to force on the Scots people a prayer-book modelled on the English book of Common Prayer, although the majority of the Scots were strict Calvinists. "The Popish ceremonies", indeed, had produced serious riots, as to the majority of people religion was far more important than mere earthly matters.

At the end of March 1639 the King decided to assert his authority in Scotland, and he and his army rode into York. But his own raw levies, gathered together in the royal cause, had little heart to fight, and met with fierce resistance. The campaign, mismanaged from the first, was a failure. An uneasy peace, however, was patched up and the army disbanded.

During this period of crisis, Evelyn had been ill with malaria, and did not recover for four months, after which he left Oxford. It had been decided that he and his brother should study law at the Middle Temple, and their father had purchased for them a "very handsome apartment". As they would both inherit country estates in due course, a knowledge of the law, as relating to land and property, was considered essential. Indeed, the majority of young men took this course of study.

But in London an ominous gloom prevailed, and to settle down to serious work was almost impossible. Matters between the King and his Parliament had come to a head, and the young lawyers and students at the Middle Temple now spoke openly of civil war. On the 11th of April,

* Between the years 1630 and 1643, 20,000 men, women, and children emigrated to New England, and 40,000 to Virginia and other colonies.

1640, in the Easter vacation, Evelyn saw the King ride through London in state, and thought it "a very glorious and magnificent sight". But on the 10th of June, the Archbishop of Canterbury's Palace at Lambeth was assaulted by the mob, and on the 30th of August the Royalist and Scots armies met again, with disastrous results. The Royalist soldiers, "without heart or discipline, were led like sheep to the slaughter", and the Scots took the towns of Newcastle, Durham, Shields, and Tynemouth.

In November the Long Parliament met, and Charles was obliged to agree to their terms—that not more than three years should elapse between Parliament and Parliament; that the Star Chamber, the High Commission, and the Council of York should be dissolved; and that men who had been confined in remote dungeons should be set at liberty. He promised never again to raise money without the consent of the two Houses or to unlawfully imprison any man, and never again to subject his people to the jurisdiction of courts martial. He promised to maintain the Protestant religion, "if need be to the hazard of my life and all that is dear to me".

Within three weeks, however, Charles had broken all his promises. He had appointed large numbers of Popish officers in the army, with the result that whole regiments were disaffected. Then, finally, some of the most distinguished Members of Parliament were thrown into prison merely for protesting. Sir John Eliot, indeed, died in the Tower.

What followed was almost a declaration of civil war, as the Lord Keeper, the Primate, and the Lord Lieutenant were impeached. The Lord Keeper saved himself by flight, the Primate (Archbishop Laud) was sent to the Tower, and Earl Strafford was imprisoned. They were accused of high treason by having endeavoured to subvert the laws and constitution of the country, and in this the Parliament acted as one man, so strong and general was the indignation excited by many years of lawless oppression.

Such was the state of the country when the year of 1640 drew to a close. Meanwhile, at Wotton there was much anxiety, as Evelyn's father had become seriously ill and the doctors were doubtful of his recovery. He was taken, therefore, to Bath to drink the waters, and John and his brother George rode down to visit him and stayed in Bath for two months. But unfortunately there was no improvement, and, finally, Richard Evelyn was brought home in his litter, accompanied by his sons. He was found to be suffering from dropsy, and on the 20th of December he died.

> He retained his senses and piety to the last, [recorded Evelyn] which he most tenderly expressed in blessing us, whom he now left to the world and the worst of times, whilst he was taken from the evil to come . . . and thus we were bereft of both our parents when we most of all stood in need of their counsel and assistance . . . especially myself, of a raw, vain, uncertain and very unwary inclination . . . who thought of nothing but the pursuit of vanity and the confused imaginations of young men. But so it pleased God to make trial of my conduct in a conjecture of the greatest and most prodigious hazard that ever the youth of England saw.

Richard Evelyn was buried by the side of his young wife; and George, the heir, who had been married a few months previously, came into his inheritance. But Wotton was still Evelyn's home, if he cared to make it so.

Meanwhile, events were moving rapidly in London, for the Earl of Strafford had attempted to escape from the Tower, and had offered the Lieutenant of the Tower £22,000 and a good marriage for his son if he would connive at his flight.* But this was refused, and menacing crowds surrounded the Houses of Parliament night and day, shouting for justice and calling for Strafford's death. Finally, on the 25th of January, 1641, he was tried for treason before the Lords and Commons and Their Majesties. Evelyn was present, and heard the Earl defend himself brilliantly. Nevertheless, he was sentenced to death, and the King signed the death warrant. Then, on the 12th of May, on Tower Hill, Evelyn saw Strafford lay his head on the execution block. It was a moving scene, yet there was a great shout of joy when the axe fell. The Earl was only forty-three years of age, but the feeling against him was tremendous, as apart from his cruelty in the Scottish campaign, he had, as the Lord Deputy in Ireland, a terrible record. Under promise of certain concessions from the Crown, he had obtained vast sums, but he had tricked and bullied the Parliament, and concessions were never given. He had broken land titles everywhere by undisguised illegality and violence, forcing verdicts for the King by threats, fines, and imprisonment; he had punished sheriffs, judges, juries, and lawyers. He had confiscated nearly all Connaught and a large part of Munster, and had illegally crushed and ruined many of the highest people in the land.

For Evelyn, the Earl's execution left "a strange and confused situation".

* *Memoirs of the Verney Family*, vol. 1, p. 359.

His was a gentle, cautious, inoffensive nature which abhorred the thought of violence. Yet civil war now seemed inevitable. In that case would not he be called upon to fight? He was a Royalist at heart; he had been reared in that tradition. But he was only twenty years of age, and he knew nothing of war or its terrible implications. There was fighting in Flanders, it is true, and many young men were going there in order to gain some experience of soldiering. Would it not be wise to do likewise and at the same time consider carefully his position? Away from England he would be able to see things in perspective. Had he been asked to defend his country against a foreign invader he would have had no hesitation in offering his services, but civil war, if it came, was very different. Actually he had an opportunity to serve as a volunteer in the Low Countries under a Captain Apsley, and this he decided to do.

His decision to go abroad, however, was not entirely approved by his friends and relatives, and his sister Jane, to whom he was much attached, was extremely dejected at the news. She begged him, at least, to have his portrait painted, so he sat to the artist Vanderborcht at Arundel House. Evelyn then obtained a pass from the Custom House, repeated his Oath of Allegiance, and rode down to Gravesend; he was accompanied by a friend and two servants. At Chatham, which they visited while waiting for a favourable wind, they saw that "glorious vessel", the newly built *Royal Sovereign*, and, finally, they embarked on a Dutch frigate, convoyed by five other ships. The following day they landed at Flushing, from whence they took wagon for Rotterdam, and a few days later Evelyn was in The Hague, where he dutifully paid his court to the Queen of Bohemia. Then, via Leyden, Utrecht, and Nimeguen, he arrived early in August at the Leaguer, where the Dutch army was encamped. Here he was received by Captain Apsley, and was able to view the trenches, the approaches, and the mines of the besiegers.

Actually, however, Evelyn's military experience lasted only a fortnight, and he then went on to Rotterdam, Haarlem, and Amsterdam. He visited castles, churches, monasteries, cathedrals, palaces, picture galleries, prisons, hospitals, and libraries. He bought books, maps, shells, atlases, curiosities, and pictures. But it was the magnificent architecture of Amsterdam, and particularly the churches, which made such a deep impression. He was amazed to see that ships of considerable size could ride at anchor "before the very doors of the merchants". He also greatly admired the well-paved streets planted with lime trees, and the charming houses. He visited the Exchange, where merchants of every nationality were congregated, he saw the dog market, and on St. Bartholomew's day he "went amongst the booksellers".

At the delightful city of Leyden he visited the colleges and schools, the physic garden ("well stored with exotic plants"), and a famous printing house. He was allowed, also, to see the celebrated Anatomy School, and he talked with some of the Jesuits. In Antwerp he was allowed to view part of the citadel, which he thought "a matchless piece of fortification".

Inevitably on his journeyings there were various adventures, but he finally arrived at Brussels where he was quite enchanted with "the sweet and delicious gardens, full of noble statues", and with the "artificial music". Eventually he called on His Majesty's Agent, who provided him with a coach and six horses, in which he drove from Brussels to Ghent, where he had arranged to meet Lord Arundel, Earl Marshal of England. Evelyn then travelled with his lordship's train to Bruges, and on to Ostend, where they viewed the river, harbour, and fortifications. Finally, they travelled by wagon to Dunkirk, and embarked "in a pretty frigate of six guns for England". From Dover the party rode post to Canterbury, and at last reached London, where they landed at Arundel Stairs. Here Evelyn took leave of the Earl, and went to his lodgings in the Middle Temple.

Evelyn's first trip abroad had been a memorable one; but like all journeys at that time there had been some hazardous moments. He therefore gave solemn thanks to God for his safe return, and received the Holy Sacrament. He had been away for three months, but to escape for a time from storm-tossed England had been a tremendous relief. He and Richard spent Christmas at Wotton, and the festival was kept in the merry, traditional style, with generous hospitality. There was much feasting, piping, and dancing; the poor were given alms; masquers and mummers entertained the guests; and carols were sung lustily. The loving cup was passed from hand to hand, and finally the boar's head, trimmed with rosemary and bays (for luck), was carried into the hall to the flourish of trumpets and the songs of minstrels.

The traditional feasting lasted for twelve days (the custom of the time), and then Evelyn returned to London, where he resumed his studies at the Middle Temple. It was a duty he owed to his dead father who had carefully arranged this plan of education. But life amongst the students was, on the whole, pleasantly entertaining. Evelyn much enjoyed browsing in the fine library, and spent many delightful hours in the lovely gardens with their handsome lime and hawthorn trees and their famous red and white roses. But for his law studies Evelyn could find little enthusiasm; there was so much of which he disapproved—"the immoderate fees, the tedious and ruinous delays, the tossing from Court to Court . . . before an easy cause can come to a final issue". Meanwhile, he and his young companions followed the natural inclinations of young men, and spent their time in "dancing and fooling". The Sword of Damocles might be suspended over their heads, but they were too young to realize the full implications of war. Besides, it was possible that even at the eleventh hour the King might compromise with his people; many men believed so.

There was only one real temptation for the young law students at the Middle Temple; at Bankside, almost adjoining, were many "disorderly houses". According to rumour, these had been erected for the convenience of the old Knights Templars. They were, however, subject to strict laws and regulations, and only a minority of students allowed their thoughts to stray in that direction.

It was their duty, as gentlemen, to attend regularly at Court, to pay their homage to their Sovereign. But these visits now brought little pleasure. For Charles's elegant Court had utterly changed. Only a few years ago there had been fine company and magnificent masques and ballets. The King and Queen had gathered round them men and women of culture and talent. The beautiful Queen was the theme of every poet, "the star of all beholders". But gloom and anxiety now pervaded the palace. The sentries paced grimly back and forth, and were continually whispering in corners. Matters were going from bad to worse.

Evelyn had purchased at The Hague a suit of horseman's armour; he felt therefore that he was ready for all eventualities. Yet the problem remained—where did his duty lie? Soon, apparently, he must make up his mind. There could be no doubt that the King, by his unconstitutional acts, had created an extremely dangerous situation. His promises had been violated without scruple or shame, and no true Englishman could stand by and see Parliament reduced to a nullity. Nevertheless, Evelyn

17

had been taught that loyalty to the throne was a matter of solemn honour; otherwise the monarchy would be destroyed. And what could take its place? He could not reject this sacred principle now. But, on the other hand, he could not murder his brethren for such a principle. That was out of the question. He abhorred violence, and he was convinced that it solved nothing.

Meanwhile, the most horrifying news was arriving from Ireland, where Evelyn had several friends. Every post brought fresh accounts of the fierce rebellion which had started on the 23rd of October. As Viceroy in Ireland, Strafford had succeeded in establishing a military despotism, but his cruelty, fines, and illegal confiscations had had their terrible effect, and the native Catholics were now taking their revenge and were burning the Protestants out of their houses. Hundreds had perished in the severe weather, and the numbers who had died in the rebellion were already estimated at 40,000. The rebels were also ruthlessly killing all the cattle, and famine therefore seemed inevitable. The English Parliament had sent reinforcements of troops, but the soldiers had received no pay for months, and were desperately short of food. As a result they were deserting in hundreds. Was this a foretaste of what was to come in England? The fear was certainly justified.

On the 4th of January, 1642, King Charles unsuccessfully attempted to seize and arrest five Members in the House of Commons, and the City immediately rallied to the side of the Parliament. The King then tried to obtain possession of the Fleet, but was unsuccessful, as the sailors declared for the Parliament. His attempts to seize magazines of arms in Leicestershire and Hull also failed; and, finally, Charles rejected the last propositions put to him by the Parliament; he declared that to grant such demands would reduce him to "the mere shadow of a King". He now therefore began to put in force the commissions of array in the Midlands and the north, and in August he set up the royal standard at Nottingham. The civil war had started.

Bewildered as he was, Evelyn felt at this time that he must assist the King, and on the 12th of July he sent his "black menage horse and furniture", through a friend, to His Majesty at Oxford.

As the weeks passed, however, it became clear that few men were responding to the King's call, and his army grew smaller every day. He was desperately short of money, artillery, and ammunition, and had therefore laid taxes on the rural districts occupied by his troops. But these produced comparatively little, and he was forced to rely principally on the generosity of the rich cavaliers who were now mortgaging their lands, pawning their jewels, and melting down their plate. Meanwhile, the Queen had sailed to Holland with the Crown jewels, in order to seek allies and to obtain guns and supplies.

The Parliament forces now controlled the Home Counties, the Fleet, the navigation of the Thames, and most of the large towns and seaports.* These were tremendous advantages, as they had at their disposal practically all the military stores of the kingdom, and were able to raise duties, both on imports and exports.

But it was a strange war, for both armies lacked experience of military matters, and most men had never seen a battle. And now, as the opposing forces fought over the land, they left behind a tragic toll of desolation and misery. Towns were taken and re-taken, beautiful houses were pillaged and burnt to the ground, the deer, cattle, and sheep were stolen, fences were pulled down, and plantations destroyed. Meanwhile, hundreds of men, women, and children were ordered to assist in making fortifications, and they dug and toiled for days on end, come wind, come weather. Soldiers, too, demanded to be housed and fed, and as many as a hundred soldiers would suddenly descend upon a country house and stay for weeks. The owners, whose husbands were generally away fighting, either for King or Parliament, wept and protested, but dare not refuse. Then the soldiers would consume all the food, wine, and ale, and finally depart with all the valuable horses. There was little fighting, as yet, in Evelyn's neighbourhood, but many of his friends were suffering. Women were terrified and exhausted by being awakened night after night, to fly from either the King's or the Parliament troops, both equally feared. Some owners of country houses, it is true, stayed on, and even helped to defend the place when attacked or besieged, but women of this courageous type were few. Many owners lost all their belongings, even their title deeds, when their mansions were burnt.

On the 3rd of October Evelyn went to see the siege of Portsmouth, and on the 12th of November he rode, fully armed, to join the King's army at Brentford. But he arrived to find that the battle was over, and the defeated Royalists were retreating. He therefore returned home, and

* Macaulay's *History of England*, vol. 1, p. 113.

it was at this time that he realized, with a tremendous shock, the serious implications of joining the Royalist forces—the estates of himself and his brothers, which all lay close to London, would immediately be seized by the Parliamentarians, and the result meant certain ruin to himself and his family. Was he justified in making this fearful sacrifice, probably without any advantage to the King? Also, in fighting for His Majesty, he, John Evelyn, must commit murder. He had friends and relatives on both sides; and was he to plunge a dagger or lance through the heart of a cousin or brother, and then watch him die in agony? The idea was unthinkable. Nor could he see what would be gained by a continuation of this cruel conflict. When both sides were exhausted, a peace would almost certainly be arranged, but at what a cost of misery and bloodshed. He had observed, also, that men were fighting—on one side or the other —for the strangest reasons. Some men fought in order to keep their possessions, which they feared might be seized by the King; others fought for the Parliament which they had elected, and which they felt bound to support. Some men were fighting merely because their friends were fighting; others fought because they did not wish to be branded as cowards.

So the dreary year of 1642 drew to a close. Neither King nor Parliament had gained any real advantage, and the majority of people were aghast at the turn of events; the whole conflict appeared to be a hideous nightmare. Brothers were fighting against brothers, and fathers against sons. Meanwhile, both sides appealed to God to justify the rectitude of their intentions. The Parliament was convinced that it fought for heaven, and the King was no less convinced that his claims were sacred. It was all too bewildering, too horrible. And Evelyn was equally perplexed. He and his brothers and friends had discussed the situation interminably. Where did his duty lie? He was tortured by indecision.

CHAPTER 2

IN EXILE

ON THE 2nd of May, 1643, Evelyn was in London and saw the "furious and zealous people demolish the stately cross at Cheapside". It was an alarming incident, and London was in a state of fearful unrest. Petitions against the unpopular bishops were being presented to the House of Commons, and apprentices were creating violent disturbances round Westminster, the Abbey being pelted with stones. "No bishops! No bishops!", roared the crowd. They had broken the windows, and, finally, "a tile cast by an unknown hand had bruised Sir Richard Wiseman that he died thereof". The bishops were obliged to protest to the King that they dared not go to the House to sit.

Evelyn returned to Wotton, as he said, "to possess myself in some quiet". He was extremely unsettled, and felt that creative work—the solace of the sensitive—was essential while he considered his position. He started work, therefore, on some classical translations, and with his brother's permission he built at this time a study, a fishpond and an island at Wotton.

Meanwhile, the Royalist troops had been successful in many encounters and were apparently gaining the upper hand, but their victories were not consolidated. On the 20th of September young Lord Falkland was killed at the battle of Newbury—a tragic waste of a valuable young life. He had flung himself into the middle of the fight because, as he said, he was "weary of the times, and foresee the misery of my country". Why were these courageous young aristocrats laying down their lives? Because they believed, with all the Englishman's conservatism, in romantic honour, the reverence due to royalty, and the traditions in which they had been reared. Few ever entered into the political question; they fought for the old banner, as their ancestors had done. They were not mere fawning courtiers, and their motives were neither base nor selfish.

As for the Parliamentary soldiers, they believed that they were risking their lives for the precious liberties and religion of England. Meanwhile, they were being moulded into one of the finest armies Europe had ever seen.

And now the Parliamentarians were pressing every man to take the Covenant, an oath which many of Evelyn's friends found utterly unacceptable. They had already gone abroad. The country squires who had left England, however, had had their estates confiscated and had been obliged to leave their affairs in other hands. Meanwhile, creditors had pressed their claims, wives and husbands had been parted, children had been sent to relatives and friends, rents could not be collected, and heavy debts had piled up. The situation was a tragic one.

Evelyn, of course, had no real home, and no dependants. He had, however, inherited several estates (from which he derived his income), but, if necessary, friends and relatives had promised to supervise these. He was not yet twenty-three, and his father had intended that, like all young men of good family, he should complete his education by making the grand tour of Europe. And this he now determined to do. The period of indecision had ended.

So the preparations were made, and Evelyn and his friend Thicknesse left England on the 6th of November for France. In Paris they were warmly received by the English Resident, Sir Richard Browne, who introduced them to his intimate circle. Indeed, Evelyn was soon playing his modest part in the life of the English exiles, and when the Earl of Norwich came to Paris as Ambassador Extraordinary, Evelyn was deputed to receive him with a coach-and-six at the Palace of Monsieur de Bassompiere. The Earl then proceeded, "with a very great cavalcade", to the Palais Cardinale, where he was received in audience by the King of France and the Queen Regent in the Golden Chamber of Presence. From thence Evelyn conducted him to his lodgings in the rue St. Denys.

Evelyn was quite enchanted with Paris, which he thought "one of the most gallant cities in the world". He was greatly impressed with the "many noble and magnificent buildings", the beautiful gardens of the

Tuileries, and the wide paved streets, which he thought infinitely superior to the pebbled streets of London.

Evelyn was now able, in fact, to satisfy, to his heart's content, his enthusiasm for gardens, sculpture, paintings, and ancient architecture. His thirst for knowledge was insatiable, and he and his friends made many excursions to the environs of Paris. Some journeys, it is true, were a little hazardous, and when he drove with a party to Fontainebleau they were warned to beware of stags, wolves, bears, and a lynx. They were also obliged to carry arms for fear of robbers. Nevertheless, the journey was well worth while, and Evelyn was utterly charmed with the exquisite gardens, with their lovely antiquities, fountains, and statues.

On the 19th of March, 1644, he toured Normandy, accompanied by Sir J. Cotton ("a Cambridgeshire Knight"), and they visited Rouen, Dieppe, Havre de Grace, where they inspected the fortifications and made their bows to the Duke de Richelieu. During the summer months, too, Evelyn and his friend Thicknesse went to the beautiful city of Tours, where they stayed for nineteen weeks. They then rode by easy stages to Marseilles, "a delicious journey" through vineyards, oliveyards, orange groves, myrtles, pomegranates, and "the like sweet plantations". Evelyn was quite enchanted with the lovely villas "built all of freestone and looking like so many heaps of snow dropped out of the clouds amongst these perennial greens". Marseilles itself, however, was thoroughly depressing, as the streets were crowded with slaves, fettered with huge chains, carrying heavy burdens, and working unceasingly.

From Aix, Evelyn and his friend went on to Cannes, and then sailed to Genoa, where again he was delighted with the "well-designed and stately palaces", the magnificent churches, and the gardens. The walls of the city, built to a "prodigious height", were 20 miles in extent, and the inhabitants were dressed "in stately garb, rather like Spaniards". They were carried along the streets in litters and sedans instead of coaches. A further acquaintance with Genoa, however, revealed the deplorable fact "that this beautiful city is more stained with horrid acts of revenge and murders than any one place in Europe, or haply in the world".

Pisa, of course, was well worth a visit, and here Evelyn met an old friend, Thomas Henshawe, who had just arrived from Spain. Livorno, however, was a depressing city, for again the streets were crowded with

23

slaves, "singing, weeping, playing, all nearly naked, and miserably chained". A few days later, Evelyn and his friends arrived in Florence, and from there they proceeded to Rome.

The time now was November, and the plan was to stay in Rome until the new year. They were determined to see everything, and they visited the hospitals, orphanages, palaces, and picture galleries. Evelyn was particularly impressed with the Vatican: "Certainly this is one of the most superb and royal apartments in the world, much too beautiful for a guard of gigantic Switzers, who do nothing but drink and play cards in it." What a magnificent sight were the elaborate religious ceremonies. The lights, the processions, the music, the cannon roaring, and the wonderful fireworks, produced an almost incredible air of excitement. All the windows of the city were lit up with transparencies—"a glorious show"—and the streets, ablaze with bonfires, were "as light as day".

On Christmas Eve, Evelyn and his friends spent the whole night walking from church to church, gazing at the gorgeous pageantry. Who could wonder at the intense religious fervour of the people? The whole thing transported one back to the colourful, musical, fanatical Middle Ages. The ghetto of the Jews, however, was a most mournful place. "The Jews dwell as in a church by themselves", he noted, "and live only upon brokerage and usury." They were "very poor and despicable", and all wore yellow hats.

Evelyn and his party made many friends in Rome, but by the end of January they were in Naples, where the most striking feature was the wonderful food. "We seldom sat down to fewer than fourteen or twenty dishes of exquisite meat and fruits", he recorded. "The very winter here is summer, ever fruitful, so that in the middle of February we had melons, cherries, apricots and many other sorts of fruits." He thought the architecture "the most magnificent of any in Europe". There were 3000 churches and monasteries, "and these the best built and adorned of any in Italy . . . The streets are full of gallants on horseback, in coaches or sedans." But the women were "excessively libidinous". Evelyn was, in fact, shocked at the courtesans "who swarm in the city to the number, we are told, of 30,000, registered and paying a tax to the State. . . . Indeed, the town is so pestered with these cattle that there needs no small mortification to preserve from their enchantment, whilst they display all their natural and artificial beauty, play, sing, feign compliment,

24

and by a thousand studied devices seek to inveigle foolish young men."

Evelyn and his friends were now a little weary of travelling ("rolling up and down"). Nevertheless, on the 7th of February they started for Rome and, taking the overland route, were there within a week. It was carnival time when they arrived, and the streets "swarmed with prostitutes, buffoons and all manner of rabble". The Easter ceremonies, however, were extremely interesting. They heard at the Vatican the sermons of the most famous preachers, and on Good Friday there was a remarkable procession in which many fanatics, wearing vizors and masks, whipped themselves till the blood stained their clothes.

After seven months in Rome, Evelyn and his party went to Venice, where they found many old friends—Mr. Henry Howard (grandson to the Earl of Arundel), Mr. Bramstone (son of the Lord Chief Justice), and Evelyn's old friend, Henshawe. The four friends rented a house, and lived "most nobly". They all worked hard at their languages, but there was time also for entertaining, and on Twelfth Night they invited all the English and Scots in the city to a highly successful feast. Life in Venice, in fact, proved extremely agreeable, although Evelyn disliked the custom of bull-baiting in the streets and piazzas and the "universal madness of the place during Carnival". From Venice he was able to make several jaunts to Padua to see the famous University and schools, and he attended the celebrated anatomy lectures, where he saw a man, a woman, and a child dissected. He also visited the hospitals "to see the cures"; and these visits, he decided, were "the very best argument against the vice reigning in this licentious country". Many of the patients were in the last loathsome stages of venereal disease. Evelyn was determined, however, not to shrink from any knowledge, however unpleasant.

At the end of March it was time to return to Paris. He therefore took leave of The Patriarch, the Prince of Wirtenberg, and Monsieur Grotius, and packed up his books, pictures, and busts. Accompanied by the poet Mr. Edmund Waller, Capt. Wray (the son of Sir Christopher Wray), and another friend, they proceeded via Verona to Milan, and from there they travelled with mules over mountains. They were warned to beware of avalanches, ferocious bears, and wolves, but they escaped all hazards until they reached Geneva, where Evelyn became seriously ill, and to his horror the disease proved to be smallpox, which he had apparently caught from an infected bed. By good fortune he was well nursed through his illness by "a vigilant Swiss matron", and after being confined to his room for five weeks he was able to continue his journey.

It was good to be back in Paris again, and his travels had been both interesting and beneficial, as he had now learnt High Dutch, Spanish, and Italian. He and his companions had seen all sides of life; sometimes they had slept in damask beds and been treated like emperors, yet occasionally they had had to accept the hospitality of wretched inns where the beds were lousy. There had been many adventures, both by land and sea, and his valet had robbed him of clothes and plate worth £60. But his travels, for the time being, were over. He had seen the sights, he had satisfied his immense curiosity; and Paris was now his home.

Sir Richard and Lady Browne had drawn round them many English exiles, but they were a sad and anxious community, for the majority were ruined and heavily in debt. Sir Richard, too, was in serious financial straits, as his salary as Resident was in arrear. Amongst the exiles was the Lord Keeper, Lord Hatton, Sir Philip Musgrave, Sir Marmaduke Langdale, Mr. Waller, Sir William Coventry, Sir George Radcliffe, the Earl of Chesterfield, and Lord Ossory. Land in England had been mortgaged, jewellery pawned, and even clothes sold to the highest French bidder. The Queen had sold all her jewels, and although she was receiving a generous allowance from the French Government, she was heavily in debt. In Sir Richard's private chapel an English Protestant service was conducted, and Holy Communion and christenings were celebrated. The exiles were determined to maintain these services.

Meanwhile, the news from England was heartbreaking, as the Royalists had suffered many defeats. At the battle of Marston Moor (July 1644), 4000 Royalists had been killed, many prisoners were taken, and hundreds of Royalist soldiers had fled overseas. Then, in the following January, Laud, Archbishop of Canterbury, who had been a prisoner in the Tower for about three years, was executed on Tower Hill. He had been tried and found guilty, although he was certainly not a traitor. He had been genuinely pious, but the main purpose of his life had been the exaltation of the Church, and for this no persecution had been too rigorous and no fine too severe. He had been a member of the Star Chamber and High Commission, and unfortunately he had known nothing of politics.

His appointment, therefore, as Archbishop of Canterbury, had been disastrous. He was seventy-one years of age. His death had been followed by increased severity against the ministers of the Church, and it was now pronounced a penal offence in England to refuse to take the Covenant, or to use the Book of Common Prayer. Some 2000 clergy, therefore, who had refused to comply, had lost their livings.

In June, news arrived in Paris of the battle of Naseby, and apparently 1000 Royalist soldiers had been killed and 5000 taken prisoner. The King had lost all his artillery and arms and nearly all his officers. But he was still fanatically adamant, and in August he wrote to Sir Edward Nicholas: "I resolve, by the grace of God, never to yield up this Church to the government of Papists, Presbyterians or Independents, nor injure my successors by lessening the Crown of that ecclesiastical and military power which my predecessors left me."*

In the following April (1646) it became known in Paris that the King had secretly left Oxford in disguise, and had wandered from place to place, living—as he said—"like a partridge that is hunted on the mountains". Often he had been without even the barest necessities of life. Finally, he had thrown himself on the generosity of the Scots covenanters, and in December he was handed over to the Parliamentarians for the sum of £400,000 on condition that he was delivered to nine Commissioners. "I am ashamed", he had said, "that my price was so much higher than my Saviour's." The King, therefore, was now a prisoner, closely guarded, and there were dark and ugly rumours to the effect that his death was already planned.

It was at this time that Evelyn decided to return to England. Many matters concerning his property needed his attention, and he had also been asked to see the King and take messages from the Queen and ministers. Evelyn held no official position at the English Court, but apparently he was regarded as the man for this delicate task. A marriage had also been arranged between himself and Mary, the only child and heiress of Sir Richard Browne. She was fifteen years of age, and therefore too young to live with him as his wife, but such an arrangement was quite usual at that time. Mary was not strictly a beauty, but was quaintly attractive, with her serene, wide-apart blue eyes, straight little nose, and

* *Diary and Correspondence of John Evelyn*, vol. IV, p. 160 (letter from King Charles I to Sir Edward Nicholas, 25 August 1645).

27

flaxen curls. Evelyn had always admired her ingenuousness, her keen sense of humour, and her sound common sense. This was the bride he had chosen, and he and Mary were married in Paris on the 27th of July, 1647, on the feast of Corpus Christi, when the streets were richly hung with tapestry and strewn with flowers.

In order to fit his young bride for the duties of a married woman, Evelyn gave her a book on the ethics of marriage, including an essay, by a French writer, on the nuptial bed. The work was beautifully bound in red leather, and bore Evelyn's arms and motto. He warned his young wife to keep it under lock and key and to show it to no one. His marriage, of course, was not consummated, but Mary was to be left in the care of her excellent mother.

Early in September, Evelyn had a long interview with Prince Charles and Queen Henrietta Maria; he had an important mission to fulfil, but his instructions were clear, and apparently he felt himself perfectly able to do what was needed. From Sir Richard Browne, too, he had received careful advice. He left Paris for London on the 6th of September.

Evelyn had been away from England for four years, and he found, of course, many mournful changes. The civil war had left the most terrible scars. Meanwhile, he had much to do. He was to report to Sir Richard Brown regularly, addressing his letters to "Mr. Peters", and signing them "Aphanos". Names were not to be used, but numbers, by a prearranged code.

It was believed that some accommodation might yet be reached between King and Parliament, even at this late hour, but Charles himself was so obstinately adamant on all points that there seemed little hope, and the prospect was terrifying.

First, Evelyn drove down to Sussex to put his estate "in some better posture than it was", and then rode to Wotton to visit his brother George. From Wotton he went to Hampton Court, "to kiss His Majesty's hand"—a very sad meeting, but they had a long talk. The King was, of course, a prisoner, although he was not forbidden to see his children and a few friends, or to hunt. It was obvious, however, that he was haunted by the fear of assassination. The regal dignity was still there, but those tragic eyes told their own pitiful story. One's heart went out to him. "The King's case", wrote Evelyn to Sir Richard Browne, "is just like the disarmed man, who whether he agrees that his antagonist shall keep

28

his weapon or not, is forced to let him have it. . . . Oh, heavens, we are now more in the dark than ever, and I protest unto you things were never more unriddleable than at this instant of time, after so many fair and promising expectations."

Evelyn had decided, for the time being, to occupy his old chambers in the Middle Temple, as he wished to meet as many influential people as possible, in order to report to Sir Richard Browne. But it would be necessary to make many journeys into the country, not only to settle his own affairs but also those of Sir Richard, who owned property in Sussex. Sir Richard was also the owner of Sayes Court, Deptford, a timbered manor-house which had for many years been owned by his ancestors. Sir Richard had greatly feared that the King would sell the place, as he owned the lease of the land. But Sir Richard's ancestors had "built the house at their own charge", and he had urgently requested Sir Edward Nicholas (Secretary of State to King Charles) to preserve it at all costs, as it was the only seat he had, and the place where he was born. He was deeply attached to it.

The winter was a dreary one, but there was much to do, and when spring arrived, Evelyn drove into the country to visit various relatives and old friends. He purchased one manor, and sold another; he sat for his portrait to "Mr. Walker, that excellent painter," and he attended the wedding of his brother Richard to a rich and charming heiress. At the end of the summer he even went to see the "celebrated follies" of St. Bartholomew Fair. Some diversion was essential.

But matters in England were going from bad to worse, and his reports to Sir Richard Browne were hopelessly depressing. The civil war had broken out again, as apparently some castles held by royalists had been fortified and were still holding out; news of bloody encounters and bitter sieges came in daily. The Royalists were making a determined last stand, and even in London they were protesting, as in April Sir John Geare had appeared in the House of Lords, where he had refused to kneel, and as he went through the Hall he had scattered quantities of printed papers in which he summoned all the free subjects of England "to stand stoutly to their ancient privileges". He had declared that they had no power to try him as a delinquent, but he had been fined £500. John Lilburne had done the same.

All these events were reported faithfully to Sir Richard Browne, and

29

Evelyn added: "But God is above all, and I hope will convert all to the best." Trade, too, was extremely bad; there was little work for the poor, and many families were destitute and starving. Food was extremely scarce, and cattle were dying everywhere; children were roaming the streets crying for bread. Fear, too, had reduced the nation to a state of utter panic, and on the 26th of April Evelyn heard "a great uproar" in London as a rumour spread that the rebel army were about to plunder the city. It was known that the Roundheads were selling the Scots prisoners as slaves "for £5 a score" to the Barbadoes and other plantations,* and this could certainly happen in England, too. Apparently no man was safe from butchery and molestation.

The ever-present fear, also, in all minds, was that the King would be murdered, and on the 28th of December, by what means is not known, Evelyn "got privately into Whitehall" and heard the Council of the rebel army discussing the fate of the King. Their plans could only be described by Evelyn as "horrid villainies". The King was now at Carisbrooke Castle in the Isle of Wight, and apparently in some of his books he had written in the blank pages *Dum spiro spero* (While I breathe I hope), and to Sir John Bowring he had confessed that he expected every hour to be murdered. His hair had turned quite grey, and he looked an old man. On the 26th of April, 1648, he had made a pathetic attempt to escape through the bars of his window, but had been unable to get through, and had had to call for assistance in order to be released. His farewell speech to the Lords Commissioners at Newport, in the Isle of Wight, left no doubt as to what he feared:

> My Lords, you are come to take your leave of mee, and I beleeve wee shall scarce ever see each other againe; but God's will be done. I thank God I have made my peace with him, and shall without feare undergoe what he shall please to suffer men to doe unto mee.
>
> My Lords, you cannot but knowe that in my fall and ruine you see your owne, and that also neere to you. I pray God send you better frends than I have found.
>
> I am fully informed of ye whole carriage of ye plott against me and myne, and nothing soe much afflicts mee as the sense and feeling I have of ye sufferings of my subjects, and ye mischief that hangs over my three kingdomes, drawne upon them by those who (upon pretences of good) violently pursue their owne interests and ends.†

---

* *Memoirs of the Verney Family During the Civil War*, vol. 2, p. 338.
† *Evelyn's Diary* (*The Nicholas Correspondence*), vol. 4, p. 185.

This speech was made "with much alacrity and cheerfulness, with a serene countenance, and carriage free from all disturbance".

The Parliamentary Army were now in complete control, and Evelyn confessed to Sir Richard Browne that the country was "in more obscurity, thraldom, error and confusion than ever we were since these wars began. They talk of treating with His Majesty, but defer it. . . . I pray God give us patience and hope, which is the only refuge of miserable men."*

A little later—in December—Evelyn again reported: "Ireton has played the devil in Hampshire, plundering and imprisoning all such as he suspects to be loyal. Since my last, the soldiers have marched into the city and seized on the public treasures." The soldiers had also stabled their horses in St. Paul's Cathedral, and made bonfires of the seats. Ireton and his Council had also drawn up an agreement, which was called "The People's Agreement": "The King and his party, having forfeited and lost their trust in the people and been fairly vanquished, the people are now in a state of absolute freedom."

"All is now in their hands", wrote Evelyn to Sir Richard Browne, "and we are an utterly lost nation, without the mercy of God. . . . Sir, I am altogether confused and sad for the misery that is come upon us." He was certain that the King would be executed, although Cromwell had apparently tried to save his life; but the King had refused even to receive the envoy, in order to discuss terms.

The year of 1649 opened in unrelieved gloom, and Dr. Denton, the King's physician, wrote: "The complexion of our confusions grows every day more sad and black than other. . . . Ye scaffolds are building for the tryall of the Kinge. . . . It is almost every man's opinion that nothing will satisfie but his head."†

Evelyn recorded: "I heard the rebel, Peters, incite the rebel powers met in the painted chamber to destroy His Majesty."

Drums and trumpets, indeed, soon announced the trial of the King, and three days later he was taken to Westminster Hall to appear before seventy "judges". Many soldiers and a "dense mass of the populace" were also present, but the King refused to plead. He declared that the Court had no power to try him. As he was leaving, the soldiers heaped

* *Diary and Correspondence of John Evelyn*, vol. 3, p. 20.
† *Memoirs of the Verney Family During the Civil War*, vol. 2, p. 396.

vile abuse upon him, and one spat in his face. He wiped it away and said: "My Saviour suffered more than this for me." Many spectators, however, cried out bravely, "God save Your Majesty!", but the soldiers brought their sticks down savagely on those within reach. Some of the bystanders also wept bitterly.

On the 27th of January the King was sentenced to death, although many Commissioners, including Sir Thomas Fairfax, refused to sign the death warrant. Lady Fairfax, in fact, had screamed from the public gallery during the trial, "Oliver Cromwell is a traitor". Nevertheless, the signatures were collected. On Saturday, the 29th, the King was allowed to see his children (the Princess Elizabeth and the Duke of Gloucester) for the last time, and with many tears he blessed them and bade them farewell. The next day he was brought out between a line of soldiers, with drums beating and colours flying. The scaffold was draped in black and the coffin was there, waiting to receive the body. The King appeared calm, dignified, and resigned, and laid his head firmly on the block. The executioner brought down the axe with a great spatter of blood, and holding up the head said, in a loud and terrible voice: "Behold, the head of a traitor." Evelyn was not present (the sight would have been unbearable), but the details of the execution were related by his brother George and several friends.

Thousands of soldiers were on guard to prevent any sympathetic demonstration. Nevertheless, many people wept, and "a dismal, universal groan" went up from the crowd assembled. The King's courage, meekness, and regal carriage had been infinitely touching. For here was a monarch reduced to the last extremity. The pitiful scene would long be remembered. The body was embalmed, and the head sewn on in the presence of many spectators, including Cromwell. "It is now the dismallest time that ever our eyes beheld", wrote Dr. Denton. "Ye confusions and distractions are everywhere so great that I know not where to wish myself but in heaven. . . . We are now in the maddest world that ever we mortalls saw, and I have great reason to fear we do now begin to drink the dregs of our bitter cup."*

The body of the dead king was buried in St. George's Chapel, Windsor, in the vault which held the remains of Henry VIII and Jane Seymour. The beautiful chapel, however, was now a mass of ruins. The ancient

* *Memoirs of the Verney Family During the Civil War*, vol. 2, p. 401.

inscriptions, the stalls, and the banners of the Knights of the Garter had all been torn down by the Roundheads and strewn on the floor. Evelyn was indescribably shocked.

Many women went into mourning for the King, but few men dared to do so. Evelyn, however, made a vow to keep the anniversary of Charles's death as a solemn fast for the rest of his life. In vain some of his friends protested that Cromwell was not to blame for the King's death. They insisted that Cromwell had meant to mediate between the throne and the Parliament, but the soldiers had clamoured fiercely for the head of the King, conspiracies had been formed, there were threats of impeachment, a mutiny had broken out, and only with great difficulty had it been quelled. Cromwell had succeeded in restoring order, but he had realized that he could not contend against the rage of his soldiers, who regarded the fallen tyrant as their foe and the enemy of their God. The soldiers had fought and won the war; now they were determined to have their say and reap their rewards. Charles's execution was regarded as the only logical ending to the strife.

As for the civil war, what had been gained for all the misery, bloodshed, and financial loss? Evelyn was bitterly disillusioned and shocked, for it was clear that in the struggle all the perfidy and falseness of which human nature is capable had been revealed; neighbour had struck at neighbour, without shame or compunction, and old scores had been paid off under the guise of public service. Many men, too, had changed their coats several times as the fortunes of the opposing sides had risen and fallen; some men had fought first for the Parliament and then for the King. The bishops had gone under, and the top Parliament men had scrambled shamelessly for the Church's lands. Parsonages had emptied and filled again, time after time. As one parson had entered, another had departed, homeless, penniless, to face an indifferent world.

Meanwhile, life under the Commonwealth was unutterably dreary, and misfortune seemed to hang particularly heavily over Evelyn at this time, as he became dangerously ill in April, and was obliged to submit to all the painful "remedies" then in fashion. He was severely blistered, and "let blood" behind the ears and forehead. Then the alarming news arrived from Paris that the city had been besieged by the Prince de Conde, and Mary and her parents were confined within the walls. A few weeks later, however, the clouds had dispersed. His health returned, and his collection of treasures from Italy arrived; the unpacking proved an absorbing and delightful task.

Meanwhile, Sir Richard Browne and the Royalists in France were anxious to know if the monarchy could possibly be restored through the young King. Could he not make a bid for the throne? Evelyn, however, who had consulted many prominent Royalists, advised extreme caution. He confessed that he himself, even in corresponding with Sir Richard, ventured both his life and fortune. "Burn, therefore, this paper", he urged. As for young King Charles, he referred to Cromwell and his Council as "the present barbarous and bloody usurpers".

With regard to the future, Evelyn had now decided on his course. England was his native land, and when the country was more settled, he and Mary would return and make a life there together. They had many good friends, and many dear relatives. First he must return to France, and for this purpose he was obliged to obtain a pass (from "Bradshaw, the rebel") to leave the country. Then, after receiving the Blessed Sacrament—a duty he never neglected before a journey—he drove down to Wotton and to Godstone to take leave of relatives. There was a perfect orgy of dining-out and leave-taking. But the promise of return softened the farewells, and in a few days his preparations were made and all business affairs settled.

CHAPTER 3

THE COMMONWEALTH

SAYES COURT was at about this time seized by the Parliamentarians, and although later it could probably be regained, obviously the negotiations would be protracted. On the 12th of July, therefore, Evelyn returned to France. He sailed in a barque guarded by a pinnace of eight guns, and although they were chased for some time by a pirate ship, they were not attacked. On the way to Paris they were stopped several times and forced to alight from the coach and walk separately on foot with their guns on their shoulders. But the journey was completed.

In Paris, Evelyn was welcomed by Mary and her parents, and by Sir Edward Hyde, the Chancellor, Sir Edward Nicholas, the Secretary of State, Sir George Carteret, Governor of Jersey, and Dr. Earle. Evelyn went almost immediately to St. Germains, to kiss His Majesty's hand, and in the coach was the young King's mistress, Mrs. Barlow, by whom the King had had a son. Evelyn thought her "a brown, beautiful, bold, but insipid creature". The following day Evelyn went to salute the French King and the Queen-Dowager of France, and returned in one of the King's coaches. A few weeks later he again made the journey to St. Germains with Mary and his cousin, to kiss the Queen's hand. Evelyn had messages from the deceased King, and every detail of the death had to be related. But the interview with the desolate Queen was a mournful one, and Queen Henrietta Maria wept bitterly.

During Evelyn's absence it had been rumoured in Paris that he had been knighted. But actually, like his father before him, Evelyn had firmly refused that honour "several times". Titles meant nothing to him. His friends in France were desperately anxious for every scrap of news regarding affairs in England and the welfare of their friends and relatives. But he had little cheer to impart. He could only describe the new regime under Cromwell and its awful austerities. It had been declared a capital crime to "speak, preach or write" against the Government, and an Act of Parliament had been passed which stated that "the people of England . . . are hereby constituted, made, established and confirmed to be a Commonwealth and Free State . . . and that without any King or House of Lords". His Majesty's statues had been thrown down from St. Paul's portico and the Exchange by the soldiers, and churches, tombs, and fine works of art had been wantonly defaced. All pictures in the royal collection which contained representations of the Virgin or Jesus had been burnt, and all sculptures destroyed as "idolatrous". The Collegiate and Cathedral libraries had also been sacked by the Roundheads, and they had torn up and burnt the rails of the communion tables, torn the prayer-books to pieces, broken the hour-glasses, and torn the surplices off the parsons' backs. They had even hired men at 2s. 6d. a day to break the lovely stained-glass windows. In London the copes of St. Paul's had been burnt to extract the gold, the silver vessels had been sold to buy artillery for Cromwell, the graves had been desecrated, while the pulpit and cross had been entirely destroyed. The Puritan soldiers, in fact, had been utterly carried away by their fanaticism.

The possibility now of the restoration of the monarchy seemed hopeless, as young King Charles had visited Jersey, where he was still regarded as King, but he had soon been obliged to fly for safety.

That autumn in Paris proved to be a "very sickly and mortal one", and the fearful news from Ireland added to the gloom and despondency, as apparently Cromwell had laid seige to Drogheda and had finally ordered the entire garrison to be put to the sword. "I forbade my soldiers to spare any that were in arms in the town, and I think that night they put to the sword about two thousand men. . . . I believe all the friars were knocked on the head promiscuously but two." These were said to be Cromwell's own words, and it was recorded that for five days the streets of Drogheda had run with blood. Then from the garrison the soldiers had turned their swords against the inhabitants, and a thousand unresisting victims who had sought sanctuary within the walls of the great church were killed.* Hundreds of prisoners, too, including

* Lingard's *History of England*.

women and children, had been shipped to the West Indies as slaves. This terrible news produced fearful anxiety amongst the Royalists, as many had friends and relatives in Ireland, and to obtain first-hand information from that stricken country was almost impossible.

Evelyn, as always during periods of anxiety, took refuge in creative writing, and he compiled at about this time, at the request of an English friend, a most interesting account of *The State of France*. It was an exhaustive and detailed account of the people, the Government, the Army, the Navy, the Orders of Chivalry, the Church, and the Nobility. It was printed and published privately. Evelyn had now lived in France for some years, and had had time to digest his opinions and impressions. Indeed, there was much to admire, and he had come to the conclusion that Paris, with its "hundreds of magnificent noblemen's houses", was the finest and most beautiful city in the world. In addition, every nobleman's palace possessed its own fine library and laboratory. Here, indeed, was culture.

But what had surprised Evelyn most in France were the powers invested in the Sovereign. The King had the power to start and stop wars, to impose taxes, and to nominate all church appointments; the French Parliament had no real power. "The French", wrote Evelyn, "are the sole nation in Europe that do idolise their Sovereign, unto whom they have likewise a more free and immediate access—without much ceremony —than in other Courts."

Evelyn had been particularly struck by the fact that the majority of French people "looked forty at the age of twenty. . . . The women then are extremely decayed, when ours, if not beautiful, are yet very tolerable." The "women of quality", however, were, for the most part, "as exquisite beauties as any the whole world produces. . . ." The wealthy French people, he had decided, "ate like Princes, and far exceed our tables; the common people, worse than dogs. . . . They are exceedingly courteous, and have generally their tongues well hung, so they are for the most part of jovial conversation."

Evelyn thought the French children charming, "yet though they be angels in the cradle, yet they are more like devils in the saddle, age generally showing that what she so soon bestows, she takes as fast away".

As for the French doctors, Evelyn declared that although some were "able and accomplished", the majority were "pretenders to physic", and he would rather risk his life with one English physician than "to a whole College of these French leeches".

Finally, Evelyn pointed out that the French people had "a natural dread and hate to the English, as esteeming us, for the most part, a rude, fierce and barbarous nation".

On the 27th of June, 1650, Evelyn again left Paris for England, where he stayed for about five weeks. When he returned to Paris, he and Sir Richard Browne were frequently invited to the sumptuous French Court, and were received in audience. There was no austerity here, and the balls, masques, and operas could only be described as "stupendously rich and gorgeous".

Meanwhile, Cromwell had not been idle, and his conquests were phenomenal. He had completely subjugated Ireland, and on the 23rd of September it was known that he had been victorious at the battle of Dunbar, and had then laid siege to the city of Edinburgh. The Scottish Parliament had retired to Perth, and young King Charles II had been crowned a covenanted king at Scone. Some two weeks later, however, it became known that he had succeeded in making a miraculous escape after the flight at Worcester. "This news", said Evelyn, "exceedingly rejoiced us." Almost all the Royalists, in fact, were convinced that it was only a matter of time before the monarchy was restored, and Sir Edward Hyde, Chancellor of the Exchequer to Charles I (later the Earl of Clarendon), wrote to Sir Richard Browne that there was "no reason to despair of better days, or that we may not eat cherries at Deptford again".

On the 6th of February, 1652, Evelyn said a final farewell to France and sailed to England. But what a sad home-coming it proved, as his dearly loved young sister Jane had died in "childbed" a month earlier, and she could not be there to welcome him. On every side, too, he was met by mournful faces; people had forgotten how to smile. England was now supposed to belong to "the people", the rabble, the ignorant, the levellers. Courtesy, culture, and respect for authority had all gone by the board; nobles and gentlemen were regarded as despicable tyrants, and kings were anathema. The new theory was that all should be brought to the same plebeian level, except, of course, those whom the Army had elected to power. They were the new masters, and would live in magnificence.

When Evelyn and his party landed at Dover, they were dressed, of course, in the French style, and as they drove to London in their coach a crowd of young hooligans ran beside them trying to frighten the horses, and hooting and crying "French dogs! French dogs!" At Rochester, where Evelyn stayed the night, the landlord of the inn sat down at the same table, and proceeded to belch and puff tobacco smoke in the faces of Evelyn and his friends. In London, the coach was again beset by little ruffians who viciously pelted them with squibs, soil, and stones. The carmen, too, had caught the general tone, and cursed the coaches loudly for daring to use the public highway. "You would imagine yourself", said Evelyn, "among a legion of devils, and in the suburbs of hell." He barely recognized the England of six years ago.

London had sadly deteriorated, and the noble buildings had been grossly neglected and defaced. Round the beautiful edifice of St. Paul's and the Banqueting House in Whitehall, for instance, many hideous sheds, warehouses, and shops had been erected, and the streets, through indiscriminate building, had become dangerously narrow. The paving had become "ruinous", and was full of holes. The spouts and gutters had also been allowed to deteriorate. After a heavy shower, therefore, the streets were flooded, and almost impassable. Many wharfs and magazines of wood, coal, etc., had been erected at random, and all idea of artistic planning or beauty had been abandoned.

The use of coal had also greatly increased owing to the scarcity of timber for fuel. During the war, wood had been used extensively for the building of ships. But now the smoke from thousands of coal fires made the London air in winter "hell upon earth". It left "a soot" on everything, and on all sides one heard ceaseless coughing and barking. On a damp day the fogs in winter were "intolerable", and this was quite a new horror in the capital. "I have been in a spacious church where I could not discern the minister for the smoke, nor hear him for the people's barking."

But the saddest change was to be observed in the churches, where, according to Evelyn, the prayers were "insipid, tedious and unmethodical", and intoned "in an affected and mysterious manner . . . like the gibberish of beggars and vagabonds". The service was unrecognizable, and the sermons painfully long and uninspiring. They were generally read from a book, and in some churches, to Evelyn's dismay, the scriptures were no longer read.

The beautiful church organs had all been ripped out by the Puritans, and many had been set up in taverns, where drunken revellers sang raucously to their music. In the taverns, incidentally, there was far more drunkenness, as it had become the custom to drink a health to everyone separately at the table. In France, as in England before the war, "the guests saluted the table with a single glass only, and thus temperate and decent behaviour was observed". "It is esteemed a piece of wit to make a man drunk", he wrote. The conversation at table, therefore, was "heavy, dull, insignificant . . . loud, querulous and impertinent". When the ladies retired the men would drink heavily and quarrel. And, indeed, at one party, Evelyn was horrified to see one of the male guests enter the room "all bloody and disordered", and his companions "pursuing him and dragging him by the hair". Finally, he shattered a beautiful mirror and two valuable pieces of porcelain.

Evelyn attended one or two balls at this time, and although he saw "many great beauties", he could not approve of ladies dancing with their dancing masters, "a custom quite unknown in France".

Apparently Hyde Park was now the fashionable promenade. But where was the delightful elegance of the past? It was depressing to see such a poor "assembly of wretched jades and hackney coaches". Adjoining were the Spring Gardens, where "one could dine on neats' tongues, salacious meats, trifles, tarts, etc.", and in the thickets of the gardens the amorous visitors often stayed until midnight.

All these comments on "The state of England" were written to a friend in France, and Evelyn also pointed out one very unhappy change: in many instances, family ties had broken down irreparably; the effect of the Rebellion had been to set parents against their children, and children against their parents; the time-honoured filial piety was no longer the fashion; it did not belong to the new freedom. Even in the upper classes this was noticeable, as the ruined fortunes of the Royalists had prevented them from educating their children according to their social positions.

Yet in describing England to his friend, Evelyn pointed out certain features which were unchangeable: "It must be avowed that England is a sweet and fertile country . . . the fields, the hills and the valleys are perpetually clad with a glorious and agreeable verdure." Evelyn did not forget to mention, either, the delightful bowling greens, the horse races, "the incomparable parks of fallow deer, the horses and hounds and the fox hunting". There was nothing like these in France. Evelyn had, however, one more comment to make: "All Englishmen ride so fast upon the road that one would swear there were some enemy in the area, and all the coaches in London seem to drive for midwives."

CHAPTER 4

UNDER CROMWELL'S RULE

EVELYN believed that Cromwell had assumed power without claim or title, and to him "the new tyranny" was almost unbearable. In the Capital itself, "the insolences were so great in the streets", and it was clear that although Cromwell had fought against a tyrannical monarchy, he had now become the most inflexible despot. Possibly this was inevitable, but Evelyn had little talent for speculative thought; he could only see the facts as they were.

By an edict of the mighty Cromwell, the Royal Arms in halls, churches, and public buildings all over England had been taken down, and the Puritans had ordered all maypoles to be destroyed, all sports forbidden on Sundays, and soldiers given power to enter private houses to see that the Sabbath was not profaned, and that the Parliament fasts were observed. Bells had been torn down from steeples, and vestments, organs, and musical instruments had all been banned from church services. Fiddlers were put in the stocks, and dancing and games were fiercely prevented. It was forbidden, also, to chant the psalms, and an Act had been passed which punished adultery with death, a penalty that had actually been inflicted in some cases.

But it was the Puritans' attempt to forbid the traditional gaiety of Christmas which roused the greatest indignation. Christmas, from time immemorial, had been celebrated as the season of joy, feasting, and goodwill, when families and friends met in love and affection, and quarrels were forgotten. The poor had always been entertained by the rich, and it was a festival which had always been particularly welcome during the dark days of winter.

The general opinion was that many Puritans were utterly insincere. They declared, for instance, that they disapproved of bowling, yet (as John Aubrey observed) "these hypocrites did bowl in a private green at their College every Sunday after sermon". The Puritans would not be seen drinking in taverns, either, yet would buy drinks and tipple at home. As for fine clothes, which they thought it a sin to wear, one Puritan had certainly ordered a splendid cloak of "French scarlet cloth at two guineas a yard, as good as any in London, trimmed with eight and a half dozen rich buttons".

It was obvious to Evelyn that ambitious men had discovered that the way to preferment and riches was to conform to Puritan ideas, and even to excel them in zeal, for no man could hope to rise to eminence except through Puritan favour. The sincere Puritans, therefore, were surrounded by men who paid them lip service but who were not honestly of their faith. And from these hypocrites, who were many in number, the nation had formed its opinion, thus bringing the whole regime into disrepute.

There was, however, one reason for thankfulness—one of the chief "rebels", Henry Ireton, Cromwell's son-in-law, had died of plague in Ireland, and Evelyn saw his splendid state funeral in London. He was buried like a prince.

Cromwell was frequently seen in London in a fine coach-and-six, and there were eighty guards, "in stately habits", with trumpets sounding. But when Evelyn met the great man being carried in his sedan chair through St. James's Park, "to take the air", he could not repress a shudder. The Protector's red nose seemed symbolical of the blood he had shed.

This, however, was the world one had to face, and Evelyn's plan now was to "compound with the soldiers" and settle at Sayes Court, which although "sequestered" by the Government, could apparently be bought back or leased through the Trustees of Forfeited Estates. Sayes Court was a picturesque old manor-house containing about fifteen rooms. There was a courtyard, good stables, an orchard, and a garden of about 2½ acres. Evelyn planned to repair and enlarge the house and to buy an adjoining 100 acres, in order to extend the garden. Already he had wonderful plans. Deptford was an attractive village, and only 5 miles from Whitehall, so was in every way convenient for London.

It was early in May that Evelyn heard from Paris that his wife Mary was expecting a child. Sir Richard Browne wrote quaintly:

Dear son,
   . . . I am now to acquaint you that your wife will (God blessing her with safety) bring you a depositum you left behind you here, of far greater value, viz. . . . a young cavalier, who hath within these few days unexpectedly discovered his vivacity, and plainly manifests his intention, within a few months, to come forth and be a citizen of the world. . . . And if grandfathers love more tenderly their remote offspring, you will not, I hope, envy me my share in the great contentment, who so passionately wish you and yours all happiness. . . . Your ever dearly-loving father, to serve you, R. Browne.

Mary was to sail from France shortly, and Evelyn hoped, by that time, to have the house and garden in some semblance of order. He also ordered, from a design he had brought from Paris, a handsome coach.

Mary sailed from France early in June, and Evelyn rode to Rye to await her arrival. Sailing was very unsafe, as England and Holland were still at war. Nevertheless, Mary's ship successfully evaded the Dutch fleet, and at about 4 in the afternoon, as he was playing bowls, the vessel appeared on the horizon, sailing into harbour at about 8 that evening, to his "great joy". Mary was accompanied by her mother, and had brought with her seventeen bails of furniture; she had been away from her native land for twelve years.

They stayed for a few days in Rye, and then went on to Tunbridge Wells, where Lady Browne wished to remain for a time in order to drink the waters. Here Evelyn left them, and rode back to Sayes Court; he was anxious to superintend the repairs and alterations still in progress. The day was hot, and having sent his servant on ahead, Evelyn rode at his leisure, in the shade. But suddenly, as he approached Bromley, two cut-throats sprang at him from the hedge, striking with long staves. They threw him down, took his sword, and dragged him into a nearby thicket, about a quarter of a mile from the highway, where they robbed him of two valuable rings, a pair of buckles set with rubies and diamonds, and his silver-hilted sword. They then bound him, set him up against an oak, and threatened to cut his throat if he cried out. Both were carrying pistols. Having tied the horse to a tree, they departed, and apparently did not take the horse as he was marked and cropped on both ears and was well known on that road. In this very unhappy position, tormented by flies, ants, and the sun, Evelyn remained for two hours, but at last succeeded in freeing his hands. He rode to a Colonel Blount, a Justice of the Peace, who immediately sent out a hue and cry. The next morning Evelyn went to London and ordered 500 tickets to be printed and dispersed by an officer of Goldsmiths' Hall. As a result, within two days, the stolen property, with the exception of the sword, had been recovered. A few weeks later one of the robbers was tried, but Evelyn, "not willing to hang the fellow", refused to give evidence. (Later the man was charged with some other crime, and, refusing to plead, was "pressed to death".)

And now began for Evelyn that admirable family life, the details of which he so carefully set down in his diary. Within a very short time he was the leasehold owner of Sayes Court, and had settled down as a country gentleman. His first son, Richard, was born on the 24th of August, 1652, and was a source of great pride and pleasure. Life under the Commonwealth was irksome but bearable. Indeed, there was no alternative.

But the year 1653 dawned with happier prospects, as Cromwell, who had become "The Lord Protector", was endeavouring to establish peace everywhere. He was now called his "Highness", and although a House of Commons and a new House of Lords had been formed, his rule was absolute. Nevertheless, justice was maintained, the law was fairly administered, and property was secure. It was clear, too, that he had made England the most formidable power in the world. She was now supreme on the ocean, and able to dictate peace to the United Provinces; the Pope himself had been forced to preach humanity to Popish princes, for Cromwell had said that unless favour was shown to the Protestants, the English guns would be heard in the castle of St. Angelo.

The ceremony of Cromwell's installation had taken place at Westminster Hall, and the judges in their robes, the Council of the Commonwealth, the Lord Mayor, Aldermen, and Recorder of London, and the chief officers of the Army had all been present. Later, seated in a splendid chair of state in the Banqueting House at Whitehall, he had received congratulations from foreign ambassadors. Cromwell was king, therefore, in all but name. But "the public had given no sign of approbation". He had delivered the nation from tyranny, but they were not grateful, as the religious upheaval, to the majority of men, was wholly unacceptable. Everything had changed. Communion services—so

45

dear to the truly pious—were forbidden, and Evelyn was obliged to ask a friend to take the service in his own private chapel. In fact, Evelyn now seldom went to church, as the parish churches were "filled with sectaries of all sorts, blasphemous and ignorant mechanics usurping the pulpits everywhere".

Evelyn had formed a close friendship with that gifted author and splendid parson Dr. Jeremy Taylor, who had fearlessly and with a complete disregard for his own safety propounded from the pulpit the principles in which he believed. But he had already been imprisoned for attacking the Puritan preachers in the preface to his collection of prayers. "It is an evil time and we ought not to hold our peace", wrote Jeremy Taylor to Evelyn, and Evelyn had replied, "Julianus Redivivus can shut the schools indeed and the temples, but he cannot hinder our private intercourses and devotions, where the breast is the chapel and the heart is the altar. . . . God will accept what remains, and supply what is necessary. The purest ages passed under the cruelest persecution."

On Sunday afternoons Evelyn frequently stayed at home in order to catechize and instruct his household. But he was really alarmed when Cromwell decreed that ministers of the Church of England should no longer teach or preach in any schools, on pain of imprisonment or exile. "So this", wrote Evelyn in his diary, "was the mournfulest day that in my life I had seen, or the Church of England herself since the Reformation. . . . The Lord Jesus pity our distressed Church and bring back the captivity of Zion."

The fearless Jeremy Taylor, at about this time, was again sent to the Tower because he had included in his new book a picture of Christ praying, contrary to a recent Act concerning "scandalous pictures". A few weeks later he was released, but during his imprisonment his "two sweet hopeful boys" died of smallpox, and there was no one to comfort his poor bereaved wife. This was a great grief. The gentle and kindly parson was also "much shaken by his imprisonment". But from this time Evelyn allowed him a pension. "Sir, you are too kind to me", wrote Jeremy Taylor. "I can only love you, and honour you, and pray for you. I am a debtor for your prayers, for the comfort of your letters, for the charity of your hand, and the affections of your heart."

The strict Puritan regime, however, could not seriously interfere with that delightful pastime, travel, and Evelyn was now determined to show to Mary the beauties of her native land. She had left England when she was five years old, and her many relatives were anxious to meet them both. On the 4th of June, 1654, therefore, Evelyn and Mary set out in their coach-and-four. They dined at Windsor, and inspected St. George's Chapel and the castle; then, having stayed the night at Reading, they went on to the house of Lord Craven. From Newbury they proceeded to the mansion of Mary's uncle, Sir Edward Hungerford, where they were hospitably entertained for some days. Bath and Bristol came next, and from there they drove to Oxford, where they were handsomely entertained, met many old friends (including "that miracle of a youth, Christopher Wren"), and visited all the colleges. After staying for two weeks in Oxford they drove to another uncle of Mary's, Sir John Glanville, formerly Speaker of the House of Commons. This patriot had actually burned down his mansion to prevent the rebels making a garrison of it. A King's man, indeed!

Salisbury was the next port of call, and they visited Wilton, the handsome seat of the Earl of Pembroke. They then stayed for a time with Mary's grandfather, Sir John Pretyman. From thence they drove to Gloucester, Worcester, Warwick, Coventry, Nottingham (where many of the poor lived in rocks and caves), York, Hull, Beverley, Lincoln, and Grantham.

It was not until the end of the month that Evelyn and Mary set their faces towards home, visiting Cambridge on the way. And here, indeed, was a feast of architecture. They visited all the colleges, and some were highly praised by Evelyn, but others he found disappointing. As for the town of Cambridge itself, he condemned it at once as a "low, dirty, unpleasant place, the streets ill-paved, the air thick and infected by the fens. Nor are its churches anything considerable in comparison with Oxford."

After Cambridge, the travellers drove to "that goodly palace, Audley End . . . one of the stateliest in the kingdom", and when, finally, they arrived back at Sayes Court, they had completed a round journey of some 700 miles, all by coach.

There was, of course, no Court now to which one owed a duty, but on the 11th of February, 1656, Evelyn "ventured" to go to Whitehall, which he had not seen for many years. He found it "very glorious and well-furnished". Cromwell, however, was not, from all accounts, a happy man; he went constantly in fear of his life. He spent £60,000 a year on "intelligence", and postmasters and secretaries were all in his pay; nothing escaped him. Nevertheless, he had realized that both the Levellers and the Royalists were anxious to hurl him from power, and he had a guard of 150 men, he wore armour under his clothes, and he never slept for more than three nights in the same bed. He wore daggers on his person, and his bodyguard carried not only swords but pistols. His mother never heard the sound of a pistol shot without exclaiming dramatically "My son is shot!" In addition, his health had deteriorated, he was in debt, and many of his friends had proved treacherous. His dearly loved daughter, Mrs. Claypole, was a staunch Royalist, and during her illness she had blamed him severely, in her delirium, for the blood he had shed.

Evelyn had seen Cromwell "riding in triumph through the city to feast at the Lord Mayor's", and this seemed "in contradiction to all custom and decency". Evelyn had also been present at the launching of one of Cromwell's ships, and to Evelyn's disgust, in the prow was a representation of the Protector, crowned with laurels, on horseback, "trampling six nations under foot—a Scotsman, an Irishman, a Dutchman, a Frenchman, a Spaniard and an Englishman". The inscription was "God be with us".

But the severity of the Puritans was unhappily brought home to Evelyn on Christmas Day, 1657, when during a church service in London the building was suddenly surrounded by soldiers. Some members of the congregation were sent to prison, while Evelyn and his party were taken to a room and examined. They were told that the law forbade the use of the Common Prayer, and the prayers for King Charles. The next day Evelyn was released, but the incident had angered him, and he wrote in his diary, "Such a dangerous, treacherous time!" A little later he visited Eltham Palace, and found the chapel in "miserable ruins, the noble woods and park having been destroyed by the rebels". But was not this typical of soldiers? They cared nothing for lovely medieval architecture, although such buildings could never be replaced. When, therefore, a number of Puritan soldiers were billeted on him, Evelyn could barely bid them welcome. Fortunately ("thank God!") they "departed the next day for Flanders".

Evelyn still corresponded with the exiled King Charles and the Queen Mother, and through his acquaintance with the Holland Ambassador he was sometimes able to send important items of news. The restoration of the Monarchy seemed unlikely, but it was his fervent hope. Meanwhile, the best solace for this austere existence was creative work, and as books on architecture were scarce, Evelyn was compiling a monograph on the subject and translating from the French, Italian, and Latin. His essay on Lucretius, his first publication, had been printed, but the result was bitterly disappointing, as in his absence he had had to rely on a friend for the correction of the proofs, and there were many errors. "Never was book so abominably misused by the printer", recorded Evelyn, "never copy so negligently surveyed by anyone who undertook to look after the proof-sheets with all exactness and care." For his first attempt at authorship it was a minor tragedy.

Evelyn was also writing various pamphlets—his thoughts on certain subjects, and some of these would certainly be printed. At the same time he was repairing Sayes Court, and rebuilding the chapel, kitchens, buttery, walls, still-house, and orangery. He was planting new orchards—choosing his time carefully when the moon was new—and he was planning with immense enthusiasm a wonderful garden, the dream of his life. It was to be the epitome of all the glorious pleasure grounds he had seen in France and Italy.

His extensive garden, indeed, soon took shape, and became celebrated, not only for its magnificent show of flowers, trees, and shrubs, but for its salads, vegetables, and choice fruit. His hothouses were famous, and every detail of the work was planned and executed with passionate enthusiasm. He was a perfectionist, and set the standard for his staff. Labour was cheap and plentiful, and to work in "Mr. Evelyn's garden" was considered a coveted honour.

One day, rather to his surprise, the President of Cromwell's Council and a party of his friends arrived on a visit to Sayes Court, and they made an extensive tour of the house and grounds. They greatly admired the rare and beautiful birds in the aviaries, the handsome library, the picture gallery, and Evelyn's collection of rare coins, porcelain, ivories, and medals. Samuel Pepys also paid a visit to Sayes Court, and declared that it was "a most beautiful place".

At about this time Evelyn made several tours of the country, as most of his friends were now extending and rebuilding their mansions which had been wholly neglected during the war; there was a perfect passion

49

for building, and Evelyn was already regarded as an expert on such matters; they were all anxious for his advice. But when the country seat he visited was "naked" (devoid of trees), or badly sited, and when the inevitable avenue of trees was "ungraceful", Evelyn, the soul of tact, found it hard to hide his disapproval. He could so easily have put matters right had he been consulted in time.

Mary rarely accompanied him on these journeys, as she usually presented him with a child each year, and a journey by coach or on horseback over rough roads was out of the question. It was a sad fact that very few of his children lived long. "A most likely child" would suddenly develop convulsion fits and sigh out its tiny life. Others seemed to die for no reason at all; so many weird diseases lay in wait for the innocent young. But his friends and relatives all suffered such losses constantly. "Children are such blossoms as every trifling wind deflowers", he said.

Yet there was one loss at this time which brought a very heavy grief to Evelyn and Mary. His first-born, Richard, a beautiful, brilliant child, aged five, died after much suffering. He had been ill for some time with a mysterious disease, and apparently nothing could be done. Richard was an infant prodigy, and Evelyn had been so anxious to make him a scholar that the child had been urged to learn, probably beyond his capacity. He could read before he was five, decline all the nouns, "conjugate the verbs regular, turn English into Latin, construe and prove what he read, and had a strong passion for Greek". He had "a wonderful disposition for mathematics" and could demonstrate propositions of Euclid. He had been "all life and prettinesse", and to see him suffer was torture. "Sweet Jesus, save me, deliver me, pardon my sins, let Thine angels receive me", he cried in the agony of his pain. "Such a child I never saw", said Evelyn. "For such a child I bless God, in whose bosom he is. . . . In my opinion he was suffocated by the women and maids that tended him and covered him too hot with blankets as he lay in a cradle, near an excessive hot fire in a close room. . . . The Lord Jesus sanctify this and all my other afflictions. Amen. Here ends the joy of my life, and for which I go even mourning to the grave."

But apparently "the afflicting hand of God" was still upon Evelyn, as his youngest son died less than three weeks later; he was not yet a month old. "God's holy will be done", said Evelyn resignedly, and both boys were buried in Deptford church. Dr. Jeremy Taylor, and many friends and relatives, came to offer their condolences, but it was Dr. Taylor who brought such wonderful comfort. "Remember, sir", he said, "your two boys are two bright stars; their innocence is secured, and you shall never hear evil of them again. Their state is safe. . . . Strive to be an example and a comfort to your lady . . . and make it appear that you are more to her than ten sons." What a good friend Dr. Taylor was! But the loss of little children, on whom one had lavished such tender care, was very puzzling. Why did God bring them into the world if only to snatch them away again? Even the children embroidered on their samplers

> He's most in debt who lingers out the day.
> Who dies betimes has less and less to pay.

It was at this time that Evelyn translated, from the Greek, *The Golden Book of St. Chrystostom on the Education of Children*. It was dedicated to his brothers George and Richard, who were also mourning the loss of children. Evelyn felt that this book might be a consolation. "But my tears mingle so fast with my ink", he wrote, "that I must break off here and be silent. . . . Dear brothers, indulge me these excesses."

The winter had been an extremely cold one, and the spring which followed was "a sickly time" with many serious epidemics. Evelyn and his family spent the summer at Wotton as Evelyn was advising and assisting his brother with improvements to the gardens, always an enjoyable task.

But on returning to Sayes Court in September, Evelyn was shocked to find that a tremendous hurricane in August had caused widespread damage to his trees and fruit. Many of the handsomest trees had been blown down. And the storm, apparently, had driven up the Thames, to Deptford, an enormous whale, 58 feet long. This was regarded as a definite omen of some significant event, and on the 3rd of September Cromwell died. Gorgeously he lay in state in the Great Hall of Somerset House, where the ceilings and walls were covered with black velvet and hung with escutcheons. Five hundred candles burned, and the effigy, seated on a raised dais, wearing robes of crimson velvet trimmed with ermine, held a golden sceptre in one hand and a globe in the other. On the head was a glittering crown, the crown he had never dared to wear during life.

Evelyn attended the superb funeral—though not as a mourner; merely as a spectator—and apparently the cost was £60,000. The body was carried on a velvet bed of state drawn by six horses, the pall being held by his new lords. Again the effigy was there, in royal robes, and there were banners and hatchments, heralds in their gorgeous uniforms, and richly caparisoned horses "embroidered all over with gold". There were guards, soldiers, and innumerable mourners. "Yet", recorded Evelyn, "it was the joyfullest funeral I ever saw, for there were none that cried but dogs, which the soldiers hooted away with a barbarous noise, drinking and taking tobacco in the streets as they went." Certainly Evelyn could not mourn for Cromwell, and he recorded in his diary that there was "a wonderful and sudden change in the face of the public".

Indeed, what did the future hold in store? Surely it might now be possible to restore the monarchy. Evelyn had kept in touch, by pre-arranged cipher, with the young exiled King, his ministers, and the widowed Queen, and his loyalty to the royal house was unshakable. This was his dream, and he foresaw, if it could be achieved, the return of sanity, gracious living, religious freedom, an end to persecution, and the restoration of that happy era before the Puritans had assumed power. The literary activity of the clergy, in spite of rigid censorship, had never flagged during Cromwell's time, and pamphlets and treatises had prepared the way.

The future, in fact, was at long last showing some glimmerings of light, for the successor to Cromwell was his son Richard. And could this young man ever take the place of such a mighty man as Cromwell? Could he rule England, and control those freedom-loving, outspoken, intensely individual Englishmen? Men of all classes had been toughened and stirred by war. Whatever their convictions, they would make their voices heard. It had not been an easy task for Cromwell. It would be a far more difficult one for his unwarlike and inexperienced successor.

CHAPTER 5

THE RESTORATION

THE Great Protector was dead, and his son Richard had succeeded him. Richard's claims had been freely admitted, accompanied by the most fulsome addresses, and he was accorded the same state and ceremony which had attended his father. Yet it was soon clear that this amiable, modest young man, who had no enemies and was popular even with the Cavaliers, could not rule England. As the months passed, a powerful army cabal formed against him, and they insisted that the Parliament should be dissolved. Later, the officers angrily besieged his palace, and, finally, an armed group entered his apartment and threatened him with violence if he refused their demands.

"The nation is in extreme confusion and unsettled", recorded Evelyn. "Several pretenders and parties strive for the government . . . the poor Church of England, as it were, breathing her last, so sad a face of things has overspread us." And, he added, "Lord have mercy upon us".

After considerable hesitation, Richard Cromwell dissolved the Parliament, and shortly after signed a formal abdication of the supreme authority. He was in debt, he knew little of government, and he was not ambitious. He was surrounded by false friends and powerful enemies. But the country was now indubitably in danger.

It was at this juncture that Evelyn endeavoured to test the attitude of Holland towards the Restoration of the Monarchy, and the matter was discussed when he dined one day with the Dutch Ambassador. But the Ambassador (as Evelyn records in his diary) said guardedly that his nation did nothing out of gratitude, but "mind only their own profit".

53

The English nation, therefore, must not expect assistance towards the restoration of their banished King. "This was to me", wrote Evelyn, "no very grateful discourse, though an ingenuous confession." It seemed obvious to Evelyn and his friends, however, that the old constitution could not be re-established under a new dynasty. There were therefore only two alternatives—either the restoration of the Stuarts or the Army. But surely the Stuarts were preferable to a succession of military dictators raised to power by bloody revolutions. The banished royal family had expiated its faults, and the King, if restored, would certainly take warning from the fate of his father. The country passionately desired peace and freedom, and the urgent cry of the people was for a free Parliament. The Army still strongly opposed the idea of a monarchy, but they were now divided, and had no leader.

At the "great hazard of his life", therefore (as he recorded in his diary), Evelyn went to see his old school friend, Colonel Morley, who was one of the five Commissioners of the Army. Morley was also Lieutenant of the Tower of London and in command of the city; his brother-in-law was Governor of Portsmouth. Colonel Morley was a man of parts, and extremely influential in Sussex, as he had "good credit" with many of the officers of the Fleet. Evelyn felt certain that he would not betray him. On the 12th of January, 1660, Evelyn wrote again to Morley, and on the 22nd, at an interview, handed to him a pamphlet written by himself entitled *An Apology for the Royal Party*. This apparently convinced the Colonel that a restoration of the monarchy might be the only solution to the country's problems, but he himself could promise nothing. Should the restoration be achieved, however, he asked Evelyn to obtain the King's pardon for him and for some of his relatives. This Evelyn was able to promise, and also to assure Morley that the King would reward his services if he was restored. "We have now no government in the nation", recorded Evelyn. "All in confusion; no magistrates, either owned or pretended, but the soldiers, and they not agreed." About a week later he became dangerously ill with malaria. Malaria was extremely common, owing to the many miles of undrained fens in the country, where the malaria mosquito bred extensively. But he himself believed that the cause of his illness was "the cruel effects of the spleen, and other distempers". Certainly he had had a most anxious time. He had believed that Morley was capable of bringing about the restoration of the King, which "lay entirely in his hands". "What did I not undergo of danger in this connection?" he recorded. "O, the sottish omission of this gentleman!"

Meanwhile, events were moving swiftly. General Lambert and his forces were scattered, and on the 3rd of February, 1660, General Monk marched into England from Scotland with his army of 7000 veterans. This remarkable man was a brilliant soldier, and had been Commander-in-Chief to Cromwell. It was generally believed that he held the key to the future of England, and most people were looking to him alone "to recall the old long-interrupted Parliament, and settle the nation in some order". On the 10th of February he broke down the gates of the city of London, and on the following day marched to Whitehall and dissolved the Rump Parliament. All day and night the streets were crammed with people shouting "A free Parliament! A free Parliament!" And Monk had ridden calmly past. "Pray be quiet. Ye *shall* have a free Parliament", he said. This was late at night, but cheers had gone up, and soon the sky was red with the light of bonfires. The church bells began to ring, and thousands of rumps were roasted in the streets. There was "universal jubilee." The crowds went wild with delight, and wherever Monk appeared he was surrounded by people, shouting and blessing his name. The next day maypoles were set up in every crossway and on all village greens. An enormous one was erected in the Strand, near Drury Lane. Soon, too, writs were issued for a general election. It was clear that the Restoration of the Monarchy was imminent.

Evelyn, lying on his sick bed, drank in every scrap of news with thankfulness. He had hoped to have arranged the Restoration through Colonel Morley, and he had been disappointed. Yet he had certainly played his part in the drama that was now taking place. He had the satisfaction of knowing that General Monk had been influenced, when he entered the city of London, by the fact that he was assured of Colonel Morley's support in the fortress of the Tower of London and of support from the important counties of Surrey, Sussex, and Hampshire with their seaports. But this was not all. Evelyn had also contributed to the Restoration by a timely piece of propaganda, as a certain Marchmont Needham had published a coarse attack on the character of Charles II, and Evelyn had printed a complete refutation—*The News from Brussels Unmasked*. He had actually risen from his sickbed to write this, and as a result had had a relapse. But the pamphlet had had its effect; Evelyn was believed and Needham discredited.

The decision to restore the monarchy was now accepted by both Houses, and King Charles was to be asked to return to England. By the 14th of April Evelyn was convalescent and able to travel down to Wotton where, in his "sweet native air", he hoped to recover his health. Meanwhile his timely *Apology for the King* was widely read and praised.

Enthusiasm for the Restoration of the Monarchy was now whipped up, and as is the way with crowds, enthusiasm grew like a snowball. The exiled King had actually done nothing to merit the affections of his people, yet Parliament decided to send him £500 "with which to buy a jewel", and "£50,000 for his present use". The twelve City Companies also gave £1000 each as a present. Evelyn was jubilant, and he and Lord Berkley were asked to go to Holland to hand to the King the official address inviting him to return. Unfortunately Evelyn was as yet too unwell to undertake the journey. Nevertheless he received a gracious message from King Charles, and an offer of the Order of the Bath. This was politely refused.

The royal arms were now set up everywhere, and the King was proclaimed in every town and village. In front of the Royal Exchange an enormous bonfire was lighted; there were frenzied shouts of "God bless King Charles the Second", and men knelt in the streets to drink his health. They wept with emotion. Incidentally, the King had agreed to an Act of Oblivion to all who had taken part in the rebellion.

Early in May a gallant fleet set sail for Holland, its sole purpose being to bring home King Charles, the man with the genuine title. With pendants loose, guns roaring, and caps flying, the cry of *Vive le Roys!* echoed from one ship's company to another; the excitement was tremendous.

The King finally arrived at Dover on the 25th of May, 1660. He had been in exile for seventeen years, and was thirty years of age. He was accompanied by his two brothers, the Duke of York and the Duke of Gloucester, and was received by General Monk "with all imaginable love and respect". Here, too, to welcome him were crowds of horsemen, citizens, and noblemen. On the journey to London, bells rang joyfully from every steeple, and the streets of the towns through which he passed were strewn with flowers and festooned with garlands, bright scarves, and gold chains. Upon Blackheath, the Army of the Commonwealth (30,000 men) was drawn up to receive and escort the royal cavalcade, and when Charles approached Whitehall his train was met by some of the most eminent citizens, "all well mounted, all in black velvet coats with chains of gold about their necks, and every one his footman, with suit, cassock and ribands of the order of his Company". The country was mad with enthusiasm. "I stood in the Strand and beheld it, and blessed God", wrote Evelyn in his diary. "And all this was done without one drop of blood shed, and by that very army which rebelled against him; but it was the Lord's doing, for such a restoration was never mentioned in any history, ancient or modern, since the return of the Jews from the Babylonish captivity. . . ." The King declared, indeed, to his sister, that he was so "dreadfully stunned" by the acclamations of the people that he did not know whether he was writing sense or nonsense.

At the earliest opportunity Evelyn went to Court to pay his respects to the King, for whom he had letters from the Queen Mother, and the King welcomed him warmly as his "old acquaintance". Evelyn, in fact, "went to and from Whitehall all the week about business", and it was at this time that Sir Richard Browne, who had been given a post at Court, arrived in England. He was to live with Evelyn.

Charles now kept open house every day, and thousands of men, women, and children came to the Palace to kiss his hands; he insisting that "none should be kept out". Those who had been properly presented might also, without invitation, go to see him dine, sup, dance or play at hazard. His Majesty had apparently brought from the Continent a love of French music and French food, and he liked to walk up and down his long galleries, followed by his little dogs, his courtiers, and pretty women. It was observed, too, that the great fires in the Palace were kept burning all night. There was also a continual striking and chiming from the innumerable clocks.

The King, in his Declaration, had promised liberty of conscience in matters of religion, and the examination by Parliament of all claims to land with contested titles. He had agreed to satisfy the Army under General Monk with regard to their arrears of pay, and to give the same rank to his officers when they entered the King's service.* All this seemed very satisfactory.

* Goldsmith's *History of England*, vol. 2, p. 309.

Many who came to Charles's Court were, of course, strangers to this restored King, and they looked with curiosity at this swarthy, suave, indolent man. He was tall and elegant, with fine dark eyes, but the features were coarse; he had an ugly mouth, and the bold expression was decidedly unattractive. That he had a certain charm, however, was undeniable, and he was a good raconteur, although he repeated himself. Evelyn had known Charles since boyhood, but he barely recognized this man, so unlike his father, who appeared to be both shallow and frivolous. His irresponsible attitude to life, of course, had been fostered during his exile, when his position had been a most difficult one. Now, apparently, he intended to model his Court on that of King Louis XIV, which was, as Evelyn knew, opulently magnificent. Had he also learnt from the French Court some other unattractive habits? His small spaniels, for instance, "followed him and lay in his bedchamber, where he often suffered the bitches to puppy and give suck, which rendered it very offensive, and indeed made the whole Court nasty and stinking" (Evelyn). It soon became clear, too, that the King loathed business, and even the clerks tittered at his fatuous remarks when he sat in Council. Yet when he spoke to his courtiers of his escape from the battle of Worcester, how he had hidden in the oak, and had travelled four days and nights, weary and footsore, "every step up to his knees in dirt, with nothing but a green coat and a pair of country breeches on", his hearers wept.

It was observed by Evelyn, as the weeks passed, that the most worthless people were able to obtain from the King titles, places, land, state secrets, and pardons simply because it was painful for him to refuse. His bounty, in fact, went to the most shameless and the most importunate. Men who could insinuate themselves with his mistresses could also hope to rise in the world without rendering any service to the Government. One courtier would get a frigate, another a company, and another a lease of Crown lands on easy terms. Shame and honour apparently meant nothing to this king, and—perhaps inevitably—he had little faith in human nature.

Plate, hangings, pictures, and other goods which had been pillaged from Whitehall during the "rebellion" were now brought back to the Palace; it became the fashion to return the stolen goods. Then on the 23rd of June, the King revived the ancient royal ceremony of "touching for the evil" (a disease called scrofula), and hundreds of sick children were brought to the Banqueting House. They knelt before the King, and he stroked their cheeks with his hands. He then put round each neck a piece of "angel-gold" strung on white ribbon. From this date, the King "touched" about 200 children every Friday, but as these were accompanied by their friends, relatives, and hundreds of onlookers, the crowds were so great that children were frequently crushed to death. There were heart-rending scenes. It was one mad scramble for places.

On the 5th of July the King attended a splendid feast at Whitehall, and the streets were adorned with pageants "at immense cost". When he came down to Deptford, too, Evelyn arranged for a hundred young girls, dressed in white and carrying baskets of flowers, to walk before him and strew flowers in his path. Money, of course, was flowing like water, and both men and women had gone mad with gaiety. It was a violent reaction against the rigid austerity of the Puritans. The King and his licentious Court set the example, and it was said by the old Cavaliers that one half of what the King squandered on his concubines and buffoons would have gladdened the hearts of many who had been ruined in his father's cause, men who had melted down their plate, given of their lands, and advanced large sums of money. They expected some recompense, and many put forward their claims, but they were too proud to go down on their knees and beg. There had been a sudden fall in rents, and the income of every landed proprietor had diminished by 5s. in the £. Meanwhile, thousands of pounds in gold changed hands every night at the royal gambling tables.

The King, of course, was no fool, and had some smattering of culture. He was interested in chemistry, mechanics, and physics. He understood navigation and something of naval architecture. He enjoyed discussing these matters, and was an excellent conversationalist. Men felt at ease with him. Indeed, Charles, remembering the fate of his father, was treading very warily, and was affable and acquiescent. He gave audiences and listened patiently to many petitions. But even his most ardent admirers were a little disconcerted at the presence of his eldest illegitimate son, James Crofts, aged about eleven. He was the son of Lucy Walters, "a Welsh girl of great beauty but of weak understanding and dissolute manners", who had been one of Charles's mistresses while he was on the Continent. This boy was attended by pages, lived in the palace, and was treated like a prince. When he travelled, he was received with regal

59

pomp, and was escorted from mansion to mansion by a long cavalcade of armed gentlemen and yeomen. Watchmen were ordered by the magistrates to proclaim his arrival through the streets of the city, bonfires were lighted, windows were illuminated, and the bells rang. He "touched" for the King's evil, and on his escutcheon both the lions of England and the lilies of France were displayed. It was rumoured that the King had married Lucy Walters, but there was not the slightest evidence for this, and the King categorically denied it.

Another important member of the royal family was James, the Duke of York, who was particularly interested in naval matters. He had recently married, when she was expecting his child, Anne Hyde, the daughter of Edward Hyde, later Earl of Clarendon. Arabella Churchill, the daughter of a poor Cavalier, was also one of his mistresses,* though Charles had declared laughingly that both were so ugly that they must have been chosen as a penance.

This, then, was the Court which Evelyn frequently attended, and he strongly disapproved of much that he observed. But was it not natural that this reaction, in all classes, should occur? Was it not natural for men now to be suspicious of all pretensions to sanctity and all protestations of loyalty? For in whom could one have faith? A hereditary monarchy had been abolished and restored; a new dynasty had rapidly risen to the height of power and then suddenly been hurled down; a new representative system had been devised, tried, and abandoned. Masses of property had been violently transferred from Cavaliers to Roundheads and then back again from Roundheads to Cavaliers. In the course of a few years the ecclesiastical and civil policy of the country had repeatedly changed, and the men who had prospered had been the sycophants and time-servers. How could any ambitious man have faith in any doctrine or enthusiasm for any cause? Had he not seen so many excellent institutions swept away, so many noble ideas discarded? Politics were obviously nothing but a game of chance, and the most cunning and plausible rogues rose to the top.

The disillusionment and cynicism had now invaded all the higher ranks of society, and the lighter kinds of literature echoed the general attitude.

Another very curious change of mind was to be observed, for men at

* She later bore four children to James.

Court now spoke of Cromwell and his generals as murderers, and those who had served the great man and been rewarded were loudest in their denunciations. On the 14th of October, 1660, therefore, the men who had sentenced King Charles to death were tried, and in the following week ten were executed in the presence of the King. "I saw not their execution", wrote Evelyn, "but met their quarters, mangled and cut and reeking, in baskets, on the hurdle. Oh, the miraculous Providence of God!" The rest of the prisoners were reprieved and later sent to various prisons.

A few weeks later the Parliament voted that the bodies of Oliver Cromwell, Ireton, and Bradshaw should be taken out of their superb tombs in the Abbey and drawn to the gallows at Tyburn, there to be hanged. "Look back", wrote Evelyn in his diary, "and be astonished, and fear God and honour the King, but meddle not with them that are given to change." The bodies were hanged in their shrouds, and then cut down and decapitated and buried. Many spectators watched this gruesome ceremony. Finally, the heads were set on spikes on Westminster Hall. Cromwell, the man who had made England great, and saved her from tyranny, was treated like the most loathsome malefactor. He had founded her colonial empire, established her Navy, conquered Scotland and Ireland, and humbled Holland and Spain. This was his reward.

The Queen Mother, Henrietta Maria, who had been in exile for nearly twenty years, now returned to England, accompanied by her train and her daughter, the Princess Henrietta. Evelyn knew the Queen Mother well, and he and Mary duly attended her Court to pay their respects. It was a happy meeting of many old friends. The King himself took charge of Mary, and brought her into the Queen Mother's presence. He then showed Mary his private closet and his collection of pictures, jewels, crystal vases, ivories, coins, old maps, miniatures, medallions, and models of ships. Alas, the Queen Mother was no longer beautiful. Time and sorrow had done their work, and apparently the sight of her old apartments had caused her acute distress; she had burst into a paroxysm of weeping, calling herself the desolate widow of Charles. Her Dowager Palace of Somerset House was miserably dilapidated. "Ruins and desolation are round and about me", she sobbed. She related, too, to her Court, "divers passages of her escapes during the rebellion" and civil war, and the company wept in sympathy. But the Queen was well provided for,

61

as the Commons had settled on her an income of £60,000 a year, and they had promised to restore Somerset House with the splendid additions she required. The Queen Mother was also mourning for her son, the Duke of Gloucester, who had just died of the smallpox. Then about a month after her arrival, her daughter, the young Princess of Orange, died from the same fatal disease; she was twenty-eight and a widow.

The new Parliament, which was chiefly composed of men who had fought for the Crown and the Church, now began to legislate, and the Liturgy, which had been banished from church services during the Commonwealth, was ordered to be used again. Every Member, too, "on pain of expulsion", had to take the Sacrament according to the form prescribed by the old Liturgy. Another Act acknowledged the power of the sword to lie solely in the King, and required all officials of corporations to swear that they held resistance to the King's authority to be in all cases unlawful.

The greatest labour of government at this time devolved on the Earl of Clarendon, who was Chancellor of the Realm. Evelyn knew him intimately. Clarendon was remarkably able, and an eloquent speaker, but owing to his long exile, England, to him, was the England of his youth. He still believed in "the divine right of Kings". Evelyn much admired his tremendous ability, but often trembled for his fate; the "old school" were not in favour.

Evelyn had been appointed one of the commissioners for "reforming the Buildings, Streets, Ways and Encumbrances, and regulating the hackney carriages in the City of London". He was also on the Commission of Sewers and the Commission for regulating the Mint. For his services, indeed, the King had again offered to create him a Knight of the Bath, but Evelyn had declined the honour. Charles also frequently consulted him with regard to palace architecture and the royal gardens, and occasionally Evelyn sailed with him on his yacht and accompanied him otter hunting.

Another matter which Evelyn discussed with the King was the growing pollution of the atmosphere in London. He was convinced that the coal-smoke and gases poisoned the air and begrimed and defaced noble buildings. Evelyn also declared that they spoilt the fruit grown in London gardens, which now "tasted bitter and ungrateful". Evelyn's urgent advice was that chimneys should be built higher so that the smoke and fumes would be carried into the upper atmosphere, and he had been asked by the King to prepare a paper on the subject.

Evelyn was also protesting, whenever he found an opportunity, against the ancient custom of burying the dead in churches and churchyards, a practice he considered extremely unhealthy. He had discovered, however, that most people liked to be buried "in company" and in "*good* company".

But the King, as was now plain to all, was not genuinely interested in either the House of Commons or in legislation. He was thoroughly enjoying his splendid new life. He had a handsome mistress, a Mrs. Barbara Palmer, who, according to Bishop Burnet, was "a woman of great beauty, but most enormously vicious and ravenous, foolish but imperious. . . . His passion for her did so disorder him that often he was not master of himself, nor capable of minding business." Her husband, Roger Palmer, had just been created Earl of Castlemaine and Baron of Limerick in Ireland, and Charles appeared publicly with his mistress everywhere, her superb jewels being the envy of the Court ladies.

Triumphal arches for the coronation were now set up in the main streets of London, and on the 22nd of April the King made his traditional progress through the city. The coronation itself was costly and magnificent. "The streets were strewn with flowers, houses hung with rich tapestry, windows and balconies full of ladies, the City Companies with their banners and loud music, fountains running wine, bells ringing." Evelyn saw the whole colourful spectacle, and at the end of the day the city had "a light like a glory round it with bonfires". There were also many splendid city feasts, some of which Evelyn attended.

But the year of 1662 dawned with such gloomy prospects that a general fast was ordered throughout the whole nation, "to avert God's heavy judgement on this land". Incessant rain had fallen, and many districts were heavily flooded; hundreds of poor people had been rendered homeless. Then, on the 17th of January, a terrible storm, with violent hail, thunder, and lightning, occurred. Huge trees and many chimneys were blown down, and many thatched cottages were struck by lightning and set on fire. Sayes Court was "miserably shattered", though fortunately the family were not in residence, as they had been living in London for the winter months. This calamitous storm was regarded by Evelyn "as a sign of God's anger against this ungrateful and vicious nation and Court". Indeed, he was bitterly disillusioned with the Restoration, for which he had schemed and worked for years. Those in power seemed engulfed in the general dissipation and irresponsibility. "I came home to be private a little, not at all affecting the life and hurry of Court", he wrote in his diary.

Evelyn was anxious, too, about his great friend Jeremy Taylor, who had been obliged to accept a very poor living in Ireland, and was finding life particularly difficult. "I fear my peace in Ireland is likely to be short", he had written, "for a Presbyterian and a madman have informed against me as a dangerous man to their religion for using the sign of the cross in baptism." Taylor apparently felt forlorn and forgotten in Ireland. "The dead and the absent have but few friends", he quoted.

However, spring came at last, and was followed by a glorious summer. The gardens at Sayes Court had fulfilled their promise and were indescribably beautiful. They had been designed with vistas and groves, terraces, gravel walks, lawns, statues, fountains, and noble clumps of trees. There were fish and lily ponds and magnificent holly hedges. Evelyn had superintended every detail with superb artistry. The Duke of York had paid a visit and declared that there was nothing so magnificent in London.

But all talk now was of the coming of the Infanta of Portugal, whom Charles intended to marry shortly, a union ardently desired by the Queen Mother, who wished Charles to marry a Catholic. On the 15th of May, 1662, she arrived at Portsmouth. The church bells of London were rung and bonfires blazed. But apparently the King made no attempt to greet his royal bride as he was with Lady Castlemaine, who shortly expected to present him with a child. Not until five days later, in fact, did he journey to Portsmouth, where on the 20th he and the Princess were quietly married. "I do not see much thorough joy", wrote Samuel Pepys, "but only an indifferent one in the hearts of the people, who are much discontented at the pride and luxury of the Court, and running in debt."*

On the 30th of May the Queen arrived with her large train at Hampton Court, and Evelyn dutifully attended to pay his respects. She was a brunette—fresh, simple, and innocent, with a good figure and rich chestnut hair. Evelyn thought her "fairly handsome, though low of stature". A great crowd had assembled to pay their court to her, and the Lord Mayor and Aldermen had brought her £1000 in gold as a

* *Pepys' Diary*, 15 May 1662.

wedding present. A very beautiful gondola had also been sent from the state of Venice, and the Queen Mother had given "a great looking-glass and toilet of massy gold".

Evelyn noticed that Hampton Court had been refurnished "with incomparable splendour". There were some superb tapestries, and many rare pictures. The hangings, designed by Raphael, were extremely beautiful, and "very rich with gold". The chapel roof was now "excellently fretted and gilt", and the park had been planted with "sweet rows of lime trees". There was a pretty Banqueting House, the canal was almost complete, and the gardens had been much extended and improved.

All, in fact, was fair to outward view, but Evelyn was told that relations between Charles and his bride were already strained. The first grievance was with regard to the Queen's dowry. £500,000 sterling had been promised, and also the assignment, to England, of Tangier, a strong and important trading port. The free trade of Brazil and the West Indies (which had hitherto been denied) had also been offered, and the island of Bombay, with its spacious bay, towns, and castles. It was a magnificent dowry, but had not materialized. The Earl of Sandwich had gone to Portugal with a fleet of ships to escort the Infanta, but on arrival Catharine's mother had paid only half the dowry; the rest, she said, had been spent in raising money for troops for the defence of the country. Then, finally, the Queen and her cunning advisers had delivered the dowry not in gold but in bags of sugar, spices, and other merchandise. Lord Sandwich, aghast at the turn of affairs, had already taken possession of Tangier, so could not refuse to receive the Princess.

To Charles this was a severe blow, as he was not only burdened by the debts incurred by the Protectorate, but already, in spite of his immense income, deeply involved on his own account. Lady Castlemaine had already caused trouble, as apparently she did not intend to lose one scrap of her despotic influence. Evelyn was told that the new Queen had been told of Charles's liaison with Lady Castlemaine, so had been advised by her mother to keep the peace but to refuse to allow the lady in the Palace. To the Queen's consternation, therefore, Lady Castlemaine's name had appeared at the head of the King's list of Ladies of the Bedchamber. Catharine, naturally indignant, had struck the offensive name out of the list and burst into tears. But Charles was extremely angry and told her that he intended to be obeyed. He had also told the

Earl of Clarendon that whoever hindered him in this would be his enemy
to the last moment of his life. Clarendon, therefore, had pointed out to
the young Queen that she had no choice, and when Catharine had wept
and begged to be sent back to Portugal she was reminded that she could
not now dispose of her own person. She was, in effect, a prisoner, and
could not even leave the Palace without the King's permission. If she
quarrelled with her "lord and master" she would "certainly get the worst
of it". Finally, she was forced to submit, and Lady Castlemaine came
every day to the Palace. Also, the King supped with her—or some other
mistress—every night. It was known, indeed, that the imperious Lady
Castlemaine, in her fits of fury, threatened to tear the King's child to
pieces and to set the Palace on fire. She strongly objected to this marriage.

"At Court", wrote Pepys, "things are in very ill condition, there being
so much emulacion, poverty, and the vices of drinking, swearing and loose
amours, that I know not what will be the end of it but confusion. . . .
In short, I see no content or satisfaction anywhere, in any one sort of
people. For lack of money all things go to rack. The season very sickly
everywhere of strange and fatal fevers."*

The new Queen's retinue was proving, also, an extremely difficult one.
Her Portuguese maids of honour were for the most part "old, ugly and
proud", and some refused to lie in any bed in which a man had ever
slept. £40,000 a year had been settled on the Queen for the maintenance
of her Court, but she had brought:

    4 almoners
    A confessor
    2 preachers
    6 Benedictine fathers
   17 officers of her household
    2 cup-bearers
    2 carvers
    2 sewers
    5 ushers
    6 grooms of the Privy Chamber
    7 gentleman ushers
    6 pages of the bedchamber

* *Pepys' Diary*, Bell & Sons' edition, 1930, vol. 2, p. 93.

11 Franciscan Friars, with their musicians, servers, and porters
An apothecary
A surgeon
4 pages of the presence
12 grooms of the Great Chamber
24 watermen
A master of the Queen's Barge
1 porter of the back stairs
7 ladies of the bedchamber
5 maids of honour
6 dressers
A laundress
A sempstress
A starcher

An expensive retinue, indeed!

Evelyn was distressed by the general atmosphere at Hampton Court, and, having done his duty by the new Queen, was glad to take his leave and spend a few weeks at Albury with Mr. Henry Howard, a kinsman of the Duke of Norfolk. There was an interesting house party and some hunting, a buck being killed in the park. But Evelyn was soon back again in London as the Queen Mother was anxious to see Sayes Court and the celebrated gardens of which she had heard so much. She came with her ladies in waiting, including the new beauty, Frances Stewart, with whom the King was already head over heels in love.

The Queen Mother's visit to Sayes Court lasted until late in the evening, and she "graciously partook of a collation" before she returned to her Palace. She, too, was enchanted with the house and garden.

The following day the Lord Chancellor (the Earl of Clarendon) and his lady arrived at Sayes Court on the same errand. His purse and mace were borne before him in traditional style, and the party stayed to supper and were "very merry". A few days later there was a wonderful water festival on the Thames. It was arranged for the new Queen, and hundreds of boats and barges, "dressed and adorned with all imaginable pomp", conducted Their Majesties down the river from Hampton Court to Whitehall. They sailed in their elegant new gondola, and sat under a canopy of cloth-of-gold supported by high corinthian pillars, wreathed in flowers, festoons, and garlands. It was a splendid sight. There was lovely music, and some beautiful pageants were presented. Evelyn, in his new boat, sailed in the procession, and thought the festival "the most magnificent triumph that ever floated on the Thames".

The return of the Court to London meant that Evelyn was constantly at Whitehall; there were endless committee meetings concerning his government work. But on every hand he was told of the King's incredible debts; they were a public scandal, for few tradesmen were paid. Yet at Court there were continuous balls and masques. Then in October all England was shocked to hear that Dunkirk had been sold to King Louis XIV of France. Dunkirk had been won by Oliver Cromwell from Spain, and was justly prized as a trophy of British valour. To lose it was to add to the already formidable power of France. Evelyn frequently discussed State affairs with his friend Samuel Pepys, and Pepys declared that there was no money for the repair and maintenance of naval ships. Nor were the wages of the sailors regularly paid. In an island country this was an extremely serious matter. Yet it was clear that England was drifting into a war with Holland, and the King appeared to be utterly apathetic. The Duke of York took an interest in naval affairs, and sat in Council, but he had little power.

However, time passed. Evelyn conscientiously performed his public duties, he dined out constantly, and he entertained envoys and ambassadors at Sayes Court. Musical river parties were fashionable, and the evening would finish with "a great banquet". But Evelyn had also for some months been working on two books—*Sylva* (a manual on forestry) and *The History and Art of Chalcography and Engraving on Copper*. Both were being written at the request of the newly organized Royal Society, who believed that a book on forestry was urgently needed, as owing to the civil war thousands of acres of oak forests had been felled; the timber required for the building of ships was therefore almost exhausted. *Sylva* was intended to instruct landowners in the afforestation of their woods.

Evelyn was also taking a very keen interest in the Royal Society, and at the meetings he met some of the most brilliant men in England. The members dined together regularly and exchanged ideas, compared research, and made experiments. The transfusion of blood, the ponderation of air, the fixation of mercury, the laws of magnetism, the ebb and flow of the sea, the course of the comets, the properties of the atmosphere, the laws of statics, were merely a few of the exciting subjects discussed. The members were determined to sift all evidence, from whatever quarter, dispassionately, and there was a feeling that the great scientific secrets of the universe were about to be revealed. The King himself had become a member, and had a laboratory at Whitehall; he owned a great telescope, drawing 35 feet, and he had granted the Society the use of the Royal Arms and presented them with a silver-gilt mace. Other distinguished members were Dr. Harvey (the discoverer of the circulation of the blood), Robert Boyle (the eminent scientist), Samuel Pepys, Dr. Christopher Wren, and Sir Thomas Browne. Bishops, soldiers, and courtiers made up the numbers.

Evelyn had given to the Royal Society his remarkable *Table of Veins, Arteries and Nerves* which he had purchased ten years earlier in Padua. He had also subscribed 50,000 bricks towards building a college for the Society at Arundel House. Even the bishops were interested, although one declared that he welcomed the Royal Society provided that "the two subjects of God and the soul were foreborne". In all the rest they might "wander at their pleasure", he said.

In April the King, accompanied by the Duke of Richmond, the Earl of St. Albans, Lord Lauderdale, and "several persons of quality", came for the first time to Sayes Court to see the house and garden. His Majesty went through every room, and was elegantly entertained with "a collation". He expressed his unqualified admiration for all he saw, and departed in rare good humour. Certainly he was an excellent connoisseur.

But the following year (1664) brought its troubles, as in March Evelyn lost another child, Richard. He was a month old, and died "without any sickness or danger perceivably, being to all appearances a likely child. We suspected much the nurse had overlayne him, to our extreme sorrow, being now reduced to one. But God's will be done." Three days later Evelyn recorded in his diary: "After evening prayers was my child buried near the rest of his brothers—my very dear children." That the nurse had "overlayne" the tiny child is extremely likely, as such tragedies were only too common. As for the tragedy of infant mortality, pious resignation was the only attitude, as doctors were working in the dark. They had no modern means of diagnosis—X-rays, blood tests, etc. They knew nothing of antiseptics or of safe anaesthetics; they knew nothing of the existence of micro-organisms, and little of chemistry. Also, their knowledge of anatomy was inadequate owing to the lack of facilities for dissection. In addition, the Church's strict teaching, almost without question, was that illness and pain were "just punishments for sin, sent expressly by God". If illness was God's will, therefore, of what use was a physician? Why attempt to save a life which God apparently wished to take? Evelyn and Mary spent hours each day on their knees imploring God's mercy and protection.

But again Evelyn turned to literature for consolation and comfort, and he now published *The Gardener's Almanack. What to do monthly throughout the year*—an excellent manual on gardening. It was dedicated to Abraham Cowley, the poet, who had confessed that he had always wanted "a small house and a large garden". "Oh, let me escape thither", he had said, "and my soul shall live." He and Evelyn were old acquaintances and very good friends.

In October, too, for a change of air and scene, Evelyn went into the country with Viscount Cornbury to assist him in the planting of his park. They also visited several country seats, and finally drove to Oxford, where they were "nobly" entertained by the famous Dr. Boyle, the celebrated Dr. Wallis, and "that incomparable genius", Sir Christopher Wren. Evelyn and his friend, in fact, could hardly tear themselves away from this lively and learned company. But a return to London was essential.

CHAPTER 6

THE DUTCH WAR

EVELYN had for some time been anxious as to the possibility of war with the Dutch, and there had been many rumours. The King had been libelled in various Dutch cartoons and was furiously angry. In one he was represented with all his pockets turned inside out, begging for money from his Parliament, and in another he was led by the nose by two ladies and threatened by a third. For these insults the King and the Duke of York were anxious that "the Parliament would find reason to fall out with the Dutch". The Duke of York hated the Dutch, and longed for an opportunity to show his courage and skill as High-Admiral. Charles's irresponsible courtiers, too, were constantly urging him to "teach the Dutch a lesson". The country, of course, could not possibly afford the immense expense of a war, but kings and princes apparently thought otherwise. "For my part, I dread it", wrote Pepys.*

On the 27th of October, Evelyn's worst fears were realized; apparently war was imminent, and he was asked by the King if he would accept the appointment of one of the commissioners for the Sick, Wounded, and Prisoners of War. There were to be four commissioners, who would be given powers to appoint officers, physicians, surgeons, and provost-marshals, and to commandeer hospitals. The salary was to be £300 a year and Evelyn would be responsible for the counties of Kent and Sussex.

By November the disastrous war had actually started. "God give a good end to it", said Samuel Pepys hopefully, and soon Dutch merchant ships were being captured and brought into Portsmouth. This was considered an excellent way of obtaining valuable booty and of filling the

* *Pepys' Diary*, 30 April 1664.

empty Exchequer, but inevitably it worked both ways. The Dutch were retaliating by taking English ships.

The Commons had now voted immense sums for the prosecution of the war, but soon it was apparent that this liberality was useless owing to the extravagance, corruption, incapacity, and dishonesty of those in office. Apparently every official took bribes, and the sycophants of the Court were rapidly making fortunes; they had secured the best posts. Meanwhile, the sailors were mutinying from very hunger.

Evelyn soon realized, too, that in spite of the King's immense revenue, little money could be obtained for the wounded and sick prisoners who were already arriving in the country. A frigate had been blown up by accident, and there had been many casualties. Evelyn was also expected to make arrangements for the sailors' widows, "fortyfive of whom were with child".

Early in the year 1665 he drove by coach to Portsmouth, Rochester, Canterbury, Dover, and Sandwich in order to appoint surgeons, physicians, agents, marshals, and other officers at each of these towns. Many prisoners were temporarily lodged in Chelsea, but new batches of sick and wounded were arriving daily, many badly mutilated, having lost arms and legs. "Miserable objects, God knows!", recorded Evelyn. He was, in fact, horrified at "this bloody beginning" and the suffering and misery with which he now came face to face.

The 5th of April was ordered to be kept "as a day of public humiliation, and for the success of this terrible war", but this did not provide the money he so urgently needed, and he was therefore obliged to see the King himself and inform him "of the vast charge upon us, now amounting to no less than £1000 weekly". Evelyn had obtained the use of the Savoy Hospital and half of St. Thomas's Hospital, but this accommodation was quite inadequate, and the King seemed utterly indifferent. He merely referred Evelyn to his Ministers, who doled out small sums and then declared that they had nothing more to give.

In June came news of a naval engagement, and of the victory of the Duke of York's fleet. Bells were joyfully rung, therefore, and bonfires lighted in the city, but when the sick and wounded arrived the victory seemed doubtful. Evelyn himself went down to Chatham with Lord Sandwich (now Admiral), and they were rowed to the Fleet, then lying at anchor. It was, Evelyn decided, "the most glorious fleet that ever spread sail". They went on board *The Prince*, a ship of ninety brass ordnance and 600 men, and dined with the officers and many noblemen. After dinner, the King, Prince Rupert, and the Duke of York arrived, and a general Council was held on *The Charles* with all the flag officers. Evelyn stayed late, but finally returned in the King's yacht to Chatham with Lord Sandwich. With such a fine fleet, surely the outlook was good.

A week later Evelyn was again obliged to see the King at Hampton Court and ask for money to pay for food, lodging, medicines, and bandages for his men. Surgeons and physicians also had to be paid for their services. Evelyn and his fellow commissioners were spending heavily out of their own pockets, but obviously this could not continue.

Meanwhile, the Court had left London because of the alarming spread of the plague. Five thousand people had died in London during the second week of July, and the following week the numbers had risen to 10,000. The King had ordered "a solemn fast" to be observed "to deprecate God's displeasure against the land by pestilence and war".

But Evelyn could not expose his family to the risk of infection, so decided that they should go to live temporarily with his brother George at Wotton. George had just lost by death his second wife, and all his children except a married daughter, so was delighted to receive his relatives. Evelyn made the journey to Wotton to see them safely installed, and then returned to Sayes Court. Mary, incidentally, was expecting another child.

The situation in London was now assuming an alarming aspect, and hundreds of houses were marked with the red cross and "Lord have mercy upon us". In the streets one met surgeons, keepers, and "burriers" carrying red wands, a sign that they had been in contact with infection. But many magistrates and doctors had already fled, and thousands of plague victims therefore expired alone, unattended. "A man", said Samuel Pepys, "cannot depend upon living two days to an end", and, he added, "the people die now so that it seems they are fain to carry the dead to be buried in daylight, the nights not sufficing to do it in". (It was the custom at this time for all burials to take place at night.) Pepys had also stuck to his post, and so had the Duke of Albemarle, who was visiting the pest-houses, comforting the sick and bereaved, and arranging for their property to be guarded. The Archbishop of Canterbury and his gallant friend, the Earl of Craven, were also doing splendid work. They had opened a lazaretto for the sick, and with their own resources had staffed it with nurses and physicians, and supplied all necessities.

Meanwhile, Evelyn worked night and day over his thankless and depressing task, driving to the coast continually and organizing endless details. And how tiring his journeys were. The majority of roads in Kent were appalling and, after heavy rain, sometimes impassable. Many of the fords were extremely perilous after a storm. It was also necessary to be well armed for fear of the highwaymen and robbers who infested every piece of open country. Nevertheless, Evelyn drove on, over hill and dale, in all weathers.

Fires now burnt night and day in the streets of London by order of the magistrates, as these were believed to "consume the noxious vapours". Thousands of dogs had also been slaughtered in the belief that they carried the infection in their coats. Trade had come to a standstill, as few ships would venture up the river, and the city was almost deserted. Grass grew in the evil-smelling, unswept streets, and many houses and shops were boarded up. There was a deathly silence except for the dreary tolling of church bells and the hoarse voice of "the burrier" calling "Bring out your dead! Bring out your dead!" Men and women passed each other in the streets with averted faces and looks of terror, for who could say where and at what hour death would strike next? Would it be father, mother, sweetheart, or precious child? The very air reeked with pestilence, and in Deptford alone thirty houses were infected, one of which was close to Sayes Court.

The churches were open the whole night, and were thronged with people, praying, weeping, moaning, confessing. But another horrible feature of the plague was the rats. They had increased enormously, and they swarmed everywhere, peering with their wicked little eyes round every corner. They were enormous, and were apparently scavenging not only the dead but the dying. They had come out of the ships, and the plague had opened a new life for them.

The victims of the plague now began to fall down in the streets, as if struck by lightning, to be picked up by the "burriers" and thrown into the great communal graves. Other sick victims, in their delirium, wandered out into the streets calling for mercy and confessing their sins. "I have been a thief; I have been an adulterer", they shrieked, but no one stopped to comfort them for fear of infection. Evelyn did what he could to guard against infection, but of what use to disinfect oneself when everything one used was infected? Where were love and laughter now? The days passed like a bad dream, and the nights, alone with his gloomy thoughts and his fears for his beloved family, were almost unendurable. And ever present, also, like a nightmare, was the urgent problem of his sick seamen. It was to Viscount Cornbury that he again appealed for funds, and Evelyn declared "This nation is ruined for want of activity". Of Sir Philip Warwick he inquired why the French prisoners could not be sent home, but, he added, "I am resolved to maintain my station and refuse nothing that will contribute to His Majesty's service". He also confessed to Sir George Carteret that there were now "5000 prisoners dying for want of bread, and this barbarous measure must needs redound to the King's great dishonour". He alone was responsible. To Sir William Coventry, Evelyn wrote: "Our prisoners beg us, as a mercy, to knock them on the head, for we have no bread to relieve the dying creatures. Nor does this country afford gaols to secure them in." He was trying to arrange for accommodation in Leeds Castle, which belonged to Lord Culpeper. But Evelyn was afraid that the majority would not survive the journey, and they would starve when they arrived. "As for the pittance now lately ordered us, what will that benefit to our numbers and the mouths we have to feed?", he asked. "Neither is that to be had suddenly, and will be spent before we touch it. I could assemble other particulars of a sad countenance relating to the miseries of our own countrymen. I beseech Your Honour, let us not be reputed barbarians, or if at least we must be so, let me not be the executor of so much inhumanity."

Finally, Evelyn obtained permission to use Leeds Castle, and there he "flowed the dry moat, made a new draw-bridge, brought spring water into the court of the castle to an old fountain", and arranged for repairs to be carried out.

By September, 10,000 people a week were dying of the plague in London, and unfortunately many of the sailors had also caught the disease, so Evelyn was obliged to ask the Duke of Albemarle for the loan of a pest ship for the sick men. Evelyn and his brother commissioners had each spent about £6000 of their own money, and in spite of repeated requests to the King they were still in desperate need. Finally, on the

25th of September, Evelyn told the Duke of Albemarle that unless he had £10,000 immediately the prisoners would actually starve. Only then was the proposal made that the money should be raised out of the East India prizes taken by Lord Sandwich. First, however, His Majesty's permission and the permission of the Council had to be obtained, so an "express" was sent to the King. Meanwhile, Evelyn had put the sick prisoners, who were in "a deplorable state", on five vessels, well guarded. A few days later another 3000 prisoners arrived, and he had no accommodation whatever for these men. It was a most serious situation, and almost in despair Evelyn wrote to Sir Philip Warwick:

> One fortnight has made me feel the utmost of miseries that can befall a person in my situation and with my affections—to have 25,000 prisoners, and 1500 sick and wounded men to take care of, without one penny of money, and above £2000 indebted. . . . Sir, I am in hopes of touching the £5000 some day this week, but what is that to the expense of £200 a day? Is there no exchange, or pecuniary redemption to be proposed? Or is His Majesty resolved to maintain the armies of his enemies in his own bosom, whose idleness makes them sick, and their sickness redoubles the charge? I am amazed at this method, but must hold my tongue.

By the 30th of September the sick and wounded were lying in the streets outside the door of Pepys' office, night and day. The captains would not receive them on board, and Pepys had no ships for them and no money with which to pay them. "They died like dogs in the street unregarded", recorded Evelyn, "although they had adventured their lives for the public." Could injustice and mismanagement go further than this? The King and his frivolous Court were at Oxford, away from the awful plague, spending their days and nights in uproarious gaiety. Charles had all his seraglio with him, including Lady Castlemaine, again "with child". Rumour said that her sons were to be created dukes. It was common knowledge that she was heavily in debt to tradesmen, jewellers, and silversmiths, and that they despaired of ever being paid. Was not this a scandal? And this harlot's jewels, bestowed by the King, would have provided for many of Evelyn's sick and wounded for a year. Indeed, the majority of courtiers lived in absurd extravagance and had no intention whatever of paying for their goods. Even the King owed his draper £5000, and as his servants had not been paid their wages, they "stole the royal linen and other goods, and sold them for what they could get". Pepys had seen the Lord Treasurer and the Chancellor, and had explained the tragic situation in the Navy due to lack of money, but the Ministers merely held up their hands and cried, "What shall we do?", and the Lord Treasurer said helplessly, "But what would you *have* me do? I have given all I can for my life. Why will not people lend their money? Why will they not trust the King as well as Oliver? Why do our prizes come to nothing that yielded so much heretofore?"

There were, of course, perfectly logical answers to these questions. The city merchants would not lend money to the King because they were convinced that it would be spent on his mistresses and never repaid. As for the prizes "which had yielded so much heretofore", most of the treasure was stolen before it ever left the ships. Pepys declared that the business of the Navy was "wholly standing still. No credit. No goods sold us. Nobody will trust. All we have to do at the office is to hear complaints for want of money." Sir William Coventry prophesied that "all will be undone, and all ruined", and a noted city merchant said that the city "had given over trade and the nation for lost".

By early October matters had not improved in London, and Pepys confessed that he could not work because of "the horrible crowd and lamentable moan of the poor seamen that lie starving in the streets for lack of money, which do trouble and perplex me to the heart". As Pepys and his colleagues left the office, about a hundred men followed them, "some cursing, some swearing and some praying to us".* Also, in the streets, "multitudes of poor festiferous creatures were begging alms", for trade was at a standstill and hundreds were starving. Only one gleam of light shone through the gloom—Leeds Castle was now ready for occupation, and about a week later Evelyn went down to Maidstone to see 500 prisoners installed there. "God send us peace", said Pepys.

But now, at long last, the plague was declining; every week fewer deaths were recorded. Men and women began to smile again. They shook each other by the hand in the street, they opened their lattices and called a greeting, telling the day's good news. "God be praised", they said, and wept for joy. In all, some 70,000 persons had perished, but it was almost over, and people began to return to the capital. The rich filled every room with perfume, to disinfect their houses, and the poor burnt brimstone, pitch, and gunpowder. London gradually settled down to the old routine, the shops were reopened, and again the Exchange was thronged

* *Pepys' Diary*, 7 October 1665.

with merchants. "Now blessed be God", wrote Evelyn in his diary, "for His extraordinary mercies and preservation of me this year, when thousands and ten thousands perished, and were swept away on each side of me, there dying in our parish this year 406 of the pestilence."

The Court was still at Oxford, where they had moved from Salisbury early in September, but they returned to Hampton Court after Christmas, and on the 29th of January Evelyn had an interview with the King, who ran towards him and "in a most gracious manner" thanked him for his "faithfulness in his service at a time of such danger when all had fled their employments". Other noblemen also expressed their appreciation of Evelyn's work. But Evelyn had not come to be thanked but to persuade the King to build an infirmary for sick and wounded seamen. The matter was desperately urgent, and Evelyn had in mind, as a pattern, an excellent hospital he had seen some years ago in Amsterdam. Surely this could be done; it would not be charity; it was a matter of common humanity. The King, however, with his usual careless affability, merely said that he would consult the Duke of York.

It was now possible for Evelyn to go down to Wotton to stay with his family. In October, Mary had given birth to their first daughter (after six sons), and the little girl was very welcome and tenderly loved. The two brothers and their families and guests, therefore, spent a delightful Christmas together, "with much and indeed extraordinary mirth and cheer". But Evelyn had decided that Mary and the young child should not yet return to Sayes Court, as the plague had not entirely subsided. He himself went back to Deptford, and for weeks worked incessantly over his sick and wounded men. He also drove down to Chatham several times to search for a level and suitable site for the new infirmary. Finally, a field was found, and with infinite pains, Evelyn made a careful estimate of the amounts of bricks, lime, sand, tiles, timber, and workmen which would be needed. He also estimated how many surgeons, matrons, "beds, rugs, blankets, utensils, nurses, soap, fire, candles, etc.", would be required. He was extremely anxious to get this matter settled, as many of the sick and wounded men were quartered in scattered ale-houses (a common custom at that time), two or three men in each house. But under such conditions the men were not suitably fed, and often drank too much, which "greatly retarded their recovery". Also, surgeons had to walk long distances from one patient to another. In utter desperation Evelyn had put thirty patients in a warm barn at Gravesend, and they had made excellent progress. If the plan for an infirmary was accepted, it would be the duty of Samuel Pepys to promote the scheme, and he had promised all assistance. But the chief obstacle, as usual, would be money.

It was at this time that Evelyn presented to the King his small book entitled *The Pernicious Consequences of the New Heresy of the Jesuits against Kings and States*. He was convinced that the throne was menaced by the Catholic party, and he was determined that their secret machinations should not go unnoticed and unrecorded.

Early in February Mary returned to Sayes Court from Wotton, and the happy family life was resumed. Mary, the new baby, appeared to be thriving. But Evelyn himself was very tired and dispirited. The expensive war dragged on with its tragic loss of life, its agonies of suffering, and its many problems. It was all so futile and purposeless, and his visits to the hospitals, where he saw so many "miserably dismembered men", were heartbreaking. Pepys spoke of "the melancholy posture of affairs", and Sir George Carteret confessed that he "feared a general catastrophe to the whole kingdom".

His fears, indeed, were justified, for on the 3rd of June, 1666, the well-known sound of guns "roaring very fiercely" was heard at Deptford, and two days later news arrived of a terrible naval battle with the Dutch. Apparently there had been devastating English losses both in men and ships. Sir Christopher Mings had died of wounds, and many commanders had been killed in action. The English fleet had not taken one ship of the enemy's.

Evelyn immediately dispatched more surgeons and stores of linen and medicines to the ports in his district. A week later he went down to Chatham with the King, the Duke of York, and many nobles to see the extent of the damage. And there they were confronted with the awful spectacle of more than half the English fleet "miserably shattered". Barely a ship had escaped, and many were reduced to mere wrecks. Some were burnt down to the hull. That gallant vessel, *The Prince*, was a serious loss, and in addition nine or ten ships had been sunk, 600 men had been killed, and 1100 wounded. There were 2000 prisoners. Three days later Evelyn returned home, tired, utterly depressed, and—as he said—"weary of this sight". He confessed that he could not imagine "for what reason we first engaged in this ungrateful war".

But worse news was to come, for within a few weeks it was obvious that the country was threatened with invasion, as reports arrived that the Dutch fleet of 130 sail were on the French coast, and that 6000 armed men were ready to go on board, with 12,000 more to follow. Men were therefore hurriedly pressed into service, the majority of whom were "wholly unfit for sea". The next day they were shipped off. "Lord, how some poor women did cry", said Pepys. "They ran to every group of men that arrived, looking for their husbands; they wept over every vessel that sailed, and stood gazing out over the ocean in the moonlight till nothing more could be seen. It grieved me to the heart to hear them. . . . It is a great tyranny."*

A little later, Pepys's office yard was full of women ("about three hundred") demanding money for their husbands, who were prisoners in Holland. "They lay clamouring and swearing and cursing us", said Pepys, "and they complained that their men had fought for the King, and now they and their children were starving." Pepys declared that he was powerless to help. The King alone was responsible.

Evelyn himself was equally indignant, as very little had been handed over for his sick and wounded seamen. He was utterly tired of importuning the King, yet there was no other course. The French Ambassador had made a donation, but was it not disgraceful that foreigners should have to assist? All Evelyn's plans, in fact, seemed to end in futility, for the hospital at Chatham which he had planned with such care had not materialized; the money was not forthcoming. To save expense he had suggested burning their own bricks, and procuring timber "at the best hand". This would have saved a considerable sum, but the suggestions had fallen on deaf ears. No one cared; no one took the slightest interest. His visits to the hospitals were always distressing, as he generally stayed to see some of the wounded men dressed. And their magnificent courage made him almost ashamed of his own good health.

The Court at this time was at Tunbridge Wells, where His Majesty was amusing himself with the two actresses, Moll Davie and Nell Gwynne. Nell Gwynne, a former orange girl at the Theatre Royal, Drury Lane, had been born in a night cellar, and had at one time sold fresh herrings, wandering from tavern to tavern. Lord Buckhurst, Lord Dorset, and Lacy and Hart, the actors, had all in turn been her "protectors".

* *Pepys' Diary*, 1 July 1666.

According to Bishop Burnet, she was "the wildest and indiscreetest creature". But Thomas Povey, Treasurer to the Commissioners for the affairs of Tangier, had shrewdly summed up the Court: "If there be hell, it is here. No faith, no truth, no love, nor any agreement between man and wife nor friends."

When the Court returned from Tunbridge Wells, Evelyn had several necessary interviews with the King, but Charles seemed quite unable— or unwilling—to face his country's problems. That the sailors had not been paid their wages, and hundreds were actually starving, did not appear to concern him. He was more concerned, apparently, with per- suading Evelyn, the willing horse, to shoulder even further burdens and become a Justice of the Peace. But Evelyn begged to be excused. "This", he recorded in his diary, "was the office in the world I had most industriously avoided." The appointment would have entailed a tremen- dous amount of work; so many parishes were involved. Even in Deptford there were various problems for which he felt responsible. The plague was still prevalent there, and there was much distressing poverty, especially amongst the widows and dependants of sailors. Sir Richard Browne had built and endowed some alms-houses, and he and Mary worked constantly to relieve the sufferings of the sick and indigent.

But the saddest aspect of the plague was at the small port of Deal, which Evelyn was obliged to visit frequently in connection with his work. The place had become almost depopulated. In addition to his many commitments, Evelyn had also been appointed one of the commissioners for "regulating farming and making saltpetre", and also one of the surveyors for the repair of St. Paul's Cathedral. Sir Christopher Wren had reported that the pillars were giving way, and the tower was leaning. From the start, apparently, the Cathedral had been badly designed and built. Wren proposed that a cupola should be built, with cupola and lantern to give light "and incomparably more grace". On the 27th of August, therefore, Evelyn, Sir Christopher Wren, the Bishop of London, and the Dean of St. Paul's met and discussed the matter. They decided what work should be carried out and the estimated cost.

It was at this time that Evelyn's friends, deeply concerned at his sad looks and many cares, frequently urged him to accompany them in their various diversions, and he was invited by his friend the Lord Chamberlain to see a play acted at Court before the King and Queen. Evelyn strongly disapproved of theatre-going "in a time of such judgement and calamities". He went, therefore, reluctantly, and he was, as he expected, disappointed. The play was cleverly written, but he was shocked by "the foul and indecent women now permitted to appear and act". Many had already become the mistresses of young noblemen, "to the ruin of both body and soul". But did not the King and Court set the example of immorality and lax behaviour? Evelyn believed that the influence of the theatre was incalculable, as the magic of theatrical illusion created a most powerful effect. The sentiments expressed in the plays were deplorable, as all the virtues were ridiculed, and all the great ties which bind society together were treated with contempt. The heroes were witty and amusing, but inhuman, calculating, sneering, and cruel, adultery being represented as one of the accomplishments of a fine gentleman; intrigue and seduction were merely amusing pastimes. The loosest lines were put into the mouths of women, and some of the epilogues were utterly disgusting. The dramatist was obviously the mouthpiece of a depraved section of society, and the contemporary theatre represented the outlook of fashionable London. But once the harm was done it was almost impossible to eradicate. One could not touch pitch without being defiled.

Many women of doubtful character also haunted the theatres, sitting impudently in the boxes with the highest in the land. And the majority wore masks, not to hide their maidenly blushes, but to enable them to carry on their amorous intrigues without being discovered. Yet was there not the strongest inducement for them to be there? Day after day the King was in the theatre, laughing immoderately at the cruel and coarse jokes. Had he expressed his displeasure, or withdrawn his patronage, such plays could not have continued, for the theatre depended largely on the support of the Court and the aristocracy.

Indeed, it seemed to Evelyn that the King and his Court were failing utterly in their duty. For instance, they could have set an example and proved an inspiration to all men and women. The war had created innumerable problems, and there was social work for every available pair of hands. Hospitals were tragically in need of help, and hundreds of wounded men were in need of assistance and rehabilitation. Yet apparently no one cared. The appalling apathy made one almost despair. Magistrates appeared to be equally callous; they would do nothing to assist the wounded men, insisting that they had no powers. To a disabled man, apparently, every door was closed, and many unhappy victims were being driven to crime. Evelyn, in fact, had already had his house robbed three times. He described these men as villains, yet if they were starving, as seemed highly likely, who could blame them?

CHAPTER 7

THE GREAT FIRE AND
AN INVASION

ONE evening in late summer Evelyn observed from one of the upper windows of Sayes Court that the sky over London was blood-red and huge volumes of smoke were rolling across the horizon. The city, in fact, was on fire, and he immediately took coach and, with his wife and son John, went to the Bankside, Southwark. Houses were blazing furiously in all directions. "The night", he said, "was as light as day, and the flames were leaping after a prodigious manner from house to house and street to street, at great distances one from the other."

London was, of course, particularly vulnerable to fire, as candles and tapers were used extensively for lighting, and the majority of houses were built of wood or half-timbered and thatched; such houses were extremely inflammable. As they were built close together, even a small fire spread with alarming violence. Fire engines, of course, did not exist (until later in the century), and fire-fighting appliances would have been useless without a high-pressure water supply. The water had to be drawn from wells and carried in pails. This laborious process was now being adopted, but was quite ineffective.

"Oh, the miserable and calamitous spectacle! . . . All the sky was of a fiery aspect, like the top of a burning oven. . . . God grant mine eyes may never behold the like, who now saw about ten thousand houses all in one flame"—so recorded Evelyn. "The noise and cracking and thunder of the impetuous flames, the shrieking of women and children, the hurry of people, the fall of towers, houses and church, was like a hideous storm, and the air about so hot and inflamed that at the last one was not able to approach it. . . . Thus I left it this afternoon burning, a resemblance of Sodom, or the last day."

The fire had started, apparently, in Fish Street, and fanned by a strong east wind, was sweeping through the streets with terrifying pace and violence, the wooden buildings collapsing like bundles of sticks. Wild shouts of "Fire! Fire! Fire!" were heard on every hand, and men and women rushed about the streets screaming and praying to God for assistance, the women carrying children in their arms, and the men looking utterly bewildered. Panic had seized the whole community.

Meanwhile, the King was summoning all the help he could command, and Samuel Pepys urged him to give orders for houses to be pulled down to prevent the fire spreading. The Lord Mayor explained that he had demolished many houses already, but the fire consumed them faster than he and his men could work.

"The stones of St. Paul's flew like grenados, the melting lead running down the streets in a stream, and the very pavements glowing with fiery redness." In addition, the demolition work had blocked all the narrow thoroughfares, "so that no help could be applied". The magnificent Royal Exchange burned quickly, the fire running round its galleries like a devouring dragon, and, finally, the handsome statues of kings fell down upon their faces with a fearful roar, the lead from the roof melted and ran down as snow, and the sky was lighted up with a dazzling glow.

St. Paul's met with no better fate, and soon the great bells melted, and huge avalanches of stone came crashing down from the walls, the old tombs being buried in the debris. Then, suddenly, there was a panic rumour that the French and Dutch had planned the fire and were about to sack the town. "With this dreadful outcry we did look to be killed every hour", said one poor lady. "I have almost lost my wits."

By the following day the fire had crossed Whitehall, and "Oh, the confusion there was then at that Court!", said Evelyn, "for now they begin to bestir themselves, and not till now, who hitherto had stood as men intoxicated, with their hands across." Evelyn was asked by the King to attend to the quenching of Fetter Lane, and to preserve, if possible, that part of Holborn, "while the rest of the gentlemen took their several posts". But Evelyn was particularly concerned for the hospitals of St. Bartholomew and the Savoy, where he had lodged many sick and wounded men. Finally, the command to pull down even more houses was given, and this was effective: the flames gradually ceased to spread.

The fire raged incessantly for five days, but by the 7th of September had burnt itself out. The city, however, was all in ruins; everything between the Tower and the Temple had been destroyed, and the loss was estimated at £200,000. Eighty-four of the city churches and St. Paul's were destroyed, and 373 acres had been consumed within the city walls and 63 acres outside the walls. In addition, 13,200 houses had been totally burnt out. And this in one of the noblest cities in the world. The coal and wood wharves, the magazines of oil, resin, etc., had done infinite harm, a reminder of Evelyn's warning some months earlier to the King that these places should be moved outside the city walls for safety. Many sets of chambers in the Temple had been burnt out, and the title deeds of a vast number of estates had therefore disappeared. Many rare books and manuscripts had also been consumed. "This", as Evelyn said, "was an extraordinary detriment to the whole republic of learning."

Meanwhile, the homeless poor, who now numbered some thousands, were out in the fields, some under tents, some in miserable huts and hovels, many "without a rag, or any necessary utensils, bed or board . . . now reduced to extremest misery and poverty." The very tools with which they had earned their livings had been consumed.

The next day Evelyn walked on foot to see the damage, from White-hall to London Bridge, through Fleet Street, Ludgate Hill, Cheapside, Exchange, Bishopsgate, Aldersgate, and out to Moorfields, and thence through Cornhill. He had to clamber over heaps of foul-smelling smoking rubbish, the ground under his feet being so hot that it burnt his shoes. On his return, he walked to St. Paul's Cathedral, now reduced to a charred and shapeless shell. Only a week ago he and Christopher Wren had planned its restoration. The majority of the old tombs had perished, amongst them two Saxon kings, John of Gaunt, his wife Constance of Castile, poor St. Erkenwald, and scores of bishops—good and bad, Sir Nicholas Bacon (Queen Elizabeth's Lord Keeper), Sir Philip Sydney, Walsingham, Sir Christopher Hatton ("the dancing Chancellor"), and Vandyke the artist. The manuscripts of Shakespeare and his contemporaries had also perished; they had been placed in the crypt of St. Paul's for safety, and the heat from the fire had reduced them to ashes. Six acres of lead had totally melted, and the vaulted roof had crashed into

St. Faith's, which, filled with books belonging to the Stationers and taken there for safety, were all consumed and were still smouldering. Many beautiful and rare books, quite irreplaceable, were therefore lost. The exquisite Mercers' chapel, the handsome Exchange, Christ Church, and all the rest of the City halls and splendid buildings had also been destroyed.

But saddest of all were the wretched people who walked hopelessly about the ruins. "They appeared", said Evelyn, "like men in some dismal desert, or rather in some great city laid waste by a cruel enemy, to which was added the stench that came from some poor creatures' bodies, beds and other combustible goods."

Evelyn then walked towards Islington and Highgate, where he saw "about 200,000 people of all ranks and degrees" lying beside the few belongings they had saved from the fire. The majority were utterly destitute and homeless. Evelyn was told, however, that the King and his Council had issued a Proclamation "for the country to come in and refresh them with provisions".

Evelyn had taken many notes and made many drawings during his long peregrination, so three days later he was able to present to His Majesty "a survey of the ruins and a plan for a new city". Unfortunately, Dr. Christopher Wren had forestalled him. Nevertheless, the King was interested in Evelyn's plans, and His Majesty, the Duke of York, and the Queen discussed them with him for some time. Evelyn suggested that the debris should be used for filling up the shore of the Thames to low-water mark, so that the basin could be kept always full. Before Evelyn left the Palace, the King had expressed his grateful thanks for the excellent suggestions; he considered that Evelyn had performed an important task with remarkable speed.

About a fortnight later Evelyn was again at Court, but he observed that none of the nobility had come up from the country to assist the King or to prevent "commotions". And not a priest had come "to give the King and Court good counsel or to comfort the poor people that suffer. But all is dead. Nothing of good in any of their minds." This was significant of the general apathy, and the strong disapproval of the King and his disorderly Court. He who should have set an example to the country was despised.

On the 10th of October a general fast was ordered, "to humble us", said Evelyn, "on the late dreadful conflagration, added to the plague and war, the most dismal judgements that could be inflicted, but which indeed we highly deserve, for our prodigious ingratitude, burning lusts, dissolute Court, profane and abominable lives". It seemed to him that the country was rapidly deteriorating, and "more ruin was to come". According to Pepys, the discipline in the Fleet was "as if the devil commanded it; so much wickedness of all sorts".* Pepys, too, declared that "public matters are in a most sad condition; seamen discouraged for want of pay, and are becoming not to be governed. Nor as matters are now can any fleets go out next year. Our enemies, the French and Dutch, great, and grow more so by our poverty. The Parliament backward in raising money because of the spending; the city less and less likely to be built again . . . a sad, vicious, negligent Court, and all sober men there fearful of the ruin of the whole kingdom this next year, from which, good God, deliver us." About a month later Pepys recorded: "I found that all merchants do give over trade and the nation for lost, nothing being done with care or foresight, no convoys granted, nor anything done to satisfaction." He believed that "The Dutch or French will master us the next year, do what we can . . . unless necessity makes the King to mind his business, which might yet save all." Pepys had carefully feathered his own nest, yet he had no wish to see his country ruined.

The rebuilding of London was an urgent matter as eighty-nine churches had been destroyed in the great fire and many people were unable to find a place of worship, a sad deprivation to the pious. The rebuilding of the halls of the city companies, with their schools, was also a matter of necessity, so that trade in the city could be resumed. Sir Christopher Wren had this task in hand. But Evelyn was particularly concerned with plans for the river, and early in March of the next year he saw the Lord Chancellor and proposed to him Monsieur Kiviet's extremely practical plan to wharf all the Thames with bricks from the Temple to the Tower. A few weeks later Evelyn had an audience with the King, and was able to discuss this, yet even as he spoke he felt that the project was hopeless; the empty Exchequer would decide the matter.

Another matter on which his advice was sought was the rebuilding of part of Whitehall Palace. Through the carelessness of servants there had

* *Pepys' Diary*, 20 October 1666.

been a disastrous fire, and some of the buildings had had to be blown up with gunpowder.

But the talk of the town was the King's fabulous debts, chiefly to tradesmen, and the fact that there were menial servants at Court "lacking bread, who had not for months received a farthing of wages". Sir George Carteret admitted that he thought the kingdom "wholly lost", and wished only to retire into the country.

But debts or not, the lavish expenditure and magnificent entertainments at Court continued, and on St. George's Day Evelyn attended a sumptuous feast in the Banqueting House in honour of the Companions of the Order of the Garter. Each knight had "forty dishes to his mess, piled up five or six feet high". According to an ancient custom, the public were admitted, but within a short time, "all the food was flung about the room". Evelyn, "for fear of disorder", hastily retired.

But now even the rabble were beginning to show signs of restiveness with Court and Ministers, as it was discovered one morning that the trees in front of the Earl of Clarendon's house had been cut down, the windows broken, and a gibbet erected before his gate. Here, in bold letters, was painted

Three sights to be seen—
Dunkirk, Tangier and a barren Queen.

The sale of Dunkirk had come as a profound shock to the public; Tangier was regarded as a useless burden, and that the Queen had not produced an heir was regarded as a tragedy. Hence the inscription.

A few days later, as prophesied by Pepys the previous year, news arrived at Whitehall that an invasion by the Dutch was imminent, and according to Evelyn there was "a fear, a panic and a consternation such as I hope I shall never see more". A fleet of Dutch ships had apparently ventured as high as the Nore, and were bent on mischief. Fireships were therefore hurriedly sent to the spot, but the next appalling item of news was that Sheerness was lost, and the Dutch were in complete possession.

The drums now beat for the "trainbands", and men rushed home to gather their arms. Then, on the 12th of June, it was known that the Dutch had broken the chain at Chatham, destroyed the arsenal and stores, and burnt many ships including the *Royal Charles*. This was disaster, indeed, and at Court men were weeping openly. The bankers, meanwhile, were besieged by people demanding their money, but the banks refused to pay for another twenty days. Another depressing item of news was that the English sailors were deserting the ships and going over to the enemy.

Evelyn was at Court every day during this crisis, but the only advice the King could offer was that men "should adventure themselves no further than he would himself", and he and his Council had decided to abandon the Tower when the enemy approached. Yet this was the only strong fortification in London. Finally, the Court closed the Palace gates as a particularly gay party was in progress. Apparently until the enemy actually appeared at Whitehall they were not seriously concerned.

Huge crowds of people now assembled in the streets crying out that England was "bought and sold". The houses and carriages of Ministers were attacked, and it was feared that the Government would have to deal not only with an invasion but an insurrection. Now, too, people began to speak of Cromwell, his bravery, statesmanship, and patriotism. It was remembered how, in his time, no foreign power would have dared to take such liberties, and Holland had feared him so much that at his death Amsterdam had been lighted up as for a festival.

Evelyn feared that the enemy might venture up the Thames as far as London, so he hastily packed up his most precious possessions and plate and dispatched them to a safe place. Panic still prevailed, and "everybody was flying", he recorded, "none knew why or whither". He himself went to Woolwich to see the preparations for defence. Meanwhile, on the night of the 17th of June, at about 2 a.m., some "combustible matter" in Deptford yard caught fire and caused a fearful uproar as it was believed that the Dutch had landed and fired the Tower. There was utter consternation, and again men flew to arms and prepared to fight for their lives. "These", said Evelyn, "are sad and troublesome times."

Meanwhile the Dutch fleet still blocked the river, so that no ships could come in or out, and Evelyn was commanded by His Majesty to go with some officials and search in the outskirts of the city for fuel, which had become almost unobtainable. Evelyn did, indeed, discover some stores, and eventually reported back to the Palace, but nothing was done. He then went down to Chatham "to see what mischief the Dutch had done". And there was the incredible sight of the Dutch fleet lying within the very mouth of the Thames—"a dreadful spectacle as ever Englishmen saw, and a dishonour never to be wiped off". In the river off Chatham lay an even sadder spectacle—the burnt-out carcasses of three fine English ships, still smoking. Surely Sheerness and the ferry should have been fortified as a necessary precaution. Both had been abandoned, leaving the way clear for the enemy.

Evelyn returned home the next day, utterly disgusted at the negligence of those responsible. But would this deplorable episode be a lesson? He very much doubted it.

Finally, however, an inconclusive peace with Holland was signed, and the country was at peace again. To Evelyn's immense relief an exchange of prisoners was also arranged. He had been pressing for this for some time.

I.F.F.—D

CHAPTER 8

COURT AFFAIRS

THE year of 1668 dawned with better prospects for the country, although Evelyn was still deeply concerned about the wretched condition of the poor prisoners, "the grisly objects among the wounded", who were still in urgent need of blankets, medicines, and warm clothing. The weather was bitterly cold, and many men were dangerously ill. Some prisoners had been exchanged, but many still remained in England. But in spite of all his efforts, Evelyn could not obtain the money needed. At Court there was "deep and prodigious gaming" almost every night, and "vast heaps of gold were squandered away in a profuse manner". "This", recorded Evelyn in his diary, "I looked on as a horrid vice, and unsuitable in a Christian Court." Lady Castlemaine was known to be losing as much as £15,000 a night, and on one occasion had lost £25,000. This money would have provided for Evelyn's sick and wounded men, and much pain and misery might have been saved. His heart ached for those brave sailors, many of whom were crippled for life and would never again be able to maintain themselves. They numbered some thousands, and there were no pensions for such men. They would be beggars dependent on charity, who could look forward to nothing but starvation and penury. Yet no one cared. If Evelyn discussed their plight with a courtier he met with little sympathy; the majority were entirely engrossed in the splendid new palaces they were building, the titles they hoped to receive, the perquisites which might be obtained in one way or another. The plays at Court, which were most extravagantly staged, also "ate into the revenue". "It afflicted me", recorded Evelyn, "to see how the stage was degenerated, and polluted by the licentious times." He did, however, succeed in obtaining about £12,000 from the Treasury at about this time with which to repay his own and the other commissioners' private expenditure on the wounded sailors. But what was needed was an assured income.

Another symptom of the general feeling in the country was that the apprentices had pulled down some of the bawdy houses on Bankside, and apparently they had also contemplated pulling down "The great bawdy House at Whitehall". Finally, a sham petition, "The poor Whores' Petition", addressed to Lady Castlemaine, was published. It was written by the prostitutes whose houses had been destroyed by the apprentices, and the sad result of this was that four of the apprentices were hung, drawn, and quartered at Tyburn, and their heads stuck on London Bridge. Meanwhile, Lady Castlemaine was again pregnant, but the King had declared that the child was not his as she had formed a liaison with the actor, Henry Jermyn. According to Pepys, the King was jealous of the actor, Lady Castlemaine was jealous of Frances Stewart, and Jermyn was jealous of the King. "So they are all mad", added Pepys, "and so the kingdom is governed."

Lady Byron, Mary Knight, and Moll Davie were now all known to be the King's mistresses, and all lived in luxury. "Nothing but wickness and wicked men and women command the King", said Evelyn to Pepys,* and his word for this immoral behaviour was "bitchering". It was rumoured that the King intended to imitate King Henry VIII and divorce the Queen for "barrenness", an idea of which Bishop Burnet was said to approve. But apparently Charles was highly indignant at the plan.

Another fact which produced much criticism was that men of known bad reputation were received at Court. There was, for instance, a man named Blood, "an impudent, bold fellow, who had not long before attempted to steal the Imperial crown out of the Tower". He had stabbed the keeper and gone boldly away with the crown through all the guards; only because his horse fell was he arrested. "How he came to be pardoned, and even received into favour", said Evelyn, "not only after this but several other exploits almost as daring . . . I could never come to understand. . . . The man had not only a daring, but a villainous, unmerciful look, a false countenance, but very well spoken, and dangerously insinuating." The King, of course, was no judge of character, but in no other Court of Europe would such a scoundrel have been received.

* *Pepys' Diary*, 26 April 1667.

The Duke of York, too, was known to be heavily in debt, and his amorous affairs were almost as discreditable as the King's. "Every day things look worse and worse", said Pepys. "God fit us for the worst." Evelyn feared that the country might return again to a Commonwealth, and his fear was shared by others, many of whom were taking their money and valuables out of the country. "For that we must be ruined", said Evelyn, "our case being past belief." The country was "impoverished by the greatness of the taxes", and farmers and tradesmen were going bankrupt almost every day. The city merchants, too, were threatening to go abroad, and this was a serious threat, for trade alone had always maintained the country.

But it was a severe shock to Evelyn when his old friend, the Lord Chancellor, the Earl of Clarendon, fled the country. Apparently he had been held accountable for the war with Holland, and when the Dutch fleet had sailed up the Thames it was to Clarendon that the rage of the people had been directed. The House of Commons had detested him, as he had insisted that they encroached on the sacred prerogatives of the Crown. Nor had he attempted to hide his disapproval of the vices of the Court. Finally, he had been impeached by the Commons, and the King had taken the Seals from him. Now an Act had been passed which doomed Clarendon to perpetual exile. A cruel punishment.

Clarendon and Evelyn had been friends in France during the dark days of the civil war in England, and such a bond was not easily broken. They had shared adversity together.

It was now Evelyn's turn for some official entertaining, and a few weeks later the Venetian Ambassador arrived in London and stayed at Sayes Court before he made his state entry "with a very glorious train" into London. The King's gilded barge came up the river to carry him to the Tower, and later Evelyn accompanied him to his residence, to "a noble supper".

This year, however, was uneventful except that Mary presented him with another daughter, Elizabeth, and he published his book *The Perfection of Painting*. The following year brought another addition to the family, a daughter, who was born in May 1669 and named Susanna. Evelyn was now the possessor, therefore, of three little girls and one boy. At this time he also accomplished a very worth-while task, as his friend, Henry Howard, who owned some wonderful marble antiquities which

94

had belonged to his grandfather, was persuaded by Evelyn to present them to Trinity College, Oxford, where young John Evelyn was now a student. The statues had been found in the garden of Arundel House, "abandoned, broken and defaced", and they would have been lost to posterity unless they had been removed and preserved. Some of the marbles were placed in the new theatre at Oxford, and part of Howard's library was also bestowed on the University. Then, on the 9th of July, by invitation, Evelyn went to Oxford for the opening ceremony of the splendid Sheldonian Theatre, built by the munificence of the Archbishop of Canterbury. It had been designed by Dr. Christopher Wren, and the ceremony was conducted with imposing grandeur. There were lectures in all the Faculties, and then the guests retired to the Theatre, which was then dedicated, with solemn ceremony, followed by feasting and music.

The famous marbles, in Evelyn's opinion, "were 150 of the most ancient and worthy treasures of that kind in the learned world", and were well displayed, but he noticed that some were already scratched and damaged. He therefore advised that a holly hedge should be planted at the foot of the wall, "to be kept breast-high, to protect them". And this the Vice-Chancellor promised to do. Finally, Evelyn was created a Doctor of Law along with several eminent men.

On his return to London, Evelyn started work on the arrangement of the Howard library, which had been given to the Royal Society. He also started work on a book suggested by the King, *A History of the Dutch War*. The facts were contained in a mass of treatises, journals, libels, pamphlets, state papers, and letters, and the King had asked him to "make it a little keen, as the Hollanders had very unhandsomely abused him in their pictures, books and libels". Evelyn had previously declined this task, but the King had pressed the matter, and Evelyn had felt that he could "not decently refuse".

But before Evelyn could attempt any serious work on the book he became seriously ill with his old complaint, malaria, and did not recover until the 26th of September. A few weeks later he received bad news from Epsom; his brother Richard, to whom he was devoted, had become dangerously ill with a stone in the kidney, and he had been advised to submit to an operation—a very precarious remedy at that time. But apparently Richard could not face this. In order to persuade him, Evelyn and Samuel Pepys, who had been successfully "cut for the stone" some years previously, had been to Epsom and taken with them the stone, "as big as a tennis ball", which had been extracted from Pepys. But the unhappy patient was still adamant. Soon, therefore, his condition deteriorated, and he was in great agony of pain and began to suffer from convulsion fits. When at last he consented to undergo the operation and everything was prepared, his courage again failed; death, apparently, seemed preferable. Three days later Evelyn sat up with him all night, and early in the morning, after some hours of terrible suffering, he died. He was two years older than Evelyn. At the post-mortem examination a stone about the size of a nutmeg was found in the bladder. "He was a brother whom I most dearly loved for his many virtues", wrote Evelyn. Richard was the owner of "a noble seat", he had married "a large fortune", and had left one daughter. Evelyn returned to Deptford a few days later "full of sadness".

But life had to continue. There were continual visitors to Sayes Court to be entertained, there was much dining out—official and unofficial—and there were constant visits to relatives and friends in the country. The summer was too short to waste, and someone was always needing advice as to the design or situation of a new house. Mr. Slingsby, the Master of the Mint, wished to build a house, so on the 19th of July, with a party of friends, Evelyn drove into Cambridgeshire. The old mansion, "built for ancient hospitality", was large and ample, but was "ready to fall down with age, and placed in a dirty hole, a stiff clay, no water, next an adjoining churchyard, and with other inconveniences". A new site had to be found, and finally Evelyn suggested a plot on rising ground, surrounded by venerable woods, and with a charming view. It was a mile distant from the old house. This was a task he thoroughly enjoyed—to plan, to organize, to design.

Evelyn and his party then went on to Lord Arlington's, who had lately built a new house at great expense. And from thence they proceeded to Newmarket, where His Majesty was also building. Here Evelyn was horrified to find that the house was situated "in a dirty street, without any court or avenue, like a common one". Actually the King had bought an old house from Lord Thomond and had built on the foundations—a great mistake, but one which occurred only too often. Evelyn was, however, particularly impressed by the royal stables and the magnificent race horses which were kept, at vast expense, and with the greatest possible cosseting and care. Nothing was too good for these splendid animals in which the King took such pride.

During this visit, Evelyn and his party rode over the surrounding country, though with little enjoyment, as they were "pestered with heat and swarms of gnats". On his return to London, he drove down to Windsor to see the King. Windsor Castle was to be repaired, as it was "exceedingly ragged and ruinous", and there was much discussion as to ways and means. As usual, Evelyn's advice was asked. The King also took him aside on the terrace and urged him to proceed vigorously with his *History of the Dutch War*. The Secretaries of State had been asked to provide all the necessary papers. But, as Evelyn explained to a friend, "It is a grave and weighty undertaking in this nice and captious age, to deliver to posterity a three years' war, of three of the greatest powers and potentates in Europe against one nation newly restored, and even at that period conflicting with so many calamities besides". It was a task he had tried desperately to avoid, but there had seemed no way out. What a mass of complicated labour, therefore, lay before him.

He noticed at Windsor Castle that the hall had been handsomely decorated with arms, pikes, muskets, pistols, bandoliers, holsters, drums, and armour. The walls of the steep stairs were covered with "martial furniture", all new and bright, and the King's bedchamber was hung with tapestry and "curious and effeminate pictures". The interior of the Castle was "of astonishing beauty". All these improvements had been made since the Restoration, as for eighteen years, during the period of the Commonwealth, it had been used as a garrison and a prison. Apparently the King passed his time fishing and walking in the parks, playing bowls, hawking, planting trees, and watching cock-fights. There were many exotic birds in beautiful cages, and in his dining-room there was a cockatoo—a great favourite. Cards were also a popular pastime.

Back in London, Evelyn was obliged to spend many anxious days listening to a lawsuit which was tried before Lord Chief Justice Hales. It concerned, apparently, a large sum of money, and after the lawyers had "wrangled sufficiently", the case was referred to a new arbitration. "This", recorded Evelyn, "was the very first suit at law that ever I had with any creature, and oh, that it might be the last."

It was at about this time that Evelyn was able to introduce to the King that wonderful carver, Grinling Gibbons. In January 1671 Evelyn had first discovered this remarkable genius who had previously been employed by Betterton, the actor, for decorating the theatre in Dorset Gardens. Evelyn had met Gibbons quite by chance as he was taking a stroll in Deptford. Looking through the window of a poor cottage he had seen a young man carving a crucifix from a painting by Tintoretto. It was a marvellous piece of work, so Evelyn had knocked at the door and asked if he might enter. The young carver, to whom Evelyn took an immediate liking, explained that he was merely a beginner, and would be glad to sell this piece for £100. "In good earnest", said Evelyn, "the very frame (carved) was worth the money, there being nothing in nature so tender or delicate as the flowers and festoons about it, and yet the work was very strong. In the piece was more than one hundred figures of men, etc. I found he was likewise musical and very civil, sober and discreet in his discourse. . . . So, desiring leave to visit him sometime, I went away."

Evelyn told this story to the King and asked permission to bring Gibbons and his incomparable work to Whitehall; the King would certainly be glad to employ him. A week or two later, therefore, Pepys and Dr. Christopher Wren dined with Evelyn and then walked over to the thatched cottage to see the carving. About ten days later Grinling Gibbons brought his work to Whitehall and, after the King had admired it, it was carried to the Queen. At this juncture, however, the King was called away, and "a French peddling woman, one Madame de Boord, who used to bring petticoats and fans and baubles out of France to the ladies" began to find fault with the work "which she understood no more than an ass or a monkey", said Evelyn. This was infuriating, and Evelyn was so angry to see that the Queen was "governed by an ignorant French-woman" that he ordered the crucifix to be taken away. "So", said Evelyn, "this incomparable artist had his labour only for his pains, which not a little displeased me, and Gibbons was fain to send it down to his cottage again." Later it was sold to Sir George Viner.

Dr. Christopher Wren, however, promised to employ Gibbons,* and His Majesty also promised to find work for him at Windsor.

The new favourite at the royal harem now was Mlle Querouaille, a pretty "baby-faced" French girl who had come to England with Charles's sister, Henrietta, Duchess of Orleans, the previous year, and had been appointed Maid of Honour to the Queen almost immediately. She already

* The carving in the choir of St. Paul's Cathedral was executed by Gibbons.

98

occupied beautiful apartments at Whitehall. Mlle Querouaille was a guest at Lord Arlington's "noble pile", Euston, when early in October Evelyn stayed there. Lord Arlington wanted advice from Evelyn as to the planting of his park and avenues. There was a very large house party, and for fifteen days at least 200 people were entertained, in addition to their servants, horses and guards, "at infinite expense". The King, who was staying at Newmarket for the race meeting, came over to Lord Arlington's almost every evening, and apparently on one uproarious night (though Evelyn was not present) the King was "bedded" with Mlle Querouaille "like a wedded bride". The stocking was flung, in traditional fashion, and the caudle drunk.

Evelyn saw some of the horse racing, but he and his friends spent most mornings hunting and hawking. He also spent much of his time with the French Ambassador. From Euston, Evelyn rode on to Norwich to see the ducal palace owned by his friend, Lord Henry Howard, who wanted advice as to the building of an additional wing and pavilion. But Evelyn thought the palace—which stood in the market-place—"an old wretched building", and advised his friend "to demolish all, and set it up in a better place". He also suggested that he should build a fine palace at Arundel House, the Strand, London.

Now, also, came Evelyn's opportunity to meet, for the first time, Sir Thomas Browne, the famous author and physician, with whom he had previously corresponded and long wished to know. His house and garden proved to be "a paradise and cabinet of rarities", and together they visited all the interesting sights in Norwich—the beautiful cathedral, the stately churches, and the "noble flint buildings". Evelyn was particularly impressed with the last. But he was quite horrified to see that the churchyards of Norwich were "filled up with earth, or rather dead bodies, one upon another, for want of earth, even to the very top of the walls, so that the churches seemed to be built in pits".

On his return to Euston, Evelyn found "the jolly blades racing, dancing, feasting and revelling, more resembling an abandoned rout than a Christian Court". From that scene of noisy, vulgar carousing he was glad to depart. Back in London, Evelyn began serious work on his *History of the Dutch War*, but he was cruelly hindered by the lack of documents which had been promised but which did not materialize. At Sayes Court he had every facility for work—a quiet study and an excellent library—

but the compilation of the work was extremely laborious, and he began to regret that he had ever been persuaded to undertake the task.

He had also been appointed a Member of the Council of Foreign Plantations at a salary of £500 a year, and this entailed a mass of detailed work, many meetings with other members of the Council, and many dinners. They were concerned with New England, Jamaica, the Leeward Islands, St. Christopher, and Barbadoes. Trade with Britain also came within their jurisdiction. But the work was interesting.

As a relaxation, Evelyn sometimes strolled down to the Deptford docks, where ship-building was always in progress. The King's yachts were anchored there, and Evelyn much enjoyed watching the carpenters at their work. Here he frequently met Pepys and Captain Cocke, and they would generally dine together at the local tavern. Pepys, of course, was always excellent company; one could never be dull in that jovial, exhilarating presence. Sometimes Pepys would call on Evelyn at Sayes Court and stay to drink a glass of wine. Evelyn would read to him some of his poetry—of which secretly he was rather proud—and parts of several plays he had written. But Pepys, in his diary, confessed that the plays were "very good, but not as he conceits them, I think, to be". The poems, too, were read "with too much gusto". But Pepys added, with regard to Evelyn, "In fine, a most excellent person he is, and must be allowed a little for a little conceitedness, but he may well be so, being a man so much above others".*

Certainly Evelyn was distinctly original in some of his habits, for he confessed that in summer he used to bathe his head with a decoction of hot aromatic herbs, and then his servant would be asked to pour cold fountain water over his head "for half an hour at a time". This, he declared, was very refreshing, "and an incredible benefit to me the whole year after". He confessed, also, that he used to rub his eyelids with rectified spirits of wine in which a few rosemary flowers had been distilled. He believed that this treatment assisted his sight, his hearing, and his sense of smell. Many years previously, when looking at an eclipse of the sun without glasses, he had damaged his sight. He was now, therefore, particularly careful with regard to his eyes.

* *Pepys' Diary*, Bell's edition, vol. V, p. 137.

CHAPTER 9

THE SECOND DUTCH WAR

THE peace of Breda, apparently, had been an uneasy one, for on the 12th of March, 1672, the King told Evelyn that a war with Holland was again imminent. King Louis XIV of France had persuaded Charles to unite with him in this war, and for this assistance Charles was to be paid £2,000,000 a year for four years. The Triple Alliance between Holland, England, and Sweden had been broken, at the persuasion of Louis, who had paid Sweden a very large sum. Charles, who was always in need of money, had needed little persuasion, but his sister, Henrietta, had acted as plenipotentiary in the matter. Again Evelyn was appointed one of the commissioners for the sick and wounded. A thankless task.

On the 12th of March, although there had been no declaration of war, the first blow was given to the Dutch convoy of the Smyrna fleet, and Evelyn (who was not aware of the full facts) said, with righteous indignation, "Surely this was a quarrel slenderly grounded, and not becoming Christian neighbours. We are like to thrive accordingly."

So again, as England was at war with Holland, Evelyn's grim work as a commissioner was resumed. Many sailors had been wounded in the Smyrna conflict, and accommodation, food, clothing, and medical treatment all had to be arranged. Often Evelyn wondered why he continued with the work. But who would take his place? There were no perquisites or bribes attached to this post, so few envied him his task. He had, however, gained valuable experience in the work, and the men he assisted were so pathetically grateful that he could not desert them. It was certainly a worth-while and rewarding undertaking.

He made many journeys, therefore, down to Canterbury, Dover, Deal, the Isle of Thanet, Sandwich, and Margate. Here were hundreds of "miserably wounded men", but their sufferings were almost too pitiful to describe, and "this unnecessary war" angered and distressed him beyond measure. Why should men have to suffer in this way? Yet what could he do? He was a voice crying in the wilderness. Kings and Ministers decided these matters; they had the power of life and death over men, and nothing he could say would make the slightest difference. The war was merely a money transaction so that Charles's debts and wicked extravagance could be met. And for this men must bleed and die. Indeed, the ghastly sights he had to witness made the blood run cold, and surgeons, as they performed their gruesome operations, were often white with anxiety. On one visit, in order in give courage to a sailor whose leg had to be amputated, Evelyn was present. But he was affected almost to tears by the man's tremendous courage and fine stoicism. The excruciating operation was performed without any anaesthetic— as was inevitable at that time—and the patient was merely strapped down. Unfortunately the wound became infected with gangrene (a very common complication) and after another terrible operation he died. "Lord, what misery are mortal men subject to!", said Evelyn. "And what confusion and mischief do the *avarice, anger and ambition* of Princes cause in the world!"

Evelyn returned via Rochester, where he visited a large mansion which he had hired as a prison, and here he installed a Provost Marshal and other officers, arriving back at Sayes Court in April. He was not, however, free to follow his own occupations for long, as on the 10th of May he received an urgent letter from the King *commanding* him to go immediately to the coast and to "observe the motion of the Dutch fleet and ours", the Duke and his fleet being now "under sail", coming from Portsmouth through the downs, where it was believed there might be a naval battle. Evelyn therefore started off in his coach (merely a glorified cart, like all coaches at that time), first to Chatham, then to Canterbury, and on to Dover. But the fleet did not appear until the 16th, when the Duke of York, accompanied by the French squadron (in all over 270 ships, of which 100 were men-of-war) sailed by; they were following the Dutch who had withdrawn. "Such a gallant and formidable navy never, I think, spread sail upon the sea", said Evelyn. "It was a goodly yet terrible sight, passing eastward by the straits betwixt Dover and Calais on a glorious day." They were soon out of sight, and Evelyn would have gone aboard but the wind was too high. He went instead to see his wounded prisoners and the castle, returning to London extremely tired. He then gave the King an account of his journey, and reported that all was now in readiness for "eventualities".

A week later he was again "commanded" to go to the coast, so went to Rochester, where he found many sick and wounded prisoners newly arrived from the engagement on the 28th. There had been heavy casualties, and the gallant Earl of Sandwich had been killed—a grievous loss to the Navy. Evelyn had met Lord Sandwich only a few days previously, in Whitehall. His lordship was at that time "under a cloud", and had shaken hands with him and bid him goodbye, saying that he was certain they would never meet again. "They will not let me live", he had said mournfully. "I must do something, I know not what, to save my reputation." Apparently some time earlier he had captured eight Dutch war ships and about twenty other vessels and had apportioned part of the cargo to his own use. He had also been suspected of cowardice because he had not been sufficiently rash in a previous engagement with the Dutch. But Evelyn thought him "prudent as well as valiant; he was for deliberation and reason, they for action and slaughter without either". His death was a tragedy. "He was", said Evelyn, "learned in sea affairs, in politics, in mathematics, and in music. He had been on divers embassies, was of a sweet and obliging temper, sober, chaste, very ingenious, a true nobleman, an ornament to the Court and his Prince; nor has he left any behind him who approach his many virtues." On the other hand, the Earl was heavily in debt and quite out of favour at Court. Possibly Providence had stepped in to ease him of his heavy burden, for a man who had offended the King and Council was ruined; all favour and employment came from that royal source. Pepys had also been utterly devoted for many years to Lord Sandwich, and mourned him like a brother.

While Evelyn was at Rochester he took charge of the funeral of Monsieur Rabinierre, Rear-Admiral of the French squadron, who had died of wounds. He was buried, with full naval honours, in the Cathedral. The following day Evelyn sailed to the Fleet, which was "riding at the bouy of the Nore", where he met the King, the Duke, Lord Arlington, and all the senior officers of *The Charles*, now "lying miserably shattered".

At Sheerness, Evelyn made his report to His Majesty, and returned home; it had been an exhausting and depressing journey.

But more trouble was in store, for on the 18th of August he was again commanded by the King to go at once to Gravesend, where 800 sick and wounded men had just arrived. They were carried off the ships, soaked in blood, ashen-pale, and groaning in anguish. Some hobbled, some crawled on hand and knees; all were pitiful to see. The dead had already been thrown overboard.

After each of these tiring journeys Evelyn was obliged to see the King and ask for money, and Charles assured him, in his genial, casual way, that something would be done. The sums received, however, were hopelessly inadequate. It was a scandal, and an example of miserable ingratitude to men who had fought valiantly. Many, indeed, had been pressed into service; they were not even volunteers.

Evelyn was so harassed, weary, and depressed, in fact, that he contemplated resigning his post; but if he failed these men, to whom could they turn? No one else would undertake the work; of that he was certain.

Yet there was one consolation in his necessary attendance at Court; he had become greatly attached to one of the Queen's Maids of Honour, Margaret Blagge, a beautiful, intelligent girl of about twenty years of age. She was the youngest of the four daughters of Colonel Blagge of Horningsherth, who had been Groom of the Bedchamber to King Charles I, and one of the first to take up arms in his royal master's cause. He was Governor of Wallingford when it was surrendered in the year 1646, and after the Restoration he had been appointed Governor of Yarmouth and Languard Port, but had died shortly after.

Margaret had spent part of her childhood in France in the care of the Duchess of Richmond, but finally the little girl had been committed to the care of the Countess of Guildford. After the Restoration, Margaret had returned to her mother, and at the age of fourteen had been appointed a Maid of Honour to the Duchess of York, the daughter of Lord Chancellor Clarendon. She had stayed with the Duchess until her death.

At Court, Margaret had the reputation of a saint, and was considered "a rare example of piety and virtue". To Evelyn she seemed like some delicate, exquisite flower in a rank wilderness, and it was a miracle that she had remained pure and innocent in that "licentious and depraved Court". It was Mary Evelyn who had first recognized her remarkable

104

character, and Evelyn himself had barely noticed this young girl when she had visited Sayes Court with her older friend, Lady Berkeley. Mary had discovered that this young Maid of Honour, courted and admired by the greatest in the land, worked indefatigably for the poor. She visited hospitals and the meanest cottages in order to distribute comforts, money, and medicines, all paid for out of her own income. She would send doctors to attend the indigent sick, and parsons to administer the Holy Sacrament and to comfort the dying. She would sit for hours by their bedsides, reading and praying to them. She would take care of their children and, if possible, arrange for their education and apprenticeships. She regularly visited debtors' prisons, and would pay the debts of prisoners to effect their release. To assist in this charitable work, she employed a young woman who distributed pensions to the poor and made provision for orphan children. During Lent, Margaret spent every moment of her leisure in making garments for poor people, and these she distributed with her own hands. She was truly compassionate, and genuinely pious, but never spoke of her work. Evelyn's name for her was Electra, the bright, and he adored her charming gaiety.

Had Margaret been a Catholic she would almost certainly have become a nun. And, indeed, she confessed to Evelyn that she contemplated retiring to Hertfordshire to live alone under the direction of the Dean of Hertford (Dr. George Benson), who had "long been her spiritual father". She confessed to Evelyn, also, that she disliked Court life, but this post had been chosen for her by her mother who had considered it a great honour.

Margaret was particularly afraid of the King. In her room, therefore, she had pinned up a "scheme of devotion" to remind her of special duties and prayers. It was headed "My life, by God's grace, without which I can do nothing", and one of her resolutions was "Be sure never to talk to the King. . . . When they speak filthily, though I be laughed at, look grave." Then she had added, "Lord, assist me. . . . When I pray, Lord, hear me; when I am praised, God humble me."

It was perhaps to be deplored, but, as time passed, Evelyn became even more enamoured of this pure and lovely girl. He was irresistibly drawn to Whitehall and, when Margaret appeared in the plays at Court, he was enraptured; she was a wonderfully talented actress. It was the love of a middle-aged man for a girl of twenty, and he told himself—

as indeed he probably believed—that this was a spiritual love, utterly platonic and unselfish. He wished only to guide her now that she was an orphan. Could that be wrong? Could Mary, his wife, blame him for this?

Mary, in fact, never blamed him, and when he was absent from Sayes Court, sometimes for a week or two, nothing was said when he returned. She was the same quiet, patient Mary, the mother of his many children. Only on one occasion did she very gently rebuke him. He had been in London for five weeks, staying in his lodgings in Westminster, and Mary had written to say that she rejoiced in his happiness, and was glad that he had such a delightful friend as Margaret Blagge. But with a little forgivable sarcasm she added: "My dear, I hope you do not imagine, though I live in the country and converse with sea-nymphs, and now and then with a tarpaulin hero, that I do not apprehend the difference between this kind of felicity and that which you possess in a glorious Court amongst great beauties and wits . . . persons whose ideas are of a higher nature, whose minds are pure, and actions innocent." She then reminded him that she, his wife, also had "a little interest" in him, and she hoped he had not forgotten her. In response to this charming and touching appeal he returned home the next day. Mary knew, of course—it was common knowledge—that the Court was utterly depraved, although she rarely went to Whitehall. She was always busy with her large household, her "flock of little girls", and her old father, who was often ill with gout. In addition, she worked assiduously amongst the poor, assisted the sick, and carefully supervised her children's education.

Indeed, Mary was a typical seventeenth-century wife. Her role was to bear children, to supervise her husband's household, to nurse him in sickness, to keep his secrets, and to guard his reputation. She had no marital rights whatever. This was the state of the law between man and wife at that time, and it was accepted without question.

Sometimes, after a visit to Court, Evelyn would stay and dine with the maids of honour, and apparently they regarded him as a sort of fatherly schoolmaster, although they declared that he had "a forbidding countenance". But Margaret had now confessed to him that she was secretly betrothed to Sidney Godolphin, one of the grooms of the bed-chamber. They had been friends for nine years, but they could not marry owing to his onerous and demanding Court duties.

He hoped, however, in a few years' time, to be appointed Master of the Robes, and marriage might then be possible.

Godolphin was certainly a fine fellow—clever, cool-headed, and (according to Bishop Burnet) extremely modest and tactful. The King was reported to have said that Godolphin was "never *in* the way, and never out of the way". The perfect courtier, in fact. Samuel Pepys also thought highly of him: "I do find him a very pretty and able person, a man of very fine parts."

The wisest course was for Evelyn to keep away from Court—far, far from Margaret. But this, with his many commitments, was not possible. Yet, indeed, he was really no courtier. He was, as he confessed, "wholly unfit to converse with the knights of the carpet. Some said that I was morose and affected, others that I was plainly stupid and a fop. . . ."

The latest news at Court was that the Duchess of Richmond had had smallpox and apparently lost all her beauty, but that the French girl, Mlle Querouaille, had given birth to a son, which Charles acknowledged as his. She herself was shortly to be created Duchess of Portsmouth. One courageous parson, therefore, had startled the concubines and courtesans of Whitehall by preaching a sermon against adultery. Also, at Stoks Market a pillion had been set beside the statue of Charles II on horseback, and on the horse's breast was written: "Haste! Post haste for a midwife!"

Mlle Querouaille had been painted by Lely as the Madonna and Child, and someone had placed these lines beneath the portrait:

> Who can on this picture look
> And not straight be wonder-struck
> That such a sneaking, dowdy thing
> Should make a beggar of a King?

Another addition to the King's numerous illegitimate offspring was a daughter born to Moll Davie, the famous dancer and actress.

Yet the most disturbing and surprising news at Court was that the Duke of York had now become a Catholic. He had apparently withstood, with unswerving firmness, the attempts of his mother to change his religion when he was an exile in France, as although Henrietta Maria had promised her husband many times never to attempt to influence her children, she had broken that promise; she was entirely ruled by the Jesuits. On Easter Day, however, the Duke's apostasy was confirmed, as Evelyn and his son John took Communion, and then, "to the amazement of everyone", the Duke of York who, until the previous year had always received Communion with the King, did not on this occasion do so. "This", as Evelyn said, "gave exceeding grief and scandal to the whole nation, that the heir of it, and the son of a martyr to the Protestant religion, should apostasize. What the consequences of this will be, God only knows, and wise men dread."

Evelyn had seen, with alarm, in April, "the fopperies of the Papists at Somerset House and York House", where the French Ambassador had set up a representation of Christ at the Paschal Supper with his disciples "on figures and puppets made as big as the life in waxwork" (Evelyn). Indeed, hatred and fear of the Catholic religion was still one of the ruling passions of the community. There existed also a very real fear that England might become a Popish dynasty, allied with the dynasties of the Continent, which were at once Popish and despotic. And if so, might not England experience the terrible persecution and bloodshed which had taken place on the Continent?

In November it became known that the Duke of York was to marry the Catholic princess, Mary Beatrice D'Este, the daughter of the Duke of Modena. The Duke was now a widower with two young daughters, and had always been popular as a handsome soldier and sailor who had fought for his country. But had not Charles I married a Catholic queen with disastrous results? Was history to repeat itself? Parliament had already expressed its strong disapproval.

Nevertheless, on the 30th of September, 1673, the Duke and Mary Beatrice of Modena were married by proxy in Italy. The reluctant bride was only fifteen years of age, convent bred, and very beautiful, as her portraits show. She left Italy and landed at Dover, with her train, on the 21st of November, 1673.

108

CHAPTER 10

MARGARET GODOLPHIN

THE war with Holland had come to an end by the year 1674, as, although Louis had been successful in his war, Charles's Council had warned him that France was growing far too powerful, and her navy had become a serious menace. Charles explained the situation to the French Ambassador: "Pressed by my subjects, I am like a besieged city which can no longer defend itself." He had now consented, also, to the betrothal of his niece Mary to Prince William of Orange. Was it policy, therefore, to regard the Dutch as enemies?

To Evelyn, the cessation of hostilities was an enormous relief, as many prisoners of war and wounded sailors were still in his care. Rich friends, however, were extremely generous at this time. Lady Mordaunt frequently gave him large sums of money for the prisoners, and Margaret Blagge was equally generous, although her gifts were sent anonymously, and Evelyn only discovered the donor later. Evelyn still visited his hospitals, but less frequently. He therefore had more time for his literary pursuits. But his *History of the Dutch War* had been abandoned on the King's instructions. His Majesty explained that the Dutch were exceedingly displeased with Evelyn's treatise, the *History of Commerce*, which had been published, and was to be his preface to the *History of the Dutch War*. Evelyn had read the book to the King before it had been sent to the Press, but now the Holland Ambassador had taken exception to the book and asked that it should be called in. All copies were to be seized and sent to the printer. Another strong argument for the suppression of the book was that the Treaty of Breda was about to be signed. The King explained to Evelyn, however, that he was extremely pleased with his work. Evelyn, therefore, wrote to Pepys at this time: "I had no thanks for what I had done, and have been accounted since, I suppose, a useless fop only fit to plant coleworts, but I can't bristle, nor yet bend to mean submission. And this, sir, is the history of your historian." The matter was finished.

But Evelyn's affair with Margaret Blagge was by no means finished. She had left the Court, having declared that she was tired of Court life, and gone to live with Lord and Lady Berkeley in Mayfair. Lord Berkeley's house, built in the Palladian style, was one of the most glorious palaces in London, with its magnificent cedar staircase, its "noble" rooms, and its "princely" furniture. Evelyn thought the fore-court, stables, and garden "incomparable", and it was he who had advised the planting of the holly hedges on the terrace.

Margaret had a pretty room of her own, and here Evelyn wended his way each week, generally staying to sup or dine with her. He would bring the new devotions he had written, and together they would kneel and pray, for a long time, by candlelight. These hours were very sweet, very holy, very precious.

Margaret had written, a year or two before, that she had "never a friend in the world", and later she had added, "You are then my first friend, the first that ever I had, and ever shall be so. I thankfully accept your counsel and will endeavour to follow it." He had taken charge of her financial affairs, and was her adviser. She had confessed that Godolphin was now pressing her to marry him, secretly—a step which Evelyn could not bear to contemplate. She confessed, also, that she was afraid of marriage, of child-bearing, and of marital responsibility. He reasoned with her, very gently. Should she not be content to belong to Christ only? And he had written in one of his letters, "God Almighty knows my heart. I do love you, but it is because you love *Him*."

The deception was, indeed, perhaps natural, for his love for Margaret was utterly bound up with his love of God; he would have sworn that there was nothing sensual about it. She was incredibly innocent; she did not seem to know the meaning of passion, as between man and woman, yet vaguely she was yearning for love: that was clear.

However, she was willing to be advised by him, and he was determined not to lose her. "As for my being married", she wrote, "*you know you won't let me resolve. . . .* There is enough of this. *. . . Now to God again.*

. . . By you I will be directed." Well, he was but human. Sometimes he felt like a drowning man, struggling hopelessly against the current, and certainly in his letters he could not restrain himself; the words came pouring forth. She wrote in return: "What mean you to make me weep, and to break my heart by your love to me? Take me and all I have. Give me but your love, my dear friend. Tuesday is longed for by me, and nights and days move a tedious pace till I am near you." It was *spiritual* love, and nothing else; that he would have sworn. But sometimes it surged over him with waves of irresistible intensity.

He could not resist, either, sending her handsome presents—a beautiful jewel, a splendidly bound book. He persuaded her, too, to sit for her portrait to Matthew Dixon. But when it was finished it did not please him; she was far more beautiful. Nevertheless, he had the picture framed and hung it in his bedchamber at Sayes Court. Mary said little, but apparently she confided in her brother-in-law, William Glanville, who was a widower and one of her admirers. Glanville declared without qualification that he did not believe in "seraphic" love, and he added: "I dare not wish our friendship had begun when we first saw one another, for I am conscious I could not have trusted myself with loving you twenty years ago [his wife had died in 1651] as well as I do now. You in those days might have been safe in *your* virtue, but I could not then be sure of *my* peace. . . ."

Mary had another admirer in Mr. Bohun, who had been her son's tutor for three years. To him, also, she confessed that she was sometimes lonely. As for the portrait, to Mary's amusement, it was soon brought down by Evelyn to the best parlour.

Early in the New Year of 1674 Evelyn introduced a new feature into the Berkeley House meetings—the Spiritual Communion, an imaginary celebration of the sacrament, with his own additions and rubrics. The following day, after one such Communion, Margaret wrote: "Did not our hearts burn within yesterday, and our very spirits glow whilst we were in communion with Christ? How delightful it is. What relish it kept all the day, and even to this moment! And must we not be very careful that we lose it not this week?" She had also written: "Indeed, I love to see you, and be with you, but nothing obliges me so much as when you write to me."

Ah, what long letters he wrote. And when again she warned him that

111

Godolphin was pressing her to marry, he composed a suitable prayer for her:

> I am tossed with the tempest of my impetuous passions. . . . Oh, Thou who commandest the winds to cease and the raging billows to be still, rebuke the waves of my unruly affections. . . . I am stung and bitten with the fiery serpent of my sensual appetites. . . . Raise my affections to nobler desires . . . and quench the ardours that consume me. . . . Take my heart, sweet Jesus, take it. . . . Nothing, my Saviour, is there in this world which so bitterly afflicts me as that I had not presented it Thee sooner, and Thou hadst been my first Love, my only Love. . . .

This prayer she repeated, fervently, many times.

She wrote, a little later, with regard to marriage, "I know not *what* to determine. . . . I am in a strait and know not what to choose. Determine Thou for me, Blessed Lord." Then she wrote: "No, no. I will remain my Blessed Saviour's. He shall be my Love, my husband, my all. I will keep my virginity, present it unto Christ, and not put myself into the temptation of loving anything in competition with God."

So Evelyn had convinced her. She was to be preserved for himself—and their heavenly friendship—and, of course, for *God*. From this time she spent hours in her chamber, on her knees, weeping and praying. She began to look pale and thin, so in alarm Evelyn changed his tactics. Perhaps pity for him might move her, and he asked what would become of their precious friendship if she married. He wrote: "Whilst *you* are in the light, *I* in darkness and in a chaos; for when you are gone, what is the Court, or the country to your friend?" Later, however, when she began to look really ill and haggard, he was genuinely concerned, and wrote: "Go, go, then, my bold friend, when you please, and be happy." In reply, she thanked him for his resignation of her. "I beg of God", she wrote, "with many tears that I may love nothing but Him. Ah, that He would hear me!" If Evelyn was to lose her, then so be it; the struggle would at least be over, but it was cruelly hard. He adored her: he was hopelessly in love.

In November 1675 Margaret decided to go to Paris with Lord and Lady Berkeley, and young John Evelyn was to accompany them, Margaret having offered, in her kind way, to keep an eye on him (he was about twenty years of age). Evelyn travelled with the party down to the coast, and they set off with four coaches, three wagons, and about forty horses.

112

They went by way of Rochester and Canterbury, and were obliged to travel slowly as Lord Berkeley had had a stroke a few days previously and had not yet recovered.

In Canterbury Cathedral, Evelyn and Margaret prayed together—a blessed and lovely experience—and then at Dover she gave him her will and told him that she had made him her executor. She wept bitterly at parting, but was at last carried to the yacht, and the fort from the castle fired seventeen guns for His Excellency and was answered with five according to custom. Evelyn watched the ship until it was out of sight, and then went to church to beg a blessing on their voyage. He felt utterly desolate and heart-broken.

Margaret and he corresponded while she was in Paris, and he wrote to her: "I am often considering whether I shall evermore see you in this world. The time is short, 'tis uncertain, and when I shall see you I am still in danger of losing you again." He continually begged her to pray for him. He had thought during the last few months, that her affection was in some way changing; her letters were different, and she frequently asked him to show them to Mary. She had also asked him to return all her letters, and he had done so.

Meanwhile, Lord Berkeley's affairs took up a great deal of Evelyn's time. He had promised to collect his rents, solicit supplies from the Lord Treasurer, supervise his property and tenants, and correspond weekly. This (as Evelyn confessed) was "more than enough to employ any drudge in England; but what will not friendship and love make one do?" He had agreed to undertake this task merely to please Margaret.

Young John Evelyn also wrote long letters from Paris, and apparently he was not happy with Lord and Lady Berkeley. They had lodged him in a high, cold garret, without hangings or furnishings, next to the footmen, so that he was unable to entertain visitors. And Lord Berkeley had written critically of John: "He will never dance, or make a leg well, nor have his periwig or cravat in good order, or be a la mode, but he will prove an honest, solid and judicious man, and be very good company." Mary, too, felt that her son's position was a little ignominious: "I am sorry Jack is no better used by the Lord Ambassador, after so much profession of kindness", she wrote to Evelyn, who was in London. John was even more unhappy when he was told that Margaret was to return to England. "Pray, sir, consider", he wrote to his father, "that I am left here alone, for when she is out of that family I cannot endure the thoughts of it, and if I should put myself into it again I am sure I should die of melancholy in a little time." He confessed that he was quite in love with Margaret: "I am become most desperately her humble servant. . . . Either let me come home and settle to the law, or let me travel." He was obviously quite unaware of his father's deep affection for Margaret.

On the 3rd of April, 1676, Margaret landed at Dover, to Evelyn's "great joy", and a fortnight later he dined with her and her sister, Lady Yarborough, at Margaret's new lodgings at Covent Garden. During dinner, to his profound shock, Lady Yarborough announced that Margaret had been married for eleven months to Sidney Godolphin. Evelyn was stunned; it was like a thunderclap, and although later, when they were alone, Margaret was very penitent, he was deeply hurt. She had declared that she would never marry without consulting him first, and she had promised, also, that Evelyn should "give her away" at the ceremony. They continued to dine together, however, almost every week, as she and Godolphin had not officially acknowledged their marriage. Later, in the early autumn, while Godolphin was at Newmarket for the usual meeting, Margaret came to stay at Sayes Court for three weeks, and it was clear that she was supremely happy in her marriage. What a blessed three weeks! He was, indeed, sitting with the gods at their golden tables and tasting of earth's bliss. She would walk with him, early in the morning, while the grass was still wet, and the beautiful autumn sunlight was streaming across the trees and flowers. He would point out to her the diamond dew glittering on the thorn, the wonderful spider's web laced with opalescent beads, each one a miracle. He would show her the rare plants, the rare flowers. He would pick a peach for her, straight from the wall, and would see her eyes light up as she bit into the delicious fruit. Then they would wander down to the edge of the moat where the fish darted and the swans floated majestically. He thought that she, too, was like a swan, pure and proud, yet very modest, very unassuming. At night, in the moonlit garden, the heavenly scent of roses would drift over the grass, and they would look at the bright stars together. Then on returning to the house she would sit sipping her wine, while the delicate colour came and went in her cheeks. Her smile was heaven, her voice enchantment, and the very rustle of her silk dress had a curious fascination. Even the children adored

114

her, gazing up into her face with wonder and admiration. She belonged, of course, to another, so it was all a mockery and a farce. Yet how precious were these days and nights! How infinitely sweet! When she had returned to London, gloom descended.

Evelyn had offered to superintend the building of a small house attached to Whitehall, for Margaret and her husband, and the planning of this meant that he was able to see her frequently. Evelyn was also heavily engaged in the supervision of Lord Berkeley's affairs—a difficult and laborious task which entailed "an intolerable servitude and correspondence". Lord Berkeley had entrusted him with his seal, his keys, and his will. When His Lordship returned to England, therefore, Evelyn was immensely relieved. Evelyn had collected for him and sent to France no less than £20,000.

The time, in fact, had come for a holiday, and in July, a few weeks later, Evelyn accepted an invitation from Lord Arlington (the Lord Chamberlain) to visit Euston again. Lord Arlington had been making extensive improvements to his mansion and garden, and was anxious to show Evelyn the result of his plans. Evelyn was met at Bury St. Edmunds by his lordship's coach and six horses, and the following day they hunted in the park, killed a fat buck, and went hawking. The park was 9 miles in circumference, and here roamed a thousand red and fallow deer. Since Evelyn's last visit the mansion had been greatly improved; the King's apartments had been gorgeously furnished, there were some fine Old Masters in the picture gallery, and there was a splendid library, a pretty chapel, an orange garden, and a conservatory 100 feet long. A miniature canal ran under my lady's dressing-room window, and carp and fowl came there to be fed; it was all quite delightful.

Evelyn spent three weeks in this paradise with immense pleasure. Everything was magnificent—if a little pompous—and Lord and Lady Arlington loved dispensing hospitality; they adored beautiful things. But all this was at vast expense, and Evelyn knew for a fact that they were heavily in debt, yet "knew not how to retrench". A situation he could not but deplore.

On his journey home, Lord Arlington's coach conveyed Evelyn as far as Bury St. Edmunds, and from thence he went to Newmarket. He also paid another visit to Audley End* before returning to London. And back

* Audley End now belonged to the King.

115

in the great city he went to see the new Bedlam hospital, which he thought "magnificently built". A week later he drove, with the Lord Chamberlain, down to Windsor, to see the alterations to the Castle. Evelyn was particularly anxious to see the painted ceilings ("the rare work of Verrio") and Gibbons's "incomparable carving". From Windsor the party drove to Houndslow Heath, where the newly raised Army gave a splendid display.

During the summer Evelyn also visited the Duke of Norfolk's "palace" at Weybridge, on which His Grace had spent nearly £10,000, and Lord Thomas Howard showed Evelyn all over the mansion. But what was most interesting were the hiding-places for the Popish priests, which were cleverly constructed cupboards with the entrances cunningly concealed. In showing these, Lord Howard—who was a Roman Catholic—confessed to Evelyn that he never trusted Papists with any secrets, but "used Protestants only in all business of importance". This, surely, was a strange and significant admission.

Margaret Godolphin and her husband moved into their new house in March, and she told Evelyn that she was expecting a child in the early autumn; she was delighted. On the 3rd of September, therefore, Evelyn called to inquire after her health, and found her "in labour". He stayed until the child, a boy, was born, and was admitted to see Margaret and her baby. She seemed well, and said: "I hope you have given thanks to God for His infinite mercy to me."

Evelyn returned to Deptford, but a few days later a message from Godolphin was delivered to Evelyn while in church. Apparently Margaret was desperately ill with puerperal fever, and he begged for their prayers. Evelyn and Mary took boat immediately for Whitehall, where they found Margaret in raving delirium, and Godolphin himself so distraught that he was unable even to speak to the doctors or servants. He lay on a hard board, blaming himself, and praying and weeping. He begged Evelyn to stay. Lady Berkeley was also present, and a specialist was sent for. He could not, however, be found for some time, and when at length he arrived he declared that he could do nothing until he had consulted other physicians. Other doctors were, therefore, sent for, but it was now late at night; one doctor refused to come as he was tired out, and another "could not be prevailed to rise".

The delirium now increased, and when at last a doctor was found, the patient was "cupped", and live pigeons were put to her feet—a very old remedy. Margaret, however, grew steadily worse, and was ill all that night and the next day. A priest was sent for, and, meanwhile, Evelyn and Lady Berkeley supported her and held her hands. Finally, however, the awful paroxysms ceased and she succumbed to the agonies of death. "Oh, unparalleled loss!", wrote Evelyn. "Oh, grief indicible! By me never to be forgotten, never to be overcome."

"Having closed the eyes, and dropped a tear upon the cheek of my dear departed friend, lovely even in death, I caused her corpse to be embalmed and wrapped in lead", recorded Evelyn. "She was most dear to my wife, and affectionate to my children. But she is gone. This only is my comfort, that she is happy in Christ, and I shall shortly behold her again." The King himself, and all the Court, expressed their sorrow. Margaret was in her twenty-sixth year.

It was Evelyn, capable and resourceful, who had to arrange the funeral, as Godolphin was "struck with unspeakable affliction". Evelyn took entire charge and, according to Margaret's wishes, she was buried at Godolphin in Cornwall. Her body was carried in a hearse with six horses, and thirty mourners accompanied it on its long journey of 300 miles. In the letter she had left for her husband she had had a strange premonition of death:

> My dear,
> Not knowing how God Almighty may deal with me, I think it my best course to settle my affairs, so as that, in case I be to leave this world, no earthly thing may take up my thoughts. In the first place, my dear, believe me, that of all earthly things, you were, and are, the most dear to me; and I am convinced that nobody ever had a better or half so good a husband. I beg your pardon for all my imperfections, which I am sensible were many; but such as I could help, I did endeavour to subdue, that they might not trouble you. . . . Now, my dear, God be with thee, pray God bless you and keep you His faithful servant for ever . . . and do not grieve too much for me since I hope I shall be happy, being very much resigned to God's will.

She then asked that her child should be sent to one of her sisters, and she made careful details of bequests to servants, her cousins, and to Lady Berkeley. She then asked her husband to think of her

> with kindness, but never with too much grief. Pray, my dear, be kind to that poor child I leave behind, for my sake, who loved you so well; but I need not bid you; I know you will be so. If you should think fit to marry again, I humbly beg that little fortune I brought may be first settled upon

117

my child. . . . Now . . . farewell. The peace of God, which passeth all understanding, keep your heart and mind in the knowledge and love of God and of His son, Jesus Christ, our Lord; and the blessing of God Almighty, the Father, the Son and the Holy Ghost be with thee, and remain with thee, ever and ever. Amen.

Margaret had asked for a simple and inexpensive funeral, and she had wished to be buried at Godolphin (her husband's home) so that her ashes might be close to his. His ancestors had lived there since before the Norman Conquest, and she had loved the place. Indeed, she had often expressed a wish to retire there, far from the noise of cities and the tyranny of courts. "I believe", she had written in the letter left for her husband, "if I were carried by sea, the expense would not be very great. But I don't insist upon that place, if you think it not reasonable. Lay me where you please."

When all was over, Evelyn was almost stunned with grief, but he went in the procession as far as Hounslow. "She was", he wrote, "beloved by all, admired by all . . . for wit, beauty, good nature, fidelity, discretion and all accomplishments, the most incomparable person. She was the best wife, the best mistress, the best friend, that ever husband had. . . . To the poor and miserable her loss is irreparable." Every word came from his heart.

Margaret had carefully arranged all her domestic affairs, and had asked her husband if he would perpetuate her memory by his care of those she left behind, including the domestic servants and the poor pensioners. Later, Evelyn and her husband went through her papers, and Godolphin begged Evelyn to continue the trust his wife had reposed in him, on behalf of his motherless infant; he hoped that the friendship extended by Evelyn to Margaret would be continued to himself and his boy.

The death of Margaret was regarded by Evelyn as a punishment sent from God, and in his prayers he implored his Maker to lift His "heavy hand" and be merciful. To say that Evelyn was heart-broken is no exaggeration. Rightly or wrongly, Margaret had been for some years the light of his life. He could not help himself. Nor could be contemplate returning to Sayes Court; no one must see his grief. But Mary knew what he was suffering, and with true affection and magnanimity she wrote: "Remember all are not gone that love you, and that you still

118

have some that require your care for them; they would be comforts to you would you receive them so."

When at last he returned home he decided to write a *Life of Margaret* as a memorial. It would be a labour of love. In recalling the past and the sweet hours spent with her, that exquisite presence would be with him again, that light would illumine the darkness.

Mary wrote to Bohun at this time, and confessed that her husband lived almost entirely in his study. Evelyn called it his "new little cell and cabinet". But here he licked his wounds; here he could count on privacy. The healing process, of course, would take a long time. It would be weeks before he could face the world again with equanimity. Yet he realized also at this time that solitude was not entirely the right medicine. Communication with men was essential. "Solitude", he wrote, "produces ignorance, renders us barbarous, feeds revenge, disposes to envy, creates witches, dispeoples the world, renders it a desert, and would soon dissolve it." That was his considered opinion. He realized that he must rouse himself from this avalanche of grief; but for the time being his world was shrouded in impenetrable gloom.

The *Life of Margaret Godolphin* was written, but never finally revised, and not published during his lifetime, but he wrote this poem:

How long, Lord, ah, how long
Wait we below?
Our sodden feet stick in the clay;
We through the body's dungeon see no day.
Sorrows on sorrows throng.
Friendships (the souls of life) and friends depart
To other worlds, and new relations know.
Ah, Thou who art
The starry orbs above,
Essential Love,
Reach forth Thy gracious hand
And send me wings for flight.
Set me upon that Holy Land;
Oh bring me to that happy shore
Where no dark night
Obscures the day, where all is light;
A city there not made with hands
Within the blissful region stands,
Where we in every street
Our dearest friends again shall meet,
And friendships more refined and sweet,
And never lose them more.

CHAPTER 11

APPREHENSION AND CONSTERNATION

EVELYN'S visits to Court now were merely a dreary duty, but he was obliged to attend at frequent intervals for official audience, and Sunday was a day when the King and the Duke of York were generally accessible. This was also a favourite day for gambling, and to see the great bags of gold changing hands was an infuriating sight, for the King had just admitted to the House of Commons that he was £4,000,000 in debt, besides vast sums due to the goldsmiths and bankers. A vote had therefore been passed by the House that the "atheism, debauchery and impiety of the present age be inserted as grievances to be redressed", and some Members had suggested that the King's mistresses should be impeached because "they kept His Majesty in constant poverty". The Duchess of Portsmouth's son by Charles had been created Duke of Richmond and Lennox, and he, too, was to be "reared like a Prince", regardless of expense. Nell Gwynne had been appointed a Lady of the Privy Chamber to Queen Catharine, and Charles had purchased for her a splendid house in St. James's Square. She also owned houses in Windsor and Chelsea. Rumour said that she had obtained from the King £60,000 in a few years. And this could well be believed. The King, "to his shame", had also appropriated much of the Queen's jointure, some to Frances Stewart "and others of that crew" (Evelyn) and two leases worth £20,000 to another favourite, Lord Fitzharding. But the unhappy Queen had no remedy, although she had brought a generous dowry to Charles. There was no one to uphold her rights; every courtier was on the King's side; it was immensely to their advantage.

Meanwhile, concern with regard to the Duke of York's apostasy was steadily growing, and Evelyn had entered in his diary on the 30th of March, 1676, "This was the first time that the Duke appeared no more in chapel, to the infinite grief and threatened ruin of this poor nation." The common people echoed the general feeling, and on the 5th of November the youth of the city burnt the Pope in effigy after having carried it through the streets in great triumph in procession. The King, too, was strongly suspected of a leaning towards Rome, and the clergy, therefore, were trembling for their benefices, and the landed gentry for their Abbeys and great tithes. By October 1678 this fear reached a climax, as Sir Edmundbury Godfrey, a justice of the peace, was found murdered, and the crime was attributed to the Papists. "This", said Evelyn, "put the whole nation into a ferment against them. . . . The truth is the Roman Catholics are exceedingly bold and busy everywhere since the Duke forebore to go any longer to chapel."

The whole country, in fact, was in a state of intense fear and panic, and the trainbands were put under arms and many Catholics imprisoned. Patrols marched up and down the streets, cannon were placed round Whitehall,* and the corpse of the murdered Sir Edmundbury was exhibited to the public for several days. The Duke of York was expelled from the Privy Council, and strong resolutions were adopted against the poor, innocent Queen. Then the Commons sent the Secretary of State to prison for having countersigned commissions to "gentlemen who were not good Protestants". Finally, the Lord Treasurer was impeached for high treason.

Evelyn declared that he had never seen the nation "in more apprehension and consternation". Two conspirators had now been tried, condemned, and executed. Also, many of the Popish Peers, accused by the infamous Titus Oates, had been sent to the Tower, and all the Roman Catholic Lords were, by a new Act, excluded from Parliament "for ever". The King's, Queen's, and Duke of York's servants were banished, and the Test Act, which excluded from political or municipal offices "all who did not receive the Lord's supper according to the Church of England ceremony", was hurried through Parliament by large majorities. This was followed, owing to public pressure, by the Duke of York's resignation as Lord High Admiral of England, and his flight to Brussels.

* Macaulay's *History of England*, vol 1, p. 235.

Meanwhile, the unfortunate Samuel Pepys had been sent to the Tower on suspicion of being a Papist, and Evelyn went to dine with him, having first sent a piece of venison.

The Earl of Shaftesbury also asserted at this time that the Duke of Monmouth was the legitimate heir to the throne, so again the King stated in Council that he "had never been married to any other woman than the Queen". He later published a Proclamation to the same effect. Shaftesbury then put forward a bill for the divorce of Charles from his Queen so that "he could marry a Protestant consort", and only when the King interviewed each peer personally and urged them to vote against the measure—which he thought "a wicked design"—was it abandoned. Nevertheless, Shaftesbury's campaign in support of Charles's illegitimate son, the Duke of Monmouth, continued.

In accordance with the custom of the time, Evelyn had now arranged a marriage for his son John with the daughter of Sir John Stonehouse. In his careful, kindly, meticulous way, Evelyn had weighed every consideration—the religious views of the two young people, their backgrounds, and the financial aspect. John had now left Oxford and was to study law, but the duty of every father was, at the appropriate time, to ensure that a son was happily settled in life with a suitable partner. With regard to this marriage, Evelyn wrote in his diary: "I pray God make him worthy of it, and a comfort to his excellent mother, who deserves much from him."

On the 16th of March, Evelyn went to London and there received the sum of £3000 in gold, part of the bride's "portion". He himself had settled a generous income on the pair. They were married a few days later at St. Andrew's, Holborn, and, after the service and dancing, the bride and bridegroom were "bedded" in traditional fashion at Sir John Stonehouse's lodgings in Bow Street, Covent Garden. Evelyn was extremely happy about the whole affair, and much admired his new daughter-in-law.

In April, Evelyn paid a visit to Lord Ossory's country seat in Hertfordshire, and they spent their time in walking, riding, and discussing various improvements to the estate. Lord Ossory was particularly delighted with the new carvings by Grinling Gibbons which now adorned every room. The afternoons were spent happily in the excellent library.

The two friends had known each other for thirty years, and had been

John Evelyn. *After Kneller.*

Mary, wife of John Evelyn.

King Charles I (1600–1649). *National Portrait Gallery.*

Queen Henrietta Maria (1609–1669). *National Portrait Gallery.*

Five children of Charles I. Charles, afterwards Charles II, 1630–1685; Mary, afterwards Princess of Orange and Mother of William III, 1631–1660; James, Duke of York, afterwards James II, 1633–1701; Elizabeth, who died unmarried at Carisbrooke, 1635–1650; Anne, who died in infancy, 1636/7–1640. *After Sir A. Van Dyck, National Portrait Gallery.*

Oliver Cromwell (1599–1658).
Robert Walker, National Portrait Gallery.

King Charles II (1630–1685).

Catherine of Braganza, Queen Consort of Charles II (1638–1705).
Dirk Stoop, National Portrait Gallery.

James Scott, Duke of Monmouth (1649–1685).
National Portrait Gallery.

King James II (1633–1701). *National Portrait Gallery.*

King William III (1650–1702). *After Sir Peter Lely.*

Queen Mary II (1662–1694). *Wissing, National Portrait Gallery.*

Queen Anne, as H.R.H. Princess Anne in 1685.
Wissing, Scottish National Galleries.

George Monk, First Duke of Albemarle, K.G. (1608–1670).
From the Studio of Sir Peter Lely, National Portrait Gallery.

Edward Hyde, 1st Earl of Clarendon (1609–1674).
After Gerard Soest, National Portrait Gallery.

Sidney Lord Godolphin
Lord High Treasurer of England

Sidney Lord Godolphin, Lord High Treasurer of England (1645–1712).
After Kneller, National Portrait Gallery.

Samuel Pepys (1633–1703). *John Hayls, National Portrait Gallery.*

Eleanor Gwyn, Nell Gwyn (1650–1687).
From the Studio of Sir Peter Lely, National Portrait Gallery.

Wotton House, 1818.

Statue in the Greek Temple at Wotton, built in 1652.

The Garden at Wotton, as it is today.

Wotton House, as it is today.

Wotton Church, as it is today.

View of part of the City of Oxford in Oxfordshire.

Old Whitehall Palace from the River.

Old St. Paul's. *From a view by Hollar.*

The Tower of London. *From a view published about 1700.*

The triumphal entry into the City, 1660.

The Dead Cart.
Engraved by Davenport after a drawing by G. Cruikshank.

The Great Fire of London, 1666.

Painted by Griffier at the scene of the fire. The fire is approaching Fleet Street.

The Great Fire of London, 1666. *From an oil painting in the London Museum.*

A contemporary engraving of a 17th-century coach.

constant companions in Paris during the years in exile; they had ridden together almost daily at the Riding Academy.

But in the following July, to the great grief of his friends, Lord Ossory died, and it seemed to Evelyn that his death could have been avoided. The Earl had been extremely agitated and apprehensive because he had been appointed Governor of Tangier and General of the Forces, but he was convinced that the King was sending him to Tangier with an utterly inadequate supply of men and on "a hazardous adventure". He was expected to perform an impossible task. Lord Ossory had declared to Evelyn that he would lose his reputation and be blamed for the inevitable failure. The following day he became ill, and then delirious. Evelyn stayed with him night and day, "to his last gasp, to close his dear eyes", and apparently nothing could save him. He had died after four days' illness. Lord Ossory was an exceptionally sensitive man. "He was a loving, generous, good-natured, obliging friend . . . no one more brave, more modest; none more humble, sober and every way virtuous." So wrote Evelyn, and the loss of this dear friend was a great sorrow.

On the 30th of October, "in order to be private", Evelyn went to London. He was approaching his sixtieth birthday, and it was his custom, on this anniversary, to make a solemn survey of his life. He heard several sermons, attended Holy Communion, and spent the whole week in prayer. It was a wonderful refreshment to the spirit.

But unrest and alarm were in the air, and a few days later London was startled by the news that Lord Stafford had been arrested for "conspiring the death of the King". On the 30th of November Evelyn attended the trial, which was held in Westminster Hall, the King, Lords, and Commons being present. The trial lasted over a week, but finally the prisoner was found guilty and sentenced to death. On the 29th of December he was beheaded on Tower Hill.

And now, clearly, the King was thoroughly alarmed. The fear of assassination had to be faced, and he became gloomy and morose. "I never saw", said Sir William Temple, "any man more sensible of the miserable condition of his affairs."

It was at this time that Evelyn saw a bright "meteor" in the sky, "very much in shape like the blade of a sword", and according to the curious superstitions of his time, he was greatly alarmed. "What this may portend, God only knows", he wrote in his diary. "I pray God avert

His judgements." In his opinion the whole nation was "in the greatest ferment".

Nevertheless, the spring and summer passed pleasantly. Evelyn, as usual, visited many beautiful gardens belonging to friends. He was also watching with keen interest the rebuilding of London. A scheme of town-planning had been devised, Dr. Christopher Wren had been consulted, and new buildings had risen from the ashes of the old, stone and brick being used instead of wood. Roads had been widened, straightened, and paved, and the exquisite churches designed by Wren were beginning to rise. The lovely lace-like edifices, with their slim steeples, were appearing everywhere, a beautiful memorial to a great architect. Evelyn was also able, at this time, by special permission, to spend some days in the King's private library at Whitehall. Then, at the end of the summer, one of Evelyn's cherished hopes materialized, as he was told that plans had now been put in hand for the building of a hospital for sick and wounded soldiers and sailors, a project he had consistently urged on the King. Evelyn himself had been asked, with Sir Stephen Fox, to organize the scheme, "for its constitution and governance", and Sir Stephen was to be the "grand benefactor", having promised to settle £5000 a year on the hospital. So together, in his study, he and Evelyn drew up the plans, including the staff and officers that would be required, and their salaries. A few days later Evelyn went to Chelsea to survey the foundations.

About a week later Evelyn had another attack of malaria and did not recover for some weeks. But this time he tried a somewhat original cure —he sat, covered with blankets, with his legs immersed in hot milk up to the knees, and at the same time drank a posset. He then retired to bed to sweat. When he recovered, many friends came to congratulate him, and by May he was well enough to drive out to Chelsea with Sir Christopher Wren (the architect) and Sir Stephen Fox to see the plot and plans for the new hospital. All that was needed now was the approval of the Archbishop of Canterbury. The King was to lay the foundation stone, and the hospital would accommodate 400 men. Evelyn had "cast his bread upon the waters" and it had "returned to him after many days".

Sir Christopher Wren had been knighted in 1672, and was now one of Evelyn's intimate friends. They frequently dined together. "A wonderful genius had this incomparable person", recorded Evelyn. Wren was design-ing the new halls for the city companies, and he was hoping to rebuild

London on a magnificent scale, but even in his plans for the new St. Paul's he was thwarted and impeded. Ignorance, envy, jealousy, and selfishness met him at every point. He and Evelyn also dined frequently at the Lord Mayor's, where the feasts were truly magnificent. So recorded Evelyn. His life, in fact, was still remarkably full of interest. Through the Royal Society he had made many new friends, and as a result he corresponded regularly with several antiquaries and scientists. The Royal Society were anxious to improve the English tongue, and Evelyn had suggested a lexicon of pure English words. People also frequently sent him their books and poems for his comments—a service gladly given. Advice on gardening and forestry was also readily forthcoming. Gardening was still one of the passions of his life, and would remain so to the end. "Is there", he wrote, "under the heavens a more glorious and refreshing object of the kind than an impregnable holly hedge of about 400 feet in length, 9 ft. high and 5 in diameter . . . glittering with its armed and variegated leaves, the taller standards, at orderly distances, blushing with their natural coral. . . ." Such a magnificent hedge he had in his own garden at Sayes Court, and it was the admiration of every visitor. How much pleasanter it was to sit in a beautiful garden, surrounded by singing birds, running water, flowers, and trees, than to sit watching a cock-fight or a bear-baiting. Some years ago he had been persuaded, against his will, to attend such a "sport" in London, and he had denounced the spectacle strongly as "butcherly sports and barbarous cruelties. . . . I was most heartily weary of the rude and dirty pastime." The King, obviously, took great delight in these sports, but there was no accounting for taste.

CHAPTER 12

THE END OF A REIGN

THE year of 1683 began with a sad bereavement at Sayes Court, as in February Sir Richard Browne became seriously ill and died. He was seventy-eight years of age, and the last of his line. He had served King Charles I as Gentleman of the Privy Chamber, then as Clerk of the Council, and later as Resident in France. After the Restoration he had become Clerk of the Council to King Charles II. His father had been Clerk of the Green Cloth to Queen Elizabeth and King James I, and his grandfather and great-grandfather on the maternal side had been Treasurers successively to Henry VIII, Edward VI, Queen Mary, and Queen Elizabeth I. It was a long record of honourable and loyal service to the Crown.

Sir Richard was buried at Deptford, and all the fraternity of Trinity House—of which he was Master—attended the funeral, also the Bishop of Rochester and several noblemen and knights. Sir Richard had been born at Sayes Court, and by a special clause in his will he asked to be buried in the churchyard, close to his ancestors. He disliked intensely the custom of burying bodies in the church and chancel, "as prejudicial to the health of the living, besides the continual disturbance of the pavements and seats, and several other indecencies". Sir Richard's wishes, of course, were carried out. "Lord, teach us to number our days that we may apply our hearts unto wisdom" was Evelyn's comment. His father-in-law had been an exemplary and most loyal public servant and would be greatly missed. He was a fine classical scholar and had had a good knowledge of modern languages. But as a courtier, Evelyn had often wondered how he could have submitted, year after year, to such "servitude"; the rewards were sometimes so meagre and the fall could be so great. And this was brought home to him forcibly one May evening when he was visiting Lady Arlington. The time was about 11 p.m., and barely had the company sat down to supper when a messenger arrived with the news that the Queen was going into the park to walk. The Countess rose at once, and had to leave her supper. "By this", wrote Evelyn, "one may take an estimate of the extreme slavery and subjection that courtiers live in, who have not time to eat and drink at their pleasure. It put me in mind of Horace's mouse, and to bless God for my own private condition."

About a month later he was again sadly reminded of the fickleness of royal favour when he was passing with the Earl of Clarendon the glorious palace which his father had built only a few years before. "I turned my head the contrary way till the coach had gone past", recorded Evelyn. For, indeed, he had no wish to remind the son of "how in so short a time their pomp was fallen". Evelyn had always admired the mansion, and had said when first it was built: "I went with prejudice and a critical spirit . . . but I acknowledge that I have never seen a nobler pile. It is . . . the most useful, graceful and magnificent house in England. . . . Here is taste and use, solidity and beauty. . . . Nothing abroad pleases me better, nothing at home approaches it."

But a few weeks later monarchs, too, appeared in an unenviable light, for a plot to assassinate both the King and the Duke of York was discovered. The Rye House plot was concocted by a few desperate men who aimed to place the Duke of Monmouth on the throne and frame a new Constitution with a free Parliament. The plot collapsed, and Lord William Russell, Algernon Sidney, and the Earl of Essex were arrested and sent to the Tower. Three days later, as Evelyn was visiting Sir Thomas Yarborough and his lady at Covent Garden, news arrived that the Earl of Essex had cut his throat. Evelyn knew him well. Lord William Russell and Algernon Sidney were finally executed, and Monmouth, also implicated, purchased his pardon by a humiliating confession and a cowardly abandonment of his associates.

After the executions, the countesses of Bristol and Sunderland (relatives of Lord Russell) came to Sayes Court "to condole his sad fate". The next day came Colonel Russell and Mrs. Middleton, also relatives. Meanwhile, many active politicians of lower rank who had been connected with the plot were sent to the gallows, and many quitted the country.

127

Actions were brought against persons who had defamed the Duke of York, and damages which amounted to "perpetual imprisonment" were imposed on the culprits. (At that time, until fines were paid, all prisoners remained in gaol.) The Council also forced many boroughs to surrender their privileges.

Such was the state of the country, and the King was apparently "very melancholy, and not stirring without double guards". All the entrances to Whitehall were closed, and few people allowed to walk near the Palace. Charles had at last realized that he was dangerously unpopular, and that there was "a prevailing discontent" in all classes. Propaganda, therefore, was disseminated, chiefly through the churches, and on the day of Russell's execution the University of Oxford (according to Filmer's treatises) declared that hereditary despotism was a form of government ordained by God, and that a limited monarchy was a pernicious absurdity.* A day of "public thanksgiving for His Majesty's late preservation" was also held, and a loyal sermon was preached on the divine right of Kings.

Kings, in fact, had to be placated, and Charles's wounded vanity was now to be soothed by the building of yet another palace. The site chosen was Winchester; Sir Christopher Wren was to be the architect, and this edifice, containing 160 rooms, was intended to rival, in grandeur, Versailles; no expense was to be spared. The King's house at Newmarket had been destroyed by fire, and Charles wished to have a palace near Portsmouth so that he could keep in touch with naval affairs. (Or so he said!) How this glorious palace was to be paid for was an unsolved problem, though a "collection" had been made.

For the coming winter, as Evelyn had "many important concerns to despatch", he took a house in Villiers Street, London. He also wished his daughters to be taught music and languages by London masters. Several of his friends were in the Tower, and Evelyn always made a point of visiting such prisoners regularly. But these visits were always depressing. The prisoners fretted at the loss of their liberty, and usually became ill with anxiety. One barely knew how to comfort them.

Evelyn, of course, was quite familiar with the great fortress, but he could not repress a shudder when the mighty portcullis was lowered. The

* Macaulay's *History of England*, vol. 1, p. 270.

very rats which swam across the moat seemed to be scuttling away from an evil destiny. It was a shameful fact that prisoners were sometimes deliberately forgotten and were very harshly treated.

These examples of "man's inhumanity to man" had always saddened Evelyn.

The winter in London proved a depressing one as there were epidemics of typhoid fever, malaria, and smallpox, bringing tragedy and death to many friends and relatives. News also arrived that his old friend, the Earl of Clarendon, had died in exile, and one afternoon, as Evelyn walked down Piccadilly, he observed that "that sumptuous palace", Clarendon House, was being demolished. The materials were being auctioned to the highest bidder. The sight of men with hammers ruthlessly destroying the beautiful fabric was a mournful one, for Evelyn knew every room intimately. He had spent many hours in that palace.

Trade had deteriorated, also, as by Christmas the Thames had frozen over, and the sea was so "locked up with ice" that no vessels could come in or out. The frost continued for over a month, and long rows of booths, shops, and tents were erected on the frozen river. Coaches plied along the ice between Westminster and the Temple, and there was bull-baiting, horse and coach races, puppet plays, and interludes; there was skating and tobogganing. The fowls, fish, and birds were found frozen in large numbers, and apparently many herds of deer had perished. The trees were split as if struck by lightning, and in the country districts men and cattle were dying in hundreds. Fuel was dear and extremely scarce. In London the air was filled with smoke, and one could barely see across the streets. "Every moment", recorded Evelyn, "was full of disastrous accidents, and no water was obtainable for the pipes and engines, nor could the brewers work."

The only happy event in the year, in fact, was the birth of another child to Evelyn's son John and his wife. Their first child, born the previous year, had lived only a few weeks—a bitter disappointment. But this loss of little children was universal. The Duke of York, for instance, had already lost six children, three by his first wife and three by Mary Beatrice of Modena. Lady Fanshawe had borne fourteen children, yet only four survived. Lady Temple had had nine children and only two survived. Lady Verney, before she was thirty, had lost four children. This was the tragic pattern.

But winter passed, and spring—a tardy and reluctant spring—came at last. Evelyn and his family were still in London and saw the ceremony of "touching for the evil". But, as usual, several children were crushed to death in the crowd which pressed at the surgeon's door for tickets. A sad tragedy!

In April, Evelyn and his family returned to Sayes Court and found, as was to be expected, that the garden had suffered severely from the excessive frost. Many plants and trees were dead, the rosemary and laurels barely showed signs of life, and the oranges and myrtles were "very sick". Yet when summer arrived all was well, and the garden as lovely as ever.

The dear, sad Queen came frequently to Sayes Court and always stayed for some hours. Evelyn had grown to like and admire this much-injured Queen, and had watched with heartfelt sympathy her many disappointments. She was very anxious to produce an heir to the throne but had had several miscarriages. She was particularly fond of Evelyn's children. There was Mary, the eldest, now aged seventeen, who sang well and played the harpsichord. Susanna, with her merry smile, was a good needlewoman and a fine artist, like her mother. Then there was Elizabeth, who was particularly skilled at gardening and housewifery. She, too, was musical and studious.

Family musical evenings were a great joy, and Evelyn himself had learnt to play the theorbo, a lute with two necks.

So the summer passed, happily and busily. But again the winter proved a severe one. Evelyn was obliged to go to Court on the 25th of January, 1685, and there he witnessed a scene which stamped itself indelibly on his memory. The King was, as usual, surrounded by painted and bejewelled women, and apparently the seraglio had increased, for the infamous Madame Mazarin, who had come from France, was now a formidable rival to the Duchess of Portsmouth. She had a bad reputation for intrigue and harlotry, and should never have been received at any Court. "I can never", recorded Evelyn, "forget the inexpressible luxury and profaneness, gaming and all dissoluteness, and as it were total forgetfulness of God which . . . I was witness of, the King sitting and toying with his concubines, Portsmouth, Cleveland and Mazarin, &c, a French boy singing love songs in that glorious gallery, whilst about twenty of the great courtiers and other dissolute persons were at basset round a large table, a bank of at least £2000 in gold before them." Ten days later the King was dead. Apparently in the early morning of the 2nd of February he had a stroke. A physician had quickly opened a vein, a hot iron was applied to his head and volatile salts were forced into his mouth. He was cupped, blooded again, vomited and purged, fourteen doctors attending, and by Thursday was said to be improving; the church bells were rung. But in the evening the patient relapsed, and the Archbishop of Canterbury was obliged to warn him to prepare for death. The dying King said goodbye to his children and blessed them, and also sent a message to the Queen. "She asks my pardon, poor woman", he had said, "I ask hers with all my heart." After that, the end came soon.

The King was dead and, according to solemn tradition, no time must be lost in maintaining the succession. Evelyn and others in the Privy Gallery were therefore admitted to the Council Chamber to be witnesses of what was decided, and eventually, accompanied by the lords, the Lord Marshal, and the heralds, they went to Whitehall Gate where the new King was proclaimed with trumpets and kettle-drums. The party then proceeded to Temple Bar and to the Exchange, where the King was proclaimed again. Finally, Evelyn returned to Whitehall in order to pay his homage to the new King and Queen. The great rooms were thronged, and although the Queen was in bed and the King "in undress", nevertheless both received their subjects. Meanwhile, the bells were tolling for the dead.

Evelyn was then asked by the Sheriff of the County of Kent if he would assist in proclaiming the King. Evelyn therefore drove down to Bromley, where he was met by the Sheriff, the Commander of the Kentish Troop (500 horse), and two trumpeters. They marched to the market-place with swords drawn, made a ring, and read out the Proclamation. There were shouts from the immense crowd, His Majesty's health was drunk, and all dispersed. Evelyn then returned to London.

All were asked to wear mourning for the late King, "as for a father, in the most solemn manner". But many rumours as to the cause of his death were circulated. It was said that his tongue had swelled to the size of a neat's tongue, that a cake of deletrious powder had been found in

131

his brain, that there were blue spots on his breast and black spots on his shoulder, that something had been put into his broth, that something had been put into his favourite dish of eggs and ambergrease, that the Duchess of Portsmouth had poisoned him with a cup of chocolate, that the Queen had poisoned him with a jar of dried pears.* Such rumours, however, were common at that time, and many were actually believed by the credulous and ignorant. Almost certainly none were true.

But the doctors were not surprised at the King's demise, for debauchery has always exacted its price. "What do you want?" says Nature. "Take it and pay for it." Charles had, indeed, paid for it, but one thing could be said in his favour—he had at least made himself responsible for his illegitimate children. He had not denied them and turned them out to starve.

Evelyn, who knew most of the bishops and many of the peers who had been present at his death, could certainly deny the rumours of poison. Personally he had been attached in many ways to the late King, having known him as a boy and watched the development of his character. Charles had been moulded by circumstances, yet no one could deny that the man had been likeable. "He would doubtless have been an excellent Prince", recorded Evelyn, "had he been less addicted to women, who made him uneasy and always in want, to supply their immeasureable profusion, to the detriment of many indigent persons who had signally served both him and his father. He frequently and easily changed favourites, to his great prejudice." Evelyn also felt that Charles had been "ruled by crafty men, and some abandoned and profane wretches . . . He was ever kind to me, and very gracious upon all occasions, and therefore I cannot, without ingratitude, but deplore his loss, which for many respects, as well as duty, I do with all my soul. He was a Prince of many virtues and many great imperfections, debonaire, easy of access, not bloody or cruel, his countenance fierce, his voice great, proper of person, every motion became him. . . ."

Charles's funeral caused much comment, as on the 14th of February he was "very obscurely buried in a vault in Henry VII's chapel at Westminster, without any manner of pomp." "He was hurried", said Coke, "in the dead of night to his grave, as if his corpse had been to be

* Macaulay's *History of England*, vol. 1, p. 442.

arrested for debt, and not so much as the Blue-coat boys attending it."
But Rochester wrote perhaps the most fitting epitaph:

> Here lies our sovereign lord the king
> Whose word no man relied on.
> He never said a foolish thing
> Or ever did a wise one.

"The king is dead. LONG LIVE THE KING."

So ran the old proclamations, and Evelyn was surprised to see how soon this monarch, once so popular, was forgotten. For, indeed, the rising sun had to be worshipped, and all eyes now were centred on his brother James. For the Papists, certainly, there would be many pickings from the royal basket. The Papists, in fact, were triumphant; their King had come to the throne. In Rome, too, smiles and congratulations predominated, for after an interval of 128 years England might again become a Catholic country. That was their hope. That was their fervent prayer, and all England was well aware of the fact. The fears of the Protestants might prove to be unfounded, but few could hide their anxiety and apprehension.

CHAPTER 13

THE FEAR OF POPERY

ON THE 7th of March, all apprehension on the score of religion and all business affairs were temporarily forgotten through the illness of Evelyn's dear daughter Mary. She was "taken with the smallpox" and was soon extremely ill. This was the deadliest disease, and the majority of people made their wills and prepared for death the moment they were stricken. It swept away one-tenth of the population every year, and the doctors could do nothing. Even those who recovered were generally disfigured for life and "frightful" to see. Now the fearful scourge had attacked his bright and beautiful Mary.

There was, from the first day, little hope, and she soon asked to receive the Blessed Sacrament,

> after which, disposing herself to suffer what God should determine to inflict, she bore the remainder of her sickness with extraordinary patience and piety, and more than ordinary resignation. She died on the 14th, to our unspeakable sorrow and affliction. . . . Oh, dear, sweet, desirable child, how shall I part with all this goodness and virtue without the bitterness of sorrow and reluctancy of a tender parent? Oh, how thy mother mourns thy loss! How desolate hast thou left us! To the grave shall we both carry thy memory. God alone—in whose bosom thou art at rest—give us to resign thee and all our contentments (for thou indeed wert all in this world) to his blessed pleasure.

Mary was eighteen years of age. She had been staying with Lady Falkland, and when she had been some time in the house Lady Falkland admitted that one of her servants was ill with smallpox, and indeed died the next day. From this source of infection Mary had developed the disease. Four men had wished to marry this beautiful girl, but she had

134

not wished to settle down. "I love you and this home", she had said to her father. She had never cared for Court life, as "she was not fond of that glittering scene, now become abominably licentious". Yet she was spoken of as a future Maid of Honour to Mary Beatrice of Modena.

Mary was buried in the south-east end of the church at Deptford near several of her brothers and sisters. "Thus lived, died and was buried the joy of my life", recorded Evelyn, ". . . God Almighty of his infinite mercy grant me the grace thankfully to resign myself and all I have or had, to his divine pleasure. . . . Amen."

Her grief-stricken mother, too, was almost inconsolable, and she wrote at this time, in reply to a letter of condolence from her sister-in-law:

> How to express the sorrow for parting with so dear a child is a difficult task. She was welcome to me from the first moment God gave her, acceptable through the whole course of her life by a thousand endearments, by the gifts of nature, by acquired parts, by the tender love she ever showed her father and me. . . . The seventh day of her illness she discoursed to me in particular as calmly as in health. . . . But what shall I say? She was too great a blessing for me, who never deserved anything, much less such a jewel. . . . I could ever speak of her. . . . I acknowledge, as a Christian, I ought not to murmur, and I should be infinitely sorry to incur God's further displeasure. There are those yet remaining that challenge my care, and for their sakes I endeavour to submit all I can. . . .

Mary herself was not blessed with good health, and frequently during the winter she was confined for weeks to her room.

From nine children born to Evelyn and Mary, therefore, only three now were left—John, Elizabeth, and Susanna. But the young Mary had been loved and admired by everyone. She had been extremely talented, a good linguist, a cultured scholar, a musician, and a wonderfully graceful dancer. What a comfort Evelyn's religion was at this time. "Let Him be glorified by our submission", he wrote in his diary. Religion was his mainstay, his strong rock.

Yet all through the country—and even in his sorrow it could not be ignored—was the fear of Popery. It hung like a threatening cloud over the whole horizon. For this was a new reign, and the new King was a bigoted Catholic. According to the Constitution, he was the "Defender of the Faith", but no one could say what drastic changes he might make. Evelyn was intimate with most of the bishops, and they confessed to being extremely apprehensive.

135

About half an hour after his brother's death, the new King, James II, had taken his place at the head of the Council and had made a speech in which he declared that he was well aware of the fact that he had been accused of a fondness for arbitrary power; yet he was resolved to maintain the established government both in Church and State. This speech was received with immense relief all over the country, and was quoted in many pulpits. To Evelyn's grief and amazement, therefore, within a few days, the King, for the first time in his life, attended Mass publicly in his oratory, the doors being set wide open. "This", said Evelyn, "to the great grief of his subjects." The quite unexpected innovation, indeed, had produced a strange reaction, for when the host was elevated, the Roman Catholics fell on their knees but the Protestants walked out.*

On Easter Sunday, the rites of the Church of Rome were again, after 126 years, performed with regal splendour. "To my grief", wrote Evelyn, "I saw the new pulpit set up in the Popish oratory at Whitehall for the Lent preaching, Mass being publicly said, and the Romanists swarming at Court with greater confidence than had ever been seen in England since the Reformation."

But the new King behaved oddly in many ways. He received foreign diplomats, for instance, not standing bare-headed in his bedchamber, as Charles had done, but seated in a special room with his hat on.

Evelyn was obliged to attend Court, as he was still engaged on many commissions, and he noticed that Arabella Churchill and Catharine Sedley, two of the King's mistresses, were very much in evidence. Both had borne children to James, but apparently, on his accession, James had assured his confessor that he would see Catharine Sedley no more.

The grand Coronation took place on the 23rd of April, but the Communion service was not read, and the ceremony of presenting the Sovereign with a richly bound Bible was omitted because James had been taught to regard the Bible as "adulterated with false doctrine".

It was observed that the King went through the long ritual with studied indifference, never moved his lips for the responses, and showed no signs of fervour or devotion.

Another ominous act was that the King appointed Sir George Jeffreys to be Chief Justice of the Court of King's Bench to assist with the work of the Great Seal. This man was a depraved, ferocious, merciless lawyer.

* Clarke's *Life of James II*. Barillon, 19 February and 1 March 1685.

He drank heavily, and his language was atrocious. When he was ordering a woman to be whipped he would say: "Hangman, I charge you to pay particular attention to this lady. Scourge her soundly, man. Scourge her till the blood runs down. It is Christmas, a cold time for madame to strip in. See that you warm her shoulders thoroughly."*

The appointment of this man, whose cold-blooded brutality was well known, showed that no mercy would be extended to malefactors. And this, indeed, was soon proved, for Titus Oates was tried and finally sentenced to be stripped of his clerical habit, to be pilloried in Palace Yard, and again in front of the Royal Exchange, to be whipped from Aldgate to Newgate, and two days later to be whipped from Newgate to Tyburn. If he survived this, he was to be kept close prisoner for life. Five times every year he was to be brought from his dungeon and exposed on the pillory in different parts of the Capital. This incredibly harsh sentence was executed. He was whipped till the blood ran down, and he swooned several times. James, therefore, was asked to remit the second flogging, but he said: "He shall go through with it if he has breath in his body." During many months, Oates remained in the darkest hole in Newgate, manacled and groaning. Evelyn had happened to pass while Oates was being whipped in the street, and saw the whole ghastly scene. Was this cruelty on the part of the King prophetic of what was to come?

On the 22nd of May the Commons were summoned to the bar of the Lords, and the King, on his throne, spoke to both Houses. He repeated again that he was *"resolved to maintain the established government in Church and State"*. Evelyn was present on this occasion; but he was told, too, that the King had sent his Agent to make submission to the Pope, and to pave the way for the readmission of England to the Catholic Church.

Meanwhile, in France, the Protestants were being barbarously treated. They had been commanded to christen their children within twenty-four hours of birth; otherwise Popish priests would be called in and the infants brought up as Catholics. As a result, hundreds of refugees had fled from France. Was this an example of what would happen in England under this Popish King? The prospect was terrifying.

But trouble was already on the way for James, as news arrived in London that King Charles's illegitimate son, the Duke of Monmouth, had landed

* Christmas Sessions paper of 1678.

at Lyme Regis on the 11th of June with 150 armed followers and ammunition and provisions. He was making a bold bid for the English throne. "I pray God deliver us from the confusions which these beginnings threaten", recorded Evelyn. The news was that the Duke was rapidly enlisting supporters. In London, therefore, all was panic and confusion, and 200 persons who were suspected of being concerned in a Whig movement were arrested.

On the 1st of July, the city of Winchester was reported to be in the hands of the rebels, and the battle of Sedgemoor took place on the 6th of July. But the rebel army, hastily gathered together, proved no match for the professional soldiers, and finally 1000 rebels lay dead on the moor. Many hundreds were wounded and 500 taken prisoner. Some prisoners had already been hanged on hastily constructed gibbets. Meanwhile, Monmouth had fled, accompanied by a few friends.

At Whitehall, men met in excited groups to discuss the news. The rebellion had failed, and Evelyn wrote in his diary: "Blessed be God". Soon it was known that the Duke of Monmouth had been found, by the aid of bloodhounds, crouched in a ditch. He was brought to London, and he and his chief accomplice, Lord Grey, were sent to the Tower. Then, finally, on the 15th of July, Monmouth was executed on Tower Hill.

To punish the rebels, the King now sent Colonel Kirke to Taunton, and many men were hanged by the military, without trial. Evelyn was also told that the gaols of Shropshire and Somersetshire were packed with prisoners, most of whom were starving. But worse was to come, for early in September the infamous Judge Jeffreys, accompanied by four other judges, set out on his circuit to try the prisoners. He ordered 103 prisoners to be hanged without delay, and in Somersetshire 233 men were hanged, drawn, and quartered during the course of a few days, the bodies being displayed on village greens and country markets. A dreadful sight! But the dead rebels were less to be pitied than some of the survivors, as many were sentenced to terrible scourging.

In all 841 prisoners were sold as slaves and sent abroad, but apparently one-fifth of those who were sold were flung to the sharks before the end of the voyage, as the prisoners were so closely confined in the holds and many suffering from unhealed wounds. Of 99 prisoners carried on one ship, 22 died before they reached Jamaica. Meanwhile, Jeffreys traded in pardons, and made a fortune with which he purchased an estate.* Yet when he returned to London, the King gave him the Great Seal for his "eminent and faithful services". The King had carefully followed the proceedings in the west, and meticulously recorded the details of the trials.

Evelyn, at this time, was profoundly disturbed, and feared greatly for the future. He was a loyal patriot, and his King's commands were almost sacred, but the terrible aftermath of this rebellion had revealed an aspect of the King's character which could only be described as devilish. Unlimited power in the hands of such a man could only mean diabolical tyranny.

This apprehension was shared by most of Evelyn's friends, and the terrible news from France added considerably to their fears, for King Louis XIV was again cruelly persecuting the Protestants, and there had been widespread massacres. The Edict of Nantes had been revoked, and children had been torn from their parents and sent to be educated in convents. In spite of the military police, 50,000 families had quitted France for ever. Protestant libraries had been destroyed, and thousands of men and women banished, imprisoned, and sent to the galleys as slaves. As a result, France had become almost depopulated. King James had said that he deplored this persecution, yet a translation of a book describing the massacres of the Protestants in France was ordered to be burnt by the common hangman. Also, in opening Parliament, James asked for a standing army instead of the militia; he obviously needed this army for the furtherance of his policy. By May of the following year it seemed to Evelyn that "all engines are now at work to bring in Popery, which God in mercy prevent". The corporations were being filled with Catholic officials, and 300 Protestant officers and 5000 soldiers had been dismissed from their regiments and replaced by Papists.

But the new Lord Chief Justice Herbert now startled all England by declaring on the Bench that the power to govern the country lay entirely in the King. The Crown was absolute and the King's power unlimited. "Everyone was astonished", said Evelyn. For had not the civil war been fought for this very principle?

Courageous divines, therefore, now began to preach against Popery, but they were immediately dismissed from their livings. "I will make no concessions", announced the King. "My father made concessions and he

* *Commons Journal*, 9 October, 10 November, and 26 December 1690.

was beheaded." James II was a curious character, and, according to Bishop Burnet, he had "the strange notion" that no regard was to be had "to the pleasing of the people". James had no love for the arts, no sense of humour, and certainly no common sense. Clearly he believed that he was the divine instrument destined to bring about the reunion of England with the See of Peter. Was not the death of his brother at a comparatively early age a sign of the Divine will? He had waited for this for years, all the years of his brother's kingship. Now the time had come. He possessed that unyielding intensity of fervour, that passion for the extreme and the absolute, which is the very lifeblood of the Church of Rome. Power had come to him at last and he had seized it with all the avidity of a born autocrat whose appetite for supreme dominion had been whetted by long years of enforced abstinence and the hated simulations of submission. He was now the ruler of England and *he would rule*. The Roman Church had never had the reputation of being an institution to be trifled with.

Meanwhile, Evelyn had been appointed one of the commissioners of the Privy Seal to execute the office during the absence of Lord Clarendon in Ireland. This meant that Evelyn would be in fairly constant communication with the King. Yet the work was very welcome, as Evelyn had suffered another tragic loss; his daughter Elizabeth had died from smallpox. She had recently been married to the nephew of Sir John Tippett, Surveyor to the Navy, but Evelyn had strongly disapproved of the match. As a result, Elizabeth and her family had become estranged. This schism made the blow even more bitter. In six months, therefore, Evelyn and Mary had lost two daughters, and the breach with Elizabeth had never been healed.

CHAPTER 14

THE FIGHT FOR PROTESTANTISM

EVELYN'S appointment as one of the commissioners for the Privy Seal had to be approved by the King, so Evelyn was received in audience at Windsor. He assured His Majesty that he would endeavour to serve him "with all sincerity, diligence and loyalty". Later, many friends came to Evelyn to offer their congratulations.

From Windsor, Evelyn drove with the King and his courtiers down to Portsmouth, to view the defences and fortifications, and Evelyn was much impressed with the King's "infinite industry, sedulity, gravity and great understanding and experience of affairs"; certainly he appeared to be "sincere and honest". That he was so oddly credulous was, however, certainly a reflection on his intelligence, for the King spoke in all seriousness of a relic which had "healed a gentleman's rotten nose by only touching it".

On the journey, a halt was made at Winchester, and Evelyn was able to see the Cathedral and the new royal palace designed by Sir Christopher Wren, which had been started by King Charles II. There had been much heart-burning over this palace, for as the building proceeded the late King had paid many visits to Winchester, accompanied by his Court, and the bishops, deans, and prebendaries had been asked to accommodate the royal party, Bishop Ken's house being chosen for the temporary accommodation of Nell Gwynne. Bishop Ken, who was one of the Court chaplains, had been highly indignant. "A woman of ill repute ought not to be endured in the house of a clergyman", he had said, "least of all in that of the King's chaplain. Not for a kingdom would I comply with the King's demands." He had therefore put his house in the builder's hands for repairs, and taken the roof off. The Dean, however, had been more compliant, and a room had been built for Nell Gwynne at the south end of the Deanery. Later, the King used to speak of Bishop Ken as "the little black fellow who refused poor Nell a lodging".

Back in London, Evelyn went to lodge in Whitehall, and one evening he dined with his old friend Samuel Pepys, who always had "one ear to the ground". Inevitably the conversation turned to Popery, and to Evelyn's astonishment Pepys asserted that the King had admitted to him in conversation a few days earlier that his brother Charles had certainly died in the Roman Catholic faith. Pepys, in fact, showed to Evelyn copies of papers written in Charles's own hand which proved the fact beyond a doubt. "I was heartily sorry to see all this", wrote Evelyn in his diary, "though it was no other than was to be suspected. . . . The emissaries and instruments of the Church of Rome will never rest till they have crushed the Church of England."

And now the whole curious story of Charles's death came to light. Apparently when the doctors had declared that he could not recover, he had been urged by the bishops to confess his sins. But he could not be persuaded to take the eucharist. The Duke of York had therefore ordered the room to be cleared except for two trusted friends and a Benedictine monk named Father Huddlestone, who had saved the King's life after the battle of Worcester. This monk was brought up the back stairs, wearing a cloak over his vestments and his shaven hair covered by a wig. He had apparently performed the last rites for the dying King. Three-quarters of an hour later the bishops had been readmitted to the bedchamber. They had then realized that they had been tricked. But nothing could be done. The Duke of York, who would shortly succeed to the Throne, had taken charge. No one had dared to disobey him. This was the strange story.

Catholic sermons were now preached regularly at the Palace, and on the anniversary of the Gunpowder Plot bonfires were strictly forbidden by King James. "What does this portend?", wrote Evelyn. Four Roman Catholic lords were also sworn in of the Privy Council, and Jesuits were quartered at several colleges at Oxford and Cambridge. Many courtiers—and others—were also apostazing, Dryden (the dramatist) and Nell Gwynne being the latest converts. "But", as Evelyn said, "they were no loss to the Church."

In December, Evelyn attended the magnificent entertainment given by His Majesty to the Venetian ambassadors. After dinner there was a glorious cavalcade to Whitehall, and from thence Evelyn attended the audience in the Queen's Presence Chamber. He was then invited to accompany the two ambassadors in their coach to supper.

On the 24th of December, Evelyn and his brother commissioners were handed the Seal by the King at Whitehall, and two days later they were sworn on their knees by the Clerk of the Crown. They then took the three oaths—of Allegiance, Supremacy, and the oath belonging to the Lord Privy Seal. Later they dined with the Lord Chancellor.

Meanwhile, from Ireland, the Earl of Clarendon, where he was Viceroy, wrote to Evelyn from Dublin Castle:

> Here is a great man [Lord Tyrconnel] who storms, foams, swaggers, swears and rants. . . . He thinks to overturn nations and governments by his look and his wind, which he finds not quite so easy as he expected. But, however, he frights the honest, industrious English husbandmen and farmers. . . . Many of these men are gone, and many more are packing up to follow, some for England and some for the plantations, where they think they can thrive most, and be most secure in what they rent or buy.

Tyrconnel was a Catholic, placed there by King James, and apparently detested.

One of Evelyn's first tasks, as Commissioner, was to seal the document which created the King's mistress, Catharine Sedley, Countess of Dorchester. But clearly the Queen, who was present, took this "very grievously", and Evelyn noticed that at dinner she could eat nothing. Some months later Evelyn was asked to put the Seal to Dr. Walker's licence for publishing various Popish books. This Evelyn refused to do, but went into the country and left it to his brother commissioners, two of whom formed a quorum. Evelyn's task was, in fact, proving somewhat distasteful. No man was more anxious to serve his King or less willing to break a solemn oath, but he had not bargained for this. It was as if the magnificent edifice of Protestantism was being hacked away at the foundations. This was the solemn faith he had learnt at his mother's knee, and, unlike so many men, he was not distracted by speculation. He had always been taught that the Protestant religion was not to be questioned, and he had always seen his duty clearly according to the strict principles instilled into him by his truly pious parents and grandmother. His hatred

143

of Popery was an honest, instinctive horror of the practices of priestcraft and the habits of superstition. As for those who went over to Rome, were they not traitors both to King and country? The intoning, the confessions, the prostrations, the burning of candles, the swinging of incense; all this, to him, was idolatry.

Roman Catholic chapels were now being built all over the country. A convent was built at Clerkenwell, and the Franciscans had occupied a mansion in Lincoln's Inn Fields. A Society of Benedictine monks was also lodged in St. James's Palace.* In the Savoy, a spacious house, including a church and a school, was built for the Jesuits, and in direct defiance of two Acts of Parliament the King had now entrusted the whole government of the Church to seven Roman Catholic commissioners. All colleges and grammar schools, including those which had been founded by private benefactors, were placed under the authority of this new board, and they had complete jurisdiction over all schools. The teachers could be dismissed, suspended, excommunicated, deprived of all civil rights, and even imprisoned for life. But this was too much, and almost immediately serious riots broke out in several parts of the country. At Coventry and Worcester the Roman Catholic worship was violently interrupted, and at Bristol a profane and indecent pageant in which the Virgin Mary was represented as a buffoon, was carried in procession.† Soldiers had to be called out to disperse the mob, blows were exchanged, and there were some casualties.

The Resident of the Elector Palatinate, encouraged by the King, now fitted up a chapel in Lime Street, and when the heads of the Corporation protested, the Lord Mayor was ordered to appear before the Privy Council. "Take heed what you do", said the King sternly. "Obey me, and do not trouble yourself about either gentlemen of the long robe, or gentlemen of the short robe." Was not this the ghost of James's royal father speaking, the fatal King who had forfeited a crown and lost his head? History, in fact, was repeating itself.

But the temper of the people was rising, and huge crowds assembled in Cheapside to attack the new Mass House. The priests were insulted, and a crucifix was taken out and set up on the village pump. The Lord

* Clark's *Life of James II*, vol. 2, pp. 79, 80, Orig. Mem.
† *Ellis Correspondence*, 27 April 1686. Barillon, 19 and 29 April. *Privy Council Book*, 26 March. Luttrell's diary.

Mayor came to quell the riot, and was received with angry cries of "No wooden gods! No wooden gods!" The trainbands were then ordered to disperse the crowds, but they hung back. "We cannot in conscience fight for Popery", they said.

The King's next step was to review at Hounslow Heath his fourteen battalions of foot and thirty-two squadrons of horse, with their artillery, amounting to 13,000 fighting men. This was a mighty display of force, and clearly intended to be so.

Evelyn had watched all these despotic measures with something approaching despair, and when he attended a Popish service, with adoration and incense, at the new royal chapel, he said: "I could not have believed that I should ever have seen such things in the King of England's palace after it had pleased God to enlighten this nation." The French Ambassador at this time wrote: "The King openly expresses his joy at finding himself in a situation to strike bold strokes. He has talked to me about it and assured me that he will not flinch."*

Men in all walks of life, in fact, were now turned out of office and replaced by Papists. Popish Justices of the Peace were appointed in all counties, many more Protestant judges were dismissed, and others "more subservient" substituted. "So furiously do the Jesuits drive", wrote Evelyn. The High Commission also warned all prelates that if they refused to assist in destroying the Protestant Church they would in an hour be reduced to beggary. "The Lord Jesus defend his little flock and preserve this threatened Church and nation", wrote Evelyn. He feared that religious persecution was inevitable. The example was just across the Channel.

The King now turned to the universities, the place where youth could be influenced for life. University College, Oxford, had already been turned into a Roman Catholic seminary, and Christ Church governed by a Roman Catholic Dean. Mass was said daily in these colleges, although the undergraduates hooted and chanted satirical ditties under the windows of the Dean and Chancellor's rooms. The King had therefore ordered one of the newly raised regiments to be quartered at Oxford to prevent trouble.

The Oxford and Cambridge colleges, as ancient foundations with their

* Barillon, 19 and 29 July 1686. Macaulay's *History of England*, vol. 2, p. 112.

own charters and rights, were alone empowered to elect their presidents, but the President of Magdalen College, Oxford, had died, and the King intimated that he wished Parker, the Bishop of Oxford, who was notoriously drunken, riotous, and profligate, to be appointed to the vacancy. Parker was a convert to Roman Catholicism, and was in fact disqualified for office by the law of the land. The Fellows, therefore, would not agree to his appointment, so were cited to appear before the Commission at Whitehall, and were interviewed by Judge Jeffreys, who, after some vulgar abuse, suspended one of the Fellows from his Fellowship.

On the 3rd of September the King visited Oxford, and the Fellows of Magdalen College were ordered to appear before him. They immediately fell on their knees and presented a petition, but the King refused even to glance at it. "Is this your Church of England loyalty?", he asked. "Go home. Get you gone. I am King. I will be obeyed. Go to your chapel this instant and admit the Bishop of Oxford. Let those who refuse look to it. They shall feel the whole weight of my hand." The Fellows, still kneeling, again offered their petition, but the King flung it down.

On the 20th of October, to the amazement of all Oxford, a special Commission arrived from the King, escorted by three troops of cavalry with drawn swords. The following morning they took their seats in the hall of Magdalen College, and one of the commissioners demanded the key of the President's lodgings. This was refused, so Parker was installed by proxy, and the Commission ordered the doors to be broken open with iron bars.* Finally, all the Fellows were dismissed, and the Commission pronounced them to be incapable of ever holding any ecclesiastical preferment. Their careers were at an end.

Evelyn had many friends at both universities, and was indescribably shocked at these illegal measures. Eventually, however, Magdalen College was turned into a Popish seminary, and the Roman Catholic Bishop of Madura was appointed President. Then in one day twelve Catholics were admitted as Fellows; the work of spoliation was complete.

The King's next move was on the 3rd of July, when a Papal Nuncio was consecrated at St. James's Palace, and here the King fell on his knees before the whole Court. The Nuncio was then received in state at

* Macaulay's *History of England*, vol. 2, p. 302.

Windsor. Also, in October, twelve earls were deprived of their lord lieutenancies, and others of high military commands.

The year closed in darkness and depression as the King pursued his infatuated course. Then, to the surprise of all, he suddenly announced that his Queen was pregnant. Apparently in August he had been to St. Winifred's holy well and implored her to intercede for him for a son and heir, so that he might "continue to propagate the true faith".

The year of 1688 opened with renewed persecution of Protestants, and hundreds of fresh refugees arrived from France. "Such examples of Christian behaviour have not been seen since primitive persecutions", wrote Evelyn in his diary. Meanwhile, the Bishop of Valentia declared, "in the name of the clergy", that the French King's persecution of Protestants was "what was wished in England". He insisted that God had raised the French King to this power for that very purpose. Could fanaticism and malevolence go further? And where would it end? The general anger, in fact, threatened to burst into a revolution.

Fortunately for Evelyn there were "happy diversions" which temporarily, at least, lifted the depression. He made many delightful excursions to his country friends and their beautiful estates. Invitations to come and give advice poured in. He went in March to see Sir Charles Littleton's estate in Surrey, and then on to Sir William Temple's celebrated house and exquisite garden. He visited Sir Henry Capel's house at Kew, Lord Sunderland's seat at Althorpe, Sir Thomas Bond's "new and fine house" at Peckham, and Lord Wotton's house at Hampstead. He stayed at Sir Robert Clayton's house in Surrey for three days, and was shown all the treasures of which, through long experience, he had become a celebrated connoisseur.

Another delightful diversion at this time was a visit Evelyn paid to Christ's Hospital, the large London orphanage. He saw the children, numbering 800, at supper, and visited them in their dormitories. And when they sang a psalm in the Great Hall he was moved almost to tears. "It seemed to me a vision of angels", he wrote. "I came from the place with infinite satisfaction, having never seen a more noble, pious and admirable charity." He much admired the "order, economy and excellent government of this most charitable seminary".

Evelyn was infinitely thankful, at about this time, to be relieved of his temporary appointment as one of the commissioners of the Privy Seal.

147

Lord Clarendon had now returned from Ireland, and the King, in furtherance of his policy, gave the Seal to a well-known Roman Catholic, Lord Arundel. Ten days later the King again prorogued Parliament as the Members refused to remit the laws against Papists.

The schism between King and Parliament, in fact, was rapidly widening, but apparently the King was convinced, like his unfortunate father, that military force would, in the end, be the deciding factor. He was blind to the immensity of the opposition he was creating, and the majority of his fanatical advisers were equally blind.

CHAPTER 15

THE REVOLUTION

From the moment Charles II had been restored to the throne Evelyn had always offered his services willingly to the Government. He had worked unsparingly on many commissions, often at the risk of his health, and usually with little thanks for his trouble. He had strongly disapproved of the debauchery, mismanagement, and extravagance of Charles's reign, but his loyalty to His Majesty had never wavered. To this new King, James II, he also felt a strong traditional loyalty, but as a staunch Protestant he was shocked at the unconstitutional and autocratic methods now being employed by the King in his determination to force Roman Catholicism on the country. But Evelyn did not foresee the extraordinary crisis which now arose.

On the 27th of April the King issued a Declaration stating that his purpose was immutably fixed, and that he was resolved to employ only those who would concur in his plans. He intended holding a Parliament in November, at the latest, and he asked his subjects to choose representatives who would assist him in the task of destroying Protestantism.* This Declaration was to be read on two successive Sundays during divine service in every church in the kingdom.

But the clergy, almost without exception, decided that they could take no part in this serious violation of the laws of the realm. A consultation, therefore, took place at Lambeth amongst the bishops, and the Declaration was declared to be illegal, a statement that was signed by the Archbishop of Canterbury and six of his suffragans. This statement was presented to the King, who immediately pronounced it to be "a standard

* *London Gazette*, 30 April 1688. Barillon, 26 April and 6 May 1688.

of rebellion", and although the bishops protested their loyalty, and Bishop Trelawny fell on his knees and reminded the King that his family had fought for the Crown, the King said furiously: "Go to your dioceses and see that I am obeyed. . . . God has given me the dispensing power, and I will maintain it."* The bishops, therefore, retired; they had no choice.

That evening the document they had prepared was printed—by what means is not known—and was read in all the coffee houses and "cried about the streets". The sale was enormous, and the conduct of the prelates was widely praised. Samuel Wesley, the father of John and Charles, preached on the text "Be it known unto thee, O King, that we will not serve thy gods, nor worship the golden image which thou hast set up".† Even in the chapel of St. James's Palace the officiating minister disobeyed the order, and in Westminster Abbey the Bishop of Rochester, who read the Declaration, trembled so violently that the paper shook in his hand. The congregation, too, walked out except for a few officials.

A week passed, and the following Sunday the churches were thronged with people, but the Declaration was read in only one or two places, so the minister at St. James's Palace was dismissed and a more obsequious man installed. He certainly read the Declaration, but he trembled so much that he could barely articulate.

The King was apparently amazed at the tempest he had raised, and now realized that he must either advance or retreat. But his advisers told him to stand firm, and Judge Jeffreys, now Lord Chancellor, suggested that the bishops should be brought before the Court of King's Bench on a charge of seditious libel. The refractory bishops would then be heavily fined and given long terms of imprisonment, and would be glad to ransom themselves by promoting in and out of Parliament the King's policy.‡ The bishops were therefore commanded to appear before the King in Council, and after some angry discussion they were ordered to the Tower. But by this time thousands of people had gathered in the surrounding streets, and as the bishops passed, under guard, men and women fell on their knees and prayed aloud. From the boats rose cries of "God bless Your Lordships! God bless you!" The King, in alarm,

* Macaulay's *History of England*, vol. 2, p. 352.
† Southey's *Life of Wesley*. Macaulay's *History of England*, vol. 2, p. 355.
‡ Macaulay's *History of England*, vol. 2, p. 358.

ordered the Guards to be ready for action, the garrison of the Tower to be doubled, and two companies to be detached from every regiment and sent up to London.

All day coaches drove up to the Tower prison, while thousands of people congregated on Tower Hill. Evelyn himself went to visit the bishops of Ely, St. Asaph, and Bath and Wells, all personal friends. He was full of admiration for their courageous stand.

It was at this dramatic juncture that the Queen gave birth to a son, prematurely. But rumours were soon spread that the child was spurious and had been secretly brought into the Palace in a warming pan. The Jesuits had desired, above all things, a Roman Catholic heir, and it was believed that they would stop at nothing.

Five days later the bishops were brought before the King's Bench, and the 29th of June was fixed for their trial.

To pack a jury was now the main object of the King, and the Crown lawyers did their utmost. Four "Court" judges were on the Bench, and all were either Roman Catholics or tools of the Government. Nevertheless, after a trial which lasted all day, the bishops were acquitted, and when the verdict of "Not Guilty" was given, there were loud cries of "Huzza!" in Court. The news spread quickly, and people in the streets wept for joy. By the waterside, thousands were lined up on their knees, imploring the blessings of the bishops as they passed. The jury, too, were warmly congratulated, and were forced to shake hands with hundreds of people. "God bless you! God prosper your families. You have saved us all today", they cried.

Bonfires blazed that night all over England, and church bells were rung with frantic enthusiasm. "But all this was taken very ill at Court", wrote Evelyn.

The judges, at this time, were ordered by the King to impress on the grand jurors and magistrates throughout the country the duty of electing only such Members of Parliament as would support his policy. Meanwhile, in the Army disaffection had rapidly spread, so early in August the camp at Hounslow was broken up and the men were sent to different parts of the country. The King had brought over from Ireland some Popish troops in order to fill up the vacancies in the English regiments; but many officers declared that they would not serve with the Popish troops. The King therefore sent a troop of Horse to Portsmouth with orders to bring six of the refractory officers before him, and they were cashiered.

During the early summer of 1688 Evelyn heard many rumours of a threatened invasion from Holland, and he was told that the Dutch were making extensive preparations. Apparently the Protestant Prince William of Orange had been invited to appear in England at the head of a strong body of troops, and call the people to arms. He had been in close touch with the English Ministers of State, the Church, and the Army, and all had expressed their entire willingness to welcome an armed deliverer. But the Prince was asked to lose no time; the nation had reached breaking-point. Protestantism must be maintained. Evelyn was in London on the 18th of September, and found the Court "in the utmost consternation" as news had arrived that the Prince of Orange had landed, and the King had issued writs for Parliament to reassemble. He had also proclaimed that he "intended to maintain the Church of England". In panic haste he then recalled the bishops and attempted a reconciliation, asking them at the same time to prepare a form of prayer against the threatened invasion. He also issued another Proclamation in which he solemnly promised to maintain the Act of Uniformity, and declared that he would replace all the magistrates and lord lieutenants who had been dismissed for refusing to support his policy; he abolished the Court of High Commission and restored the Charter of London which had been forfeited six years earlier. Restitution was also made to Magdalen College, and, finally, a Proclamation came restoring the forfeited franchises of all the municipal corporations.

But these concessions were received with scorn and sneers; they deceived no one. Calculated tyranny could not be reversed at the eleventh hour. For had not the whole structure of British justice been undermined? Judges had been stripped of their ermine for refusing to give decisions which were opposed to the whole Common or Statute Law. Besides, who could now accept "the plighted word" of this King? Like his father before him, he broke solemn promises as fast as he made them. He had forfeited the confidence of the nation long ago; he had antagonized the Church, the Navy, the Army, the merchants, the universities, and the schools.

Amongst Evelyn's friends there was a passionate desire for the Prince's intervention. Here was the solution; here was an answer to their prayers.

They regarded him as their deliverer from Popish tyranny, and were praying incessantly for an east wind, which was essential for his fleet of sailing ships. All day, therefore, crowds stood in Cheapside, gazing at the weathercock on Bow Church. And, as if by a miracle, on the 14th of October the wind became easterly. But the rabble in London had already got to work, and were pulling down the nunnery which had recently been purchased from Lord Berkeley by the Papists. On the 28th the mob demolished a Popish chapel in the city, and Evelyn on his birthday wrote in his diary: "Oh, blessed Lord, defend our Church, our holy religion and just laws, disposing His Majesty to listen to sober and healing counsels. Amen. Amen." Frankly he feared another civil war; a King's party might be formed, and again brother would fight against brother, and father against son.

Evelyn had dined with various Ministers at Sir Stephen Fox's, and there he was told that Prince William and his army had been driven back by a storm, many ships had been lost, and hundreds of horses had perished.* This was lamentable news. But a little later this was denied, and it was known that the Prince had actually landed at Torbay, accompanied by 600 ships. The wind had been so favourable to the invaders that the English Navy could not possibly have intercepted them.

The Prince had sent out a manifesto, but the King had issued a Proclamation threatening severe punishment to all who should read or circulate this document. "These", wrote Evelyn, "are the beginnings of sorrow, unless God in His mercy prevent it by some happy reconciliation of all dissensions among us." His faith in God was implicit, and, he added, "I pray God to protect and direct the King for the best and truest interest of his people." What he gravely feared was a revolution.

News now arrived that William's army was marching up country, and on the 9th of November it was known that he had arrived at Exeter. Apparently enthusiasm for his cause was immense, and in hundreds of windows shone the lighted inscription "The Protestant religion and the liberties of England". Incidentally, many peers had already gone over to William and taken their regiments with them. They were heart and soul in the movement for freedom.

But in London, panic rumours ran through the streets like wildfire,

---

* When the King heard this, he said, with great devotion, "It is not to be wondered at, for the Host has been exposed these several days".

and suddenly the cry went up that knives, gridirons, and cauldrons were concealed in the new monastery at Clerkenwell. Crowds, therefore, assembled round the building, and would have demolished it but for the arrival of the soldiers. Then, on the morning of the 26th it was known that the King's daughter, the Princess Anne, had fled from Whitehall Palace. Her bedroom was empty, and her ladies-in-waiting, screaming and wringing their hands, believed that she had been murdered by the Papists. Her husband, Prince George of Denmark, had also gone over to William. But when the King was told that his daughter had fled, he cried out wildly: "God help me! My own children have forsaken me." John Churchill,* Master of the Horse to King James, had also fled.

Again the King was urgently pressed to make concessions, to dismiss all Roman Catholics from office, to separate himself wholly from France, and to grant an unlimited amnesty to those who were in arms against him.

But it was all too late. Evelyn, still in London, saw Lord Godolphin,† who told him that most of the nobility and many towns had gone over to William, who was now on his way to Oxford. Evelyn's son, John, therefore, set off for Oxford, where he was anxious to offer his services, and Evelyn returned to London to await events.

During the following week Evelyn recorded "the great favourites at Court, priests and Jesuits, fly and abscond. . . . It looks like a revolution." Evelyn was at the Palace constantly, and he was amazed that the King did not seem to realize the danger. But the Queen at least had taken warning, as she had already fled, in disguise, with her babe, to France. The King, at about this time, left London secretly, and apparently at Lambeth he flung the Great Seal into the Thames. He then took boat for Sheerness. He had fled, and England was without a ruler.

Now the rabble really got to work. Screaming "No popery! No popery!", they demolished and set on fire more Roman Catholic buildings and chapels, one after the other. Pictures, images, and crucifixes were carried along the streets in triumph amid lighted tapers torn from the altars. The King's printing press, which had printed his Roman Catholic propaganda, was completely gutted, and the papers burnt, the mansions occupied by the Elector Palatinate and the Grand Duke of Saxony were

* Later created Earl of Marlborough.
† Husband of Margaret Godolphin, who had been created a peer.

destroyed, and the house of the Spanish Ambassador was sacked without mercy, his noble library perishing in the flames. The following morning London presented a scene of frightful devastation, and the rabble were still spoiling for mischief. Then suddenly Judge Jeffreys, the most hated man in England, was seen trying to escape, disguised as a sailor. His house was immediately surrounded by a threatening mob, and he was only saved by the soldiers, who carried him before the Lord Mayor. Jeffreys begged to be sent to prison, where at least he could not be torn to pieces, so he was taken to the Tower, escorted by two lines of militia.

It was at this time that a rumour flew round that the Irish soldiers were marching on London and massacring every man, woman, and child they met on the road. In the middle of the night, therefore, the militia beat to arms, and women began to shriek and weep, while the men searched frantically for weapons. All thoroughfares were barricaded, and 20,000 muskets and pikes lined the streets. The fear was that all Protestants would be murdered, and children would be compelled by torture to destroy their parents. Babies would be stuck on pikes or flung on to the blazing ruins. These outrages had happened in Ireland and in France, and could happen again, even in England.

The King had now returned to Whitehall, and on the way he had been threatened and insulted by the mob. "Let me go", he cried. "The Prince of Orange is hunting for my life. What have I done? Tell me the truth. What error have I committed?" To Evelyn, the blindness of the man was almost inconceivable. And it was at this juncture that the King wrote to William and asked for a conference. But this was refused. "And I must plainly tell Your Majesty", said William's envoy, "that His Highness will not confer while there are any troops not under his orders."

Evelyn, meanwhile, had received letters from John, who had served with Lord Lovelace's troop in the "taking" of Oxford. John had been presented to the Prince by Colonel Sidney and Colonel Berkeley. He was passionately enthusiastic for the Prince's cause.

Chelsea and Kensington were now occupied by Dutch soldiers, and Colonel Solmea, in command, said that his orders were to take possession of the posts round Whitehall. The Coldstream Guards were already there, but by 11 o'clock they had withdrawn, and Dutch sentinels had taken

155

their places. The King, oblivious of his danger, went to bed and to sleep. Blind, fanatical, obstinate, he could not face reality.

A little after midnight, three lords arrived from Windsor and suggested to the King that he would be well advised to leave. The following morning, at 12 noon, Evelyn was present when he took barge at Gravesend. The Prince, by this time, had actually arrived at St. James's Palace, and Whitehall was filled with Dutch guards. Thousands of people had assembled to greet him, and every hat and cane was adorned with an orange ribbon, the Prince's colours. The church bells were ringing, candles were set in the windows ready for lighting, more bonfires were being piled up in the streets, and very soon every room and staircase in the Palace was thronged with people who had come to pay their court. The Prince had saved Protestantism for the nation.

That night and the following day London was splendidly illuminated, and the theatres were a blaze of orange ribbons. Every man jack in the street was wearing the colour, and even the children had tied them to sticks; the enthusiasm was immense, the shouting and cheering deafening. "Every hour is pregnant of wonders", recorded Evelyn. The revolution was over, and by a miracle there had been no bloodshed; the nation was jubilant. But now many serious questions had to be decided. For this martial Prince was obviously going to rule, and he was here to stay. The costly invasion with 600 ships had not been planned as a naval exercise; it had come to take a kingdom. Yet what of this Prince? He had been invited here, and his wife was the daughter of King James II, but nevertheless he was a stranger. Would he assume the Crown immediately, "by right of conquest", and then, as King, call a Parliament? Many lawyers advocated this, yet in the Prince's manifesto he had declared that he had no intention of conquering England. Also, would not the English soldiers require rather careful handling? Some were already murmuring that they could have fought bravely had they been given the opportunity. After all, that was their profession. They did not wish to be accused of cowardice, the greatest insult to any soldier. As for William, he could hardly claim England as a prize of war, won in fair fight. The situation was unusual, if not unique.

On the 31st of December, however, the peers were summoned to St. James's Palace, and about seventy attended. The Prince, pale and dignified, asked them to consider the state of the country and to lay before him the result of their deliberations. He also interviewed all the Members of Parliament who had served King Charles II, and the Aldermen of London.

Evelyn's feelings at this time were very mixed. He was torn between the loyalty he had sworn to his lawful King and his passionate love of the Protestant faith. Here, therefore, was the conflict. Another fact which troubled him was that James's daughter Mary had accepted the "revolution" and seemed quite willing to take her father's place on the throne. She, too, was a firm Protestant, and she had put her duty to her husband first. But Evelyn held very strong views, like most of his contemporaries, on the obligations and duties of children to their parents.

As for the revolution, probably it had been inevitable, but Evelyn was a man of peace, and had grown a little tired of the strife, the tears, the bloodshed, the aftermath of bitterness which accompanied these drastic changes. Thank God he was not an ambitious man. He had always felt it his duty to serve his King and country in any suitable capacity; he had been reared on such a principle. But the sweetest hours he had spent were not in the halls of the great, but with his books, his family, his friends, and his garden. These were the true consolations of life.

J.E.T.—F*

CHAPTER 16

WILLIAM OF ORANGE

THE year of 1689 began with "a long frost", and on every pond the merry skaters twirled and whirled. It was a new reign, and although many thorny problems remained to be solved, the burden of tyranny which had lain so heavily on the country had been lifted as if by magic. There was a wonderful feeling of freedom.

On the 15th of January Evelyn went to London at the invitation of the Archbishop of Canterbury to discuss the new situation. Five other bishops were present, and several noblemen, also Sir George Mackenzie (Lord Advocate of Scotland) and a Scotch Archbishop. There was a long discussion, and the bishops were apparently in favour of a Regency, as they felt bound by their oaths of Allegiancy to King James. But no definite decision was taken, and after some private conversation with the Archbishop, Evelyn took his leave. Two weeks later Evelyn was present at a lengthy debate at the House of Lords, and, when a vote was taken, fifty-one peers were in favour of a Regency, and fifty-four against. Some peers wished to send for King James, "with conditions"; others said that the King could do no wrong—a piece of ancient medieval propaganda—and that "the maladministration was chargeable on his Ministers". The Archbishop of Canterbury was absent at this debate, and the clergy were apparently determined to pursue their old policy of "passive obedience". It was all very bewildering. "God of His infinite mercy compose these things", wrote Evelyn, "that we may be at last a nation and a Church under some fixed and sober establishment."

The trouble was, apparently, that many "noblemen and others" who had welcomed the revolution were now criticizing what Evelyn called "the morose temper of the Prince of Orange". He had delivered them from the tyranny of a King and the threat of enforced Roman Catholicism, but they were not grateful. They had expected, apparently, a Prince Charming, with all the graces. But William was very different; his manners gave almost universal offence; he was so cold, curt, and uncommunicative. Even to women he paid little deference. His manners, of course, were those of a soldier, but naturally at the moment he was under severe scrutiny, and a gracious manner would have worked wonders with his subjects.

The truth was that William was no dissembler and no fool. He had already realized what a mass of thorny problems faced him, and he was desperately worried. The revolution was over, and not a drop of blood had been shed, but the whole Government was in confusion. The justices of the peace had abandoned their functions, the officers of the revenue had ceased to collect their taxes, the Army—which had been hurriedly disbanded—was ready to mutiny, and the Fleet was in much the same state. Forty-five regiments had retreated precipitately before an invader, and had then, without a struggle, submitted. These fighting men felt that they had been cheated.

Large arrears of pay were also due to the civil and military servants of the Crown, and only £40,000 remained in the Exchequer. What was to be done? William could not finance the country. Besides, what did he know of these people? He had been accepted, but he was a stranger in a strange land, and soon they might resent him as a usurper. He had no illusions as to the fickleness of a nation's mood, and with characteristic caution he said: "Yes, the cry is all 'Hosannah' today, but will perhaps be 'Crucify him!' tomorrow." He alone had built up the European coalition against the French ascendancy, but to govern England, where several strong parties were in opposition, was another matter. Englishmen were, on the whole, insular in outlook; their horizons were bounded by their own little island. And what was his position? Was he to be merely a consort, the husband of a ruling Queen? That was not his line. As a soldier of rare genius and proved ability, he had been accustomed to *give* orders, not to *receive* them. William, therefore, weighed down by these heavy problems, was strangely silent. He had much to ponder over.

159

Queen Mary, meanwhile, had sailed from Holland, and on the 12th of February arrived at Greenwich. She was received with much enthusiasm and affection, and only in one particular was she criticized. Evelyn recorded that "she came into Whitehall laughing and jolly as to a wedding, so as to seem quite transported. She rose early the next morning, and in her undress . . . before her women were up, went about from room to room to see the convenience of Whitehall; lay in the same bed and apartment where the late Queen lay, and within a night or two sat down to play at Basset, as the Queen her predecessor used to do. She smiled upon and talked to everybody. . . . This carriage was censured by many. She seems to be of a good nature, and that she takes nothing to heart."

Actually Mary had been asked by William to assume a cheerful demeanour as it had been said that she thought herself "wronged". She had merely obeyed her husband, whom she adored. Mary would have died for William, and she realized, also, that his health needed the greatest care. He suffered severely from asthma, and the doctors feared the disease might prove fatal. Much, therefore, should be forgiven him, and many allowances made. Certainly Mary did her utmost to supply the graciousness which was lacking in William. She was handsome, shrewd, affable, and of a particularly sweet temper.

On the 13th of February there was a magnificent banquet at Whitehall, and the Prince and Princess of Orange took their places under a rich canopy of state. The Clerk of the House of Lords read the Declaration of Rights, whereupon Lord Halifax, in the name of all the estates in the realm, asked the Prince and Princess to accept the Crown. William replied, "We thankfully accept what you have offered us", and he assured them that the laws of England should be faithfully followed, that he would endeavour to promote the welfare of the kingdom, and would constantly ask the advice of both Houses; he would be disposed to trust their judgement rather than his own.

That William was a fine statesman there could be no doubt, and within a very short time the country was calmer. The Roman Catholics had been assured that they would not be molested, all magistrates were to be continued in their offices, the revenues were to be collected, the Army remodelled, and gentlemen who had been removed from their commands were to be reinstated. The Irish soldiers whom James had brought to

England were found employment, and the Navy was conciliated by being told that every man would receive his due. The city merchants played their part by offering to extricate the Prince from his financial difficulties, and the Common Council voted him £200,000. This was, indeed, a triumph, as only a few weeks previously James had been unable to procure a much smaller loan, although he had offered to pay higher interest and to pledge valuable property.

And now Evelyn observed that all and sundry were soliciting and thrusting for "places". But the greatest problem in the country was that bribery and corruption, which had been rampant since the time of the Restoration, had eaten into the heart of every part of the Government, utterly destroying its efficiency. Honours, peerages, titles, embassies, leases of Crown lands, contracts for clothing, provisions, and ammunition, pardons for robbery, murder, and arson, had all been bought and sold at Whitehall.* The Army and Navy all took bribes, and the keepers of the arsenals sold the public stores and pocketed the money. To check this widespread evil would be a stupendous task. William would certainly not allow the ships of the Navy to become unseaworthy, as had happened in Charles's time, merely because the money voted for their maintenance had been appropriated. He did not intend to see sailors lying in the street dying of hunger because they had not been paid their wages.

One fact in particular puzzled and irritated Evelyn at this time: the Archbishop of Canterbury and the bishops were behaving with the most curious inconsistency, as although they had "contributed with zeal to the Prince's expedition" (Evelyn) they now refused to accept the new Sovereign, insisting that they could not break their Oaths of Allegiance to King James. This illogical attitude had influenced many people who naturally reverenced the opinions of the bishops, and it certainly prevented a concensus of opinion just when it was essential for the country to be united.

On the 11th of April Evelyn was present at the splendid Coronation of William and Mary. But only five bishops attended. The feasting, however, was magnificent, and it was a day of general rejoicing. As in the past, honours and titles were liberally shared out, and three Garters were bestowed. Scotland had "declared" for King William and Queen

* Macaulay's *History of England*, vol. 3, p. 61.

Mary, and many new English Ministers had been appointed. But it was clear to Evelyn that the ambitious "thrusters" had, by fair means or foul, secured all the important posts, and he seemed to be surrounded by "stupidity, inconstancy, emulation . . . and no person of public spirit or ability in office. This threatens us with a very sad prospect of what may be the conclusion." Evelyn was not in the least envious; he wanted nothing for himself. He merely realized that there were "great discontents".

Yet, indeed, how was it possible for this new King to separate the sheep from the goats? He did not know these people, or their histories, and had he been the most brilliant judge of character he could not have discriminated at that time.

There was, for example, the Earl of Marlborough, certainly a traitor. Almost every man at Court knew that he was in constant communication with the exiled King James. Marlborough was handsome, insinuating, eloquent, and brave, but he was notoriously ambitious and avaricious. His god was power, and he himself was governed by his wife, a dominating woman who exercised a fanatical influence over Anne, Princess of Denmark, the heir-apparent. Marlborough had served with distinction as a soldier, and had for years held a high position in King James's household. He had been the first to swear undying allegiance to his master; nevertheless, at the revolution he had soon fled, with about 5000 men, to the Prince of Orange's headquarters, and left behind a lame letter of explanation. He was determined at all costs to be on the winning side. William had taken him at his face value and, wishing to conciliate all parties, had made him an earl.

But Marlborough was merely one of the traitors who had secured high posts. There were many others, men who would have turned their coats with alacrity at any moment had it been in their own interests. Evelyn could have named several.

William had also chosen, for some of the chief administrative posts, some of his old and trusted Dutch friends, a choice which was much criticized. But they were the only men on whom William could rely for loyalty and ability. The most important decisions he left to his Parliament. Meanwhile, he was living at Hampton Court Palace, which was to be enlarged. He found the damp and smoke of London intolerable, so had decided to purchase Kensington House, the residence of the Earl of

Nottingham, to be used as a London palace. The village of Kensington was famed for its pure air.

William's royal crown, in fact, was proving to be extremely uncomfortable. It had become clear to him that many Ministers who occupied the highest posts were bitter enemies.* Nor was the absent King James entirely disposed of, as he had broadcast a Declaration offering pardon to all if on his landing in England, or within twenty days after, his people "should return to their obedience". Now he had gone to Ireland, where he was endeavouring, assisted by King Louis of France and Tyrconnel's army, to restore his fallen fortunes. Apparently there were far too many Protestants in Ireland for James's peace of mind, so a campaign of insults and outrages had been instituted, and many thousands of Protestants had been forced to emigrate. Those who remained were gradually drawing together for protection in large country houses, and were accumulating arms for use in case of need.

A small army was therefore dispatched to Ireland to the seat of trouble. But tragic news now arrived from that unhappy country; apparently the natives were destroying property, and burning, pillaging, and laying waste the countryside. In Leinster, Munster, and Connaught the English settlers had been quite unable to offer any effective resistance, and Charleville, Mallow, and Sligo had fallen into the hands of the natives. "This", said Evelyn, "is a terrible beginning of more troubles, especially should an army come thence from Scotland. . . . God in mercy send us help, and direct the counsels to His glory and the good of His Church." Evelyn had many Irish friends, so was particularly anxious at this time, but fortunately he had neither friends nor relatives in Londonderry, which was besieged from the 21st of April until the 31st of July. The inhabitants suffered terribly from disease and famine, but held out valiantly for about fourteen weeks, until at last relieved by Colonel Kirk's army. The garrison, however, had been reduced from 7000 men to 3000. It was the most memorable siege in the annals of the British Isles, and a splendid example of heroism.

So even in Ireland Protestantism was being seriously threatened, and at home a plot to murder King William was discovered, the suspects being sent to the Tower. When would men, in spite of differences in religion, learn to live in amity with each other? The trouble in Ireland,

* Burnet, vol. 2, p. 5.

and the plots against William's life, had no other basis than the struggle for supremacy between Protestants and Catholics. This, to Evelyn, was one of the saddest facets of "man's inhumanity to man". It occurred again and again through the centuries, and had caused incalculable misery and bloodshed.

CHAPTER 17

WAR IN IRELAND

EVELYN was obliged to go down to Hampton Court fairly frequently on business, and he was interested to see that the Palace was being enlarged and building operations had already started. His old friend, Sir Christopher Wren, was in charge of the work. The gardens, too, were being handsomely extended, and King William, who was particularly interested in gardens and architecture, was taking an active interest. The public, however, saw little of the King; he was far from well, and Evelyn was told on good authority that he was already weary of his new kingdom. He had endeavoured, with all the patience at his command, to conciliate all parties. But the Tories hated William for protecting the Dissenters, and the Whigs hated him for protecting the Tories.*

The common people, too, were very angry because William consistently refused to "touch for the evil". "It is a silly superstition", he said. "Give the poor creatures some money and send them away." To any man of intelligence, indeed, the custom was ludicrous, but it was such an old superstition, and thousands of poor, ignorant people believed implicitly in the cures. "But my child will die", wailed the unhappy mothers. "I have tried all remedies." On one occasion William was, in fact, persuaded to lay his hands on a patient, but he said, "God give you better health . . . and more sense". Indeed, he could not dissemble; he could not pretend.

William's Ministers were angry, also, because he had not in a few months set the country to rights. They did not see that he was thwarted at every step, and that his health at times sapped all energy, even the

* Macaulay's *History of England*, vol. 3, p. 528.

will to live. Evelyn was told, indeed, that William had decided to return to his native country; this royal slavery was destroying him. The strain of bad health and the problems of government were becoming insupportable. He had suggested that Mary, who was English and understood the country better, should be left to rule. William, in fact, had secretly ordered preparations for his return to Holland, but, to his surprise, his Ministers were horrified at the news, and some in tears.* They implored him not to desert them, and protested that they fully appreciated all he had done. So at length he had been induced to cancel his arrangements, but on condition that he should himself go to Ireland and take command. Ireland was still in desperate plight. In August, William's brilliant General, Schomberg, had landed there with an army, and he had found, as he advanced, that food was almost unobtainable as the country was completely desolated. Supplies from England, too, did not arrive.

Evelyn had dined, at this time, with the Marquis of Carmarthen and Lieutenant-General Douglas (a commander who was leaving shortly for Ireland), and according to their information the clothing and food sent to the troops were both unsuitable and inadequate. Then, with the approach of autumn, heavy rain had deluged the land, and the camps had become unhealthy morasses. Apparently the troops had neglected every sanitary precaution, and the result was fearful sickness and fever. Out of 14,000 in camp at Dundalk, 1700 died there and 800 sick died in course of removal to Belfast; 3800 more died in hospital at Belfast. This was tragic news.

King William believed that the royal authority, strenuously exerted on the spot, would prevent peculation and maintain discipline.

Evelyn, at this time, wrote in his diary a fervent prayer to God to preserve and direct the country. "Grant this, O Heavenly Father, for the sake of Jesus, Thine only Son and Saviour. Amen."

On the 24th of June, 1690, King William left England on his Irish expedition, but almost immediately a plot against his life was discovered, and Lord Clarendon, William Penn, Lord Torrington, and Lord Shrewsbury—all trusted officials—were implicated and sent to the Tower. They were not, however, strictly confined, and Evelyn was allowed to see Lord Clarendon. The Council, apparently, were determined to play for safety

* Macaulay's *History of England*, vol. 3, p. 530.

during William's absence, and their suspicions of betrayal were confirmed when a fleet of about eighty French ships entered the English Channel, obviously bent on invasion. The Queen and her Council, therefore, hastily took measures for the defence of the country, and on the 29th of June the two fleets met in action off Beachy Head. But the battle was a sadly uneven one, as the English ships of the line numbered only sixty, and finally the French were left in indisputable possession of the Channel; there was a very real danger that they would proceed to destroy the dockyards of Chatham. At the same time, news arrived that the French Army had been victorious in Flanders, and so could easily proceed to Dunkirk and embark for England. At any moment, therefore, an invasion could be expected, yet in England barely 10,000 soldiers were left to defend the country. It was known, too, that the Jacobites of half the counties of England were in arms, ready to assist the French. The national danger, however, suddenly united all parties. The Lord Mayor immediately assured the Queen that he and the city merchants would support her, and that £100,000 was ready to be paid into the Exchequer; 10,000 Londoners, well armed and appointed, were prepared to march at an hour's notice, and six regiments of Foot, a strong regiment of Horse, and a thousand Dragoons could be instantly raised without costing the Crown a farthing. The same magnificent spirit was shown in every part of the country, and the Jacobites were insulted everywhere and obliged to hide.*

During the three days which followed the disastrous news of the battle of Beachy Head, the aspect of London was gloomy and agitated. Evelyn was extremely concerned for his friend, Samuel Pepys, who had been sent to the Gatehouse on suspicion of having sent information to the French Court of the English Navy. The suspicion was not confirmed, but Pepys had for some years worked closely with King James, when Duke of York, and formed a strong attachment. He had not approved of the revolution, and, unlike Evelyn, had no strong feeling for the Protestant Church. Evelyn visited him in his confinement, but both Pepys and Lord Clarendon were soon released.

Meanwhile, splendid news of King William's victories in Ireland had arrived. The battle of the Boyne had been fought on the 1st of July, and the English troops had been brilliantly successful. William had been in

* Macaulay's *History of England*, vol. 3, p. 612.

the thick of the battle continuously, and had been a tremendous inspiration. But Schomberg, the great Dutch General, had been killed in action. A day or two later, Drogheda surrendered to William without a blow, and the garrison of 13,000 strong marched out, unarmed. The victory was celebrated all over England with bonfires and the ringing of bells. But the danger of invasion was not yet over as on the 21st of July a vast French fleet of 110 sail was seen in the Channel, and many were immense galleys, suitable for the landing of an army. The beacons on all the hills of Devonshire, therefore, were lighted to give warning, and every road in the country was covered by fighting men. The nation was ready to defend itself. But the threatened invasion did not materialize, and the French Admiral merely sent his galleys to ravage and burn Teignmouth, an obscure village of about forty cottages. Then the fleet sailed away. But when the news spread that the Popish marauders had made desolate the habitations of quiet and humble peasants, the whole country was stirred to anger. The outcry against the Jacobites, who were believed to have invited the enemy to make a descent on England, was vehement and general.

On the 6th of September William returned to England, and was welcomed with bonfires and illuminations. It was Marlborough who then went to Ireland with a fleet of ships and many troops to complete the task of subjugation. Cork was taken; a little later Kinsale surrendered, and five weeks later Marlborough was back in London. And surely now the country could rest on its laurels, pursue its peaceful occupations, and re-establish trade. In December, however, another sinister Jacobite plot was discovered, and the conspirators, which again included the Earl of Clarendon (the brother of the late Earl) were sent to the Tower. Ashton, the ringleader of the plot, was executed. But the chief plotter at this time was the ambitious Marlborough, and he was betrayed by some of James's supporters. So on the 16th of January, 1692, he was dismissed from all his posts.*

Evelyn himself believed that Marlborough had been dismissed "for his excessive taking of bribes, covetoutness and extortion on all occasions from his inferior officers". But this was not the whole story.

Evelyn, indeed, was utterly weary of the Jacobite plots. He had no

---

* King James's narrative, published later, gives the full story of Marlborough's treachery, and quotes his letters.

sympathy with these malevolent traitors, the majority of whom were thirsting for power. Their fanatical schemes kept the whole nation in a ferment. The civil war, with all its miseries and bloodshed, had obviously taught them nothing. England was such a beautiful country, and the majority of its people were fine, honourable citizens, yet they were constantly led into trouble by agitators and ambitious plotters. The men who rose to the top did not represent the people in any way. And religion, which should have been such a comfort, and promote harmony, seemed to bring out the worst in human nature—hatred, intolerance, and the desire for persecution. Yet for one fact he was profoundly thankful: there was, at Court, and among the upper classes, a new outlook with regard to morals. The King and Queen had set the example. And when a terrible fire burnt down all the buildings over the stone gallery at Whitehall, Evelyn was almost thankful, for the flames had consumed the apartments of the late Duchess of Portsmouth and, as Evelyn recorded, "other lodgings of such lewd creatures, who debauched both King Charles II and others, and were his destruction". The magnificent rooms which had been the scene of so much depravity and licence had been burnt to ashes. Had not God, perhaps, had a hand in this? Evelyn certainly believed so, and he went down on his knees and fervently thanked God. Prayer was always a wonderful comfort. Was it not Dr. Jeremy Taylor, of beloved memory, who had said "Prayer is the peace of our spirit, the stillness of our thoughts, the evenness of recollection, the seat of meditation, the rest of our cares, and the calm of our tempest"? How good it was to remember that pure and holy man, long since deceased, of course, but now at rest, secure from persecution.

CHAPTER 18

TRIALS AND TRIBULATIONS

IN MAY 1692 Evelyn made a note in his diary that there was "much apprehension of a French invasion, and of an universal rising". Many suspected persons were imprisoned, therefore, and naval and military forces mustered. The exiled King James apparently believed that as King William was on the Continent, the French could successfully make another attempt at invasion.

To Evelyn, who had seen so many upheavals and so much misery and bloodshed inflicted on the nation, the persistence of the exiled King seemed almost incredible. His Irish expedition had failed lamentably, his unpopularity in England was undeniable, and his Popish policy had been sternly rejected; yet apparently he was still determined to reinstate himself. He still believed in his "divine right" and holy origin, and had persuaded himself that the English people were anxious for his return. He had, in fact, issued a manifesto stating that all the charges brought against him were unfounded, and that he would, if restored, maintain the legal rights of the Church of England. This document was laughed to scorn, as, indeed, it deserved. But the threat of invasion was a serious one.

It was fortunate that the English Fleet and Army had time to prepare, and watchmen were posted at the beacons. Then, on the 29th of April, a fine squadron of English ships appeared on the Downs and were joined by the Holland squadron, the Maes squadron, and the Zealand squadron, in all, more than ninety sail of the line, manned by about 40,000 of the finest seamen of the two great maritime nations.

But there was much uneasiness in London as it was believed that the

170

enemy was relying on the co-operation of certain Jacobites in the Navy. To forestall this, the Ministers made their plans, and on the 17th of May a large assembly of officers was convoked on board the *Britannia*, and a message from the Queen was read. She said that certain information which deeply affected the character of the Navy had reached her, but she refused to believe anything against those brave servants of the State, and the gentlemen who had been so foully slandered might be assured that she placed entire reliance on their loyalty.

This clever message roused a wave of enthusiasm, and many officers at once signed an address in which they assured their Queen that they would venture their lives in defence of her rights, of English freedom, and of the Protestant religion. "God", they added, "preserve your person, direct your counsels, and prosper your arms, and let all people say Amen."*

A few hours later, the French squadron was seen from the cliffs of Portland; obviously an invasion was imminent. But the English Fleet was ready, and, after a battle which lasted until 4 in the afternoon, the French ships were on the run. Three ships fled to Cherbourg and were there attacked with fireships and burnt to ashes, and, finally, the bay of La Hogue was blockaded and six huge men-of-war were boarded and set on fire. It was a magnificent victory.

The battle raged for five days over a wide extent of sea and shore. One English fireship was lost, but, in all, sixteen French men-of-war were sunk and burnt down to the keel.

The news was received in London with wild enthusiasm, as this was the first real check to the increasing power of King Louis XIV, and all parties in England joined in thanking God for the delivery. Flags flew from all the steeples, candles shone in all the windows, and bonfires blazed in every street.

There were, of course, many sad casualties, and the majority of these were brought to St. Thomas's and St. Bartholomew's hospitals. At the same time, to Evelyn's intense gratification, the Queen announced that a lasting memorial to those brave sailors who had fallen was to be erected at Greenwich. Charles II had started to build a vast palace there, and this was to be completed and used as a retreat for sailors disabled in the service of their country. The original idea had been Evelyn's,

* *London Gazette*, 16 May 1692.

171

and in Charles's time he had pressed for it again and again. What a tremendous relief it was, too, to know that the threatened invasion had been averted and the scheming Jacobites again thwarted.

Yet there was one occurrence which threw a wave of utter sadness over the nation at this time; in September, during a terrific storm at sea, two fine ships, the *Coronation* and the *Harwich*, were lost, and 600 brave men perished.

The year 1693 dawned with fair prospects of peace. Men could now, it was hoped, forget the Jacobites and the power-hunger of Louis. Evelyn was happy, too, in the approaching marriage of his only surviving daughter, Susanna, who was to be married to a Mr. William Draper. The wedding took place on the 27th of April, and Evelyn gave the bride a portion of £4000, her jointure being £500 per annum. Then, on the 11th of May, Evelyn and Mary accompanied Susanna and her husband to Addiscombe, near Croydon, where they were "magnificently treated" by the bride's in-laws. Her new home was "very richly adorned and furnished", and she appeared to be extremely happy. "For which God be praised", said Evelyn. Susanna, as the only daughter surviving from nine children, was very precious. But on returning to Sayes Court, the large house, intended for a family of children, seemed strangely empty. Evelyn's brother George, however, was constantly urging him to let Sayes Court and share his home at Wotton. George had lost by death two wives and all his children except a married daughter. The estate, therefore, had been settled on Evelyn as the next male heir. Wotton was a place of tremendous hospitality, and his brother, like his father before him, kept open house all the year round. There were rarely less than twenty visitors, some of whom stayed all the summer, and for the twelve days of Christmas 300 tenants were feasted every day. Evelyn was deeply attached to Wotton, not only because it was his birth-place and the home of his ancestors, but because it was superbly situated and a place of great beauty. The gardens now were magnificent.

Meanwhile, life at Sayes Court had not entirely lost its savour. Evelyn had three executorships, he dined out continually, and he took a great interest in and worked hard for the Royal Society, who had again urged him to be President, but he had refused. His book, *Sylva*, had now gone into four editions and was very popular, and the publishers were constantly asking him to revise and issue yet another edition.

172

He had also been appointed one of the commissioners for endowing the new hospital at Greenwich, and this work entailed many meetings, always in London. Mary, too, worked assiduously amongst the poor of Deptford, distributing food and medicines. Indeed, there was much distressing poverty as, owing to the wet summer, the crops had failed and therefore the price of wheat had doubled. In some counties the starving poor had attacked the granaries. Another symptom of distress was the increase in crime. House-breakers had multiplied alarmingly, and stage coaches were robbed almost every day.

The country suffered a severe setback, too, in the spring of the following year, 1694, when the French Fleet set out to capture Barcelona, subdue Catalonia, and so compel Spain to sue for peace. This attempt at world domination seriously menaced the fate of England, so the British Navy, after some preparation, attacked Brest. The troops which attempted to land, however, were mown down by devastating gunfire, and 1100 men were killed. The English Admiral, Talmash, who was killed in action, declared before he died that he had been basely betrayed.* Almost immediately, Marlborough went to Whitehall and offered his sword and his services in place of the dead Admiral. They were firmly refused by William, who had now seen Marlborough in his true colours.

Finally, with regard to Sayes Court, Evelyn came to a decision. It was far too large for himself and Mary, so they would accept George's offer and spend the rest of their days at Wotton. There would be times when Evelyn would have to stay in London, but that could be arranged.

On the 4th of May, therefore, Evelyn and Mary moved, with four personal servants (his *valet de chambre*, two maids, and a footman) to Wotton. They also brought some furniture, many books and pictures, and all their treasures. Sayes Court was left fully furnished and with servants in charge, for the use of his daughter Susanna and her husband, "to pass the summer in" whenever they felt inclined.

At Wotton, Evelyn and his family met with a rapturous reception,

---

* Not until fifty years later, when the archives of the Stuarts were explored, was it discovered that Marlborough had warned King James of the English attack some weeks before, and therefore the harbour had been immediately manned and fortified. His own letter to James is the proof.

and were given their own spacious and handsome apartments. In his library Evelyn had some 2000 volumes. His brother George also possessed a very fine library. So with books, music, and good company, what more could one ask? It was spring, too, and the most beautiful time of the year. The trees were clothed in the bright opulence of young fresh leaves, the hawthorns were white in all the pride of May, the blackbirds were fluting, the cuckoo was calling, the lilacs were in full flower, and the apple orchards were a riot of blossom. Here, indeed, was peace, away from the madding crowd. One could sit out on the terrace at twilight and hear the wren singing her evening song, and the magpie chattering in the high trees. Then, when darkness fell, the sweet nightingales would begin, piercing the night with their glorious strains. They had haunted these venerable woods and thickets for centuries, and seemed to be a part of this old Elizabethan house, with its clinging creepers, its quaint, twisted chimneys and nodding gables, its latticed windows, its inglenooks, its air of old-world kindliness. How softly the candles glowed and flickered when at night the great rooms were lit up. A little music, and a game or two of backgammon or shovel-board completed the evening. Yes, there was peace in this old house.

Mary busied herself with her own special garden, with her needlework, and her miniature painting. On fine summer evenings, bowls was the popular game, and many keen matches were played on the well-kept green. It was a good life, and the garden seemed to Evelyn more beautiful every year. He knew every tree, every flowering shrub. Indeed, much of it had been created by himself. As for the surrounding country, he loved every rustic cottage, every spinney, every winding lane. From early boyhood he remembered the tinkle of the sheepbells, and in the garden the scent of lilies, limes and damask roses. Wotton and its surroundings were very dear indeed.

The traditional villagers' festivities were always interesting, too, and in particular the age-old thanksgiving for the harvest. It was brought in with a long processional dance, the Captain of the Reapers being finally crowned with a garland of flowers. Then men and masters sat down to the harvest supper, and later the peasants danced all through the summer night. At Dorking* (the nearest town), on the Eve of St. John the Baptist, there was always a splendid procession of men dressed in

* Dorking was 3 miles from Wotton.

scarlet, with gilt chains, all carrying lanterns. There were minstrels, men in armour, torch-bearers, pageants, morris dancers, and giants. The windows of houses were illuminated with candles, coloured lamps were hung all along the streets, and every porch and doorway was decorated with green branches and flowers. On this night, too, the wealthy citizens would place tables before their doors, loaded with good food, where all were invited to sit and partake, so that neighbours should resolve their quarrels and become loving friends. A delightful custom, indeed.

Winter, of course, in the country, arrived too soon. And yet, to a man like Evelyn, who loved beauty, what a miracle was a fine winter's morning, with its frosted ivy and glittering trees. In his first winter at Wotton, however, there was an epidemic of the dreaded smallpox, not only in London but in many Surrey villages. And then the tragic news arrived that the beloved Queen had caught the disease and died on the 28th of December. The news arrived when the traditional Christmas festivities were in full swing at Wotton, and this sad loss inevitably distressed the large house party. Indeed, the public sorrow for Queen Mary was universal, for her blameless life, her charm, and her large charities had quite won the hearts of her subjects. Even some of the leading Jacobites respected William's loss, but others behaved with inconceivable callousness, and it was known that at Bristol the adherents of Sir John Knight rang the church bells as if for a victory.* One non-juring divine, too, preached on the text "Go, see now this cursed woman and bury her, for she is a King's daughter".† Other Jacobite priests declared that her death was a judgement for her crimes.

Evelyn went up to London to see the lying-in-state of the Queen and found Whitehall and the neighbouring streets filled with those who wished to pay their last respects. He supped with the Bishop of Lichfield, who told him that the Queen, during her illness, had shown remarkable courage and serenity. The moment she had realized her danger she had insisted that all her ladies and every servant who had not had smallpox should instantly leave Kensington House. The disease, however, had soon proved to be of the most virulent type, and all hope of recovery was abandoned. Evelyn attended the elaborate funeral on the 5th of March, when all the streets were heavily hung with black, and men and women were weeping

* Narcissus Luttrell's diary.
† Macaulay's *History of England*, vol. 4, p. 532.

175

openly. "Never was so universal a mourning", he recorded, and apparently King William was prostrate with grief.

During the year 1695 the country had many difficulties to face. There was much distress amongst the poor, and in various parts of the country agitators were urging the people to rebel. Riots had taken place in many towns. They had, however, been quickly suppressed, and when the judges had returned from their circuits they had reported that, on the whole, the temper of the nation was excellent. Evelyn was in London on the 15th of October when King William returned from an extensive progress. He was welcomed back by a fine display of fireworks.

Early in the summer of 1696, however, another lamentable accident added to the country's distresses, as one of the Navy's best ships, the *Royal Sovereign*, was destroyed by fire at Chatham. And then, about three weeks later, a dastardly Jacobite conspiracy to assassinate King William came to light. William was to be either poisoned or stabbed, and Kensington Palace then set on fire. When William was dead, a beacon was to be lighted on the cliffs of Kent, which would be the signal for James, who would be waiting at Calais, to dispatch his fleet to invade England.* A vast army and transports were ready and waiting, and England, Scotland, and Ireland were to be invaded simultaneously. About thirty Jacobite "gentlemen" were involved in this plot, but they were, as usual, betrayed by one of their own men, and were arrested, tried, and condemned. "This", said Evelyn, "put the nation into an incredible disturbance and general animosity against the French King and King James, who were known to be in the plot."

The knowledge that their King might have been assassinated, however, brought much sympathy to William, who went in state to the House of Lords, sent for the Commons, and from the Throne announced that but for the protection of a gracious providence he would at that moment have been a corpse. The danger of invasion, however, was still great. He had therefore given orders which he hoped would suffice for the protection of the realm.†

During March the majority of the conspirators were executed. But Parliament decided that this latest Jacobite murder plot needed firm handling, and after due deliberation they passed a law that all lawyers

* Van Cleverskirke, 25 February and 6 March 1696.
† *Commons' Journal*, 24 February 1696.

176

and officers should take an oath that they renounced the exiled King
James as "no rightful King", and that they promised to avenge King
William's death if he was assassinated. This law was intended as a
deterrent to further plots. William was given a warm welcome on his
return from his camp in the Netherlands in the autumn. And then came
the wonderful news that peace on the Continent was concluded. The
Tower guns in London proclaimed the welcome tidings, the church bells
rang out, and the general sentiment was shewn by banquets and pageants.
Men wore in their hats badges of loyalty, and the Jacobites were regarded
as cut-throats, and shunned accordingly. The people had at last taken
William to their hearts. There was indeed reason for thankfulness, as
the country had passed through severe trials. Ten years earlier her liberty
and independence had seemed to hang in the balance, but her liberty
had been vindicated by a necessary revolution, and her independence
preserved by a not less necessary war. The power of the mighty monarch
of France had been checked. Now there was peace abroad and at home,
and the country had resumed its ancient place in the first rank of
European powers. Already, too, freedom of conscience and freedom of
discussion existed to an extent unknown in previous ages. Public credit
had been re-established, trade was reviving, and a quiet optimism was
apparent everywhere. The cheerful bustle in markets and seaports
indicated the commencement of a happier age.

Evelyn had no official Court duties now, but he still had three executorships, he was on intimate terms with almost all the bishops, and he dined
with them constantly. Unfortunately, his old friend, the Archbishop of
Canterbury, who had consistently refused to take the Oath of Allegiance
to William, was now out of favour, and one evening when Evelyn called,
he observed that the furniture and books were being packed up, and the
Archbishop seemed sad and depressed. He had, in fact, been dismissed.
Evelyn had to attend regular meetings at this time of the commissioners
for the building of Greenwich Hospital, and on the 30th of June, 1696,
after the committee had all dined together, he and Sir Christopher Wren
laid the first stone. As Evelyn was living temporarily in London in order
to supervise the work of Greenwich Hospital, he took this opportunity,
at the earnest request of Pepys, to sit for his portrait to Kneller; Pepys
was anxious to add Evelyn's portrait to his private picture gallery. Evelyn
himself had declared that he was far too insignificant to be put "amongst

177

the Boyles, the Gales and the Newtons of our nation. . . . What, in God's name, should a planter of coleworts do amongst such worthies?" Pepys, however, had insisted. He was one of Evelyn's fervent admirers.

While in London, Evelyn also inspected the King's house at Kensington, which was now finished. There was "a pretty private library, a great collection of porcelain" and a fine picture gallery. The gardens were "very delicious".

When the new Archbishop of Canterbury arrived at Lambeth, Evelyn was invited to dine with him, and there he found "much company and great cheer". This man, apparently, had had no scruples about oaths.

Another new interest for Evelyn was his grandson John, who was now a scholar at Eton. Evelyn had great hopes of this boy, who was highly intelligent and studious, and according to Dr. Godolphin (the Provost of Eton) a very promising student. The boy's father (Evelyn's only surviving son) had gone to Ireland to live, having been appointed a Commissioner of the Revenue and Treasury, so the Eton schoolboy spent his holidays with his grandparents at Wotton, and they constantly visited Eton during term time. Evelyn had thoroughly disapproved of his son's move to Ireland, as he regarded that country as wretchedly unhealthy. Owing to the large areas of undrained fens and bogs, a virulent type of malaria was rife, and in the last military campaign far more men had been lost by disease than in battle. Doctors, too, were scarce in Ireland, and the Irish peasants, who were extremely poor, lived in filthy and unhygienic conditions. Disease, therefore, spread rapidly, and hospitals were almost non-existent.

John, in fact, had already become seriously ill, and Evelyn was urging him to return to England, where it might be possible to nurse him back to health. Surely fate could not be so cruel as to take away this only son, this precious heir.

CHAPTER 19

DOMESTIC AFFAIRS

EVELYN had let Sayes Court, furnished, to Admiral Benbow, and unfortunately the Admiral had sub-let the house to the Tsar of Russia, Peter the Great, one of the most capricious and eccentric monarchs who ever wore a crown. The Tsar was visiting various European courts, and apparently King William was anxious to assist him in his desire to create a Russian Navy. Such a powerful ruler, in fact, could hardly be cold-shouldered.

Evelyn had heard the most fantastic stories of his behaviour, many of which were almost incredible. "The Tsar desireth to see some good honest English gentlemen", wrote Dr. Thomas Gale, the Dean of York, to Evelyn, and he added: "I hope you will come to town." But Evelyn did not accept the invitation. He was far too level-headed to enjoy the society of cranks, whatever their rank.

The Tsar had come to Deptford to study ship-building. Apparently he had a passion for maritime pursuits, and his chief ambition was to become a good boatswain and a good ship's carpenter. News of his arrival brought crowds to see this tall man of twenty-six with the piercing black eyes, a gracious smile, and a frown like a savage. He ate like a horse, drank pints of brandy, took a monkey with him to meals, and kept a jester to amuse him. He had wished to hear a debate at the House of Lords, but as he was shy and determined not to be seen, he climbed up the leads and peeped through a small window.*

At Deptford the Tsar made the most of his time. His rooms were crowded with models of ships, and every day he navigated a yacht

* Macaulay's *History of England*, vol. 5, p. 76.

179

belonging to the dockyard up and down the river. He and his companions
would then resort to an inn in Great Tower Street, to smoke their pipes
and drink their beer and brandy. That the Tsar was extremely talented
there can be no doubt, yet he lived in squalor. One of Evelyn's servants,
who had remained with the house, reported: "There is a house full of
people, and right nasty. The Tsar is very seldom at home a whole day
. . . very often in the King's Yard, or by water, dressed in several dresses.
The King is expected here this day; the best parlour is pretty clean for
him to be entertained in. The king pays for all he has."

The Tsar remained at Sayes Court for about three months, but the
damage done to house and garden in that time was almost unbelievable.
The bowling green and fruit trees were ruined, and the famous holly
hedges, of which Evelyn was so proud, were disgracefully damaged. The
Tsar had amused himself by being driven through the hedges, as a
morning exercise, and had destroyed three wheelbarrows in the process.
He had, however, thoroughly enjoyed his visit. The Navy had shown him
a sham fight at Spithead, and he had expressed in warm terms his
gratitude to the hospitable government which had provided such an
interesting spectacle for his amusement and instruction. He had left
England in the very best of spirits, and had taken with him, by permission
of King William, some captains, pilots, surgeons, gunners, boat-builders,
mast-makers, sail-makers, compass-makers, carvers, anchor-smiths, and
copper-smiths—in all 500 men. On his departure he had presented to
the King a ruby valued at £10,000, which he brought in his waist-
coat pocket and placed in William's hand wrapped in a piece of brown
paper.

On the 9th of June Evelyn went to Deptford "to see how miserably
the Tsar had left my house after three months making it his Court".
Evelyn took with him Sir Christopher Wren and his gardener, to estimate
the damage, and finally the repairs were agreed at £150, a large sum in
those days. It was all very depressing. Later, Evelyn and Sir Christopher
went to see the new hospital at Greenwich. The foundations of the hall
and chapel had now been laid, and there was much to discuss. They had
both supervised the work continually. Sir Christopher's great task of the
rebuilding of St. Paul's was now complete in the main structure,* and
had been opened early in December 1697. The work had been in progress

* The Cathedral was finally completed in the year 1710.

for twenty years. Evelyn remembered that when they had tried to blow up the Tower, a passer-by was killed, so Wren, with his usual ingenuity, had resorted successfully to the old Roman battering ram, which soon cleared a way. "I build for eternity", Wren had said, smilingly.

On Evelyn's return to Wotton he began to plant "a handsome evergreen grove". The old house was "ready to drop", but it would serve for the remainder of his brother's life and possibly his own. Every year he became more deeply attached to the place, for the ancient house held such memories, particularly of his parents. He could not enter the old nursery without seeing his mother bending over the carved and gilded cradle. He could not walk to the stables without seeing that fine man, his father, gazing with approving eyes at a new-born foal.

So the year ended. Evelyn did not feel an old man, but he confessed to a friend that he was "every day trussing up to be gone—I hope to a better place". He was growing old, but he was still extremely active, and, on the whole, his health was excellent. His daughter Susanna had already presented him with two new grandchildren, a son and a daughter, and her marriage had proved highly successful. "They are among the happiest pairs in England", he recorded.

Evelyn's son John died on the 24th of March, 1699, after a long illness. He had returned to England, hoping that his native air would restore him to health. But he had gradually deteriorated; he was forty-two. He was the sole survivor of six sons, and John himself had lost three out of five children. That was the tragic pattern. The children of the poor fared even more grievously.

John was buried in the family vault at Wotton, according to his wish. He had made a valuable contribution to literature, as he had translated three volumes of Rapin on *Gardens*, and also, from the Greek, the *Life of Alexander the Great* by Plutarch, and from the French, the *History of the Grand Vizier, Mahomet and Achmet Coprogli*.

But the Evelyn family circle was rapidly disintegrating, as Evelyn's two cousins had died during the summer, and on the 4th of October Evelyn's excellent brother George expired at Wotton. He was eighty-two, but "of perfect memory and understanding". No man had given "more noble or free entertainment to the county on all occasions", or was more popular. Two thousand persons attended his funeral, and he was buried "rather as a nobleman than a private gentleman". But Lady

Wych, his only daughter, was the sole executrix, and this elaborate funeral was her wish.

Evelyn was now, of course, the owner of Wotton, and a country squire. But he stayed in London until the following spring so that he could continue the supervision of Greenwich Hospital.

The spring was "warm, gentle and exceeding pleasant . . . with a mixture of refreshing showers", and on the 24th of May Evelyn moved his furniture from Sayes Court to Wotton, which was in superb beauty. He intended to repair the old house, but this would be a pleasant task.

He was also at this time taking a great interest in the newly formed Society for the Reformation of Manners, the aim of which was to "suppress the growing wickedness". Crime had increased alarmingly, returned soldiers having apparently become marauders. Every newspaper contained stories of travellers being stripped, robbed, and flung into ditches. Evelyn declared also that "atheism, profaneness and blasphemy amongst all sorts" were increasing daily. King William, in fact, had written to the bishops ordering them publicly to preach against the keeping of courtesans, swearing, drunkenness, and "all other lewd, enormous and disorderly practices". Many eminent persons had joined these various societies for Reformation, including twenty-nine of the nobility, seven judges, and six bishops. Quarterly lectures were given, and a special branch of the society was dealing with disorderly houses. As a result, with the assistance of the Lord Mayor of London and the Court of Aldermen, 500 brothels had already been put down. Eight other cities had formed their own societies, and there had already been many prosecutions, the offenders being fined and the fines handed to charity.

The influence of William and Mary, indeed, and their quiet, gracious Court, had been excellent, and William was now highly regarded except by the diehard Jacobites. In his speech at the opening of Parliament in November, he had assured them in gracious and affectionate language that he was determined to do his best to merit their love by constant care to preserve their liberty and their religion, by a pure administration of justice, by countenancing virtue, by discouraging vice, by shrinking from no difficulty or danger when the welfare of the nation was at stake. "These", he had said, "are my resolutions, and I am persuaded that you are come together with purposes on your part suitable to these on mine. Since then our aims are only for the general good, let us act with confidence in one another, which will not fail, by God's blessing, to make me a happy King, and you a great and flourishing people."

Yet even in this generous speech the malevolence of faction had found matter for a quarrel. "Let us act with confidence in one another" had been distorted to imply that the King distrusted the Parliament and had shown unwarrantable distrust of the King. There had been a sharp debate, and angry resolutions had been passed. Evelyn, indeed, was thankful to be clear of politics; he was too old to take sides in their wrangling.

In July he was ill, but made a good recovery, and "praised God for it. He has again graciously advertised me of my duty to prepare for my latter end, which at my great age cannot be far off", he wrote in his diary. Nevertheless, in September he went up to London and visited Samuel Pepys at Clapham, and the two old friends had a long gossip. But on the 31st of October, 1700, Evelyn had reached his eightieth year, having outlived almost all his contemporaries, and he wrote in his diary: "I with my soul render thanks to God who of His mercy not only brought me out of many troubles but this year restored me to health. . . . My sight, hearing and other senses and faculties tolerable, which I implore Him to continue, with the pardon of my sins past . . . that I may be the better prepared for my last day, through the infinite merits of my Blessed Saviour, the Lord Jesus. Amen." The winter months which followed were exceptionally cold; there were severe and continued frosts, and in January a violent storm caused widespread damage. Many chimneys were blown down, many ships were wrecked at sea, and at Wotton more than twenty trees came crashing down. But in spite of the severe weather, in February 1701 Evelyn drove to London and laid before the Speaker of the House of Commons the particulars of subscriptions which had been received towards the building of Greenwich Hospital. The amount was just over £56,000.

In the summer of 1702 Evelyn "kept his Courts" as High Sheriff of Surrey; this took up the whole week. He admitted, however, to a friend, that he had "many infirmities" and that he "much declined, and yet of His infinite mercy retain my intellects in great measure above most of my age". One addition to the family circle, in particular, pleased him at this time; he had presented the living of Rector of Wotton to Dr. Bohun, his son's tutor, who for many years had been a close friend.

But Evelyn's hopes were now centred on his grandson, John, who was his heir; and in the fashion of the time he wrote for the boy a little treatise of advice, *Memoires for my Grandson*. Evelyn recommended "an assiduous and constant course of devotion", and advised him to maintain "a pious chaplain". Unfortunately, this boy, the only male of Evelyn's family now remaining, contracted smallpox at Oxford, and was for some time extremely ill. Evelyn was in despair, but John was "blooded" immediately, and the Vice-Chancellor then ordered him to be moved to his own house, where he was devotedly nursed and attended by the best doctors. A report of the boy's progress was sent every day by either the tutor or the Vice-Chancellor himself. Two weeks later the doctors reported that John was improving, and eventually he made a complete recovery. He was, in fact, soon well enough to see something of his native land, and, like his grandfather before him, he spent part of his vacations riding through England. He had visited Chichester and Portsmouth— to see the fortifications—and he had already ridden through most of the inland counties and through Cornwall. He was studying law, history, mathematics, and chronology, and was already a good Greek scholar. "I do not much encourage his poetry", wrote Evelyn to a friend, "my desire being to make him an honest, useful man, of which I have great hopes, being so grave, steady and most virtuously inclined."

John was also taking a keen interest in Wotton, which, of course, would one day belong to him. Were not grandchildren a joy in one's old age? And to interest his grandchildren, Evelyn had looked into his own pedigree, which apparently went back to "one Evelyn, nephew to Adrogius, who brought Julius Caesar into Britain the second time. Will you not smile at this?"

Evelyn had also related to his grandchildren how, some twenty years ago, when the family vault was being enlarged, an entire skeleton "of gigantic stature" had been found there. Was not this strange? And who now could solve the mystery?

CHAPTER 20

LAST DAYS

THE days of intense creative intellectual activity were over, and so, more or less, were the days of public service. But Evelyn's interest in people had in no way diminished. His correspondence, to friends, and admirers of his books, was as voluminous as ever. Sometimes he wrote letters which extended to many pages. It was the fashion of the day; but in any case he had never possessed the gift of expressing himself pithily; he had always been rather verbose on paper, and in his old age he was becoming, as he sometimes realized, positively garrulous. Letters of condolence, too —which were considered a solemn duty—took up a great deal of time, for life was so precarious that friends seemed to "drop away" every day.

Readers who admired his books were also continually asking his advice on every department of horticulture, forestry, sculpture, literature, prints, architecture, and medals. He was considered an authority on the treatment of orange trees and the propagation and culture of rare and exotic plants. He wrote, in fact, at about this time, a short treatise on orange trees. He frequently exchanged with friends, also, by post or messenger, rare tulip bulbs (for which there was a perfect passion), and seeds, plants, and roots. He was delighted to share his treasures in this way. Friends also sent him seeds from abroad.

Evelyn's interest in prints was also as keen as ever, and on the compiling of a library he was continually asked for advice. "I confess I am foolishly fond of these and other rustications", he wrote to a friend, and he reminded his correspondent that they had been his "sweet diversions during the days of destruction and devastation . . . whilst the rebellion lasted so long in this nation".

But the study of numismatics had become an even more absorbing interest, and he now published a small volume on the subject. The book had been extremely laborious to compile, as the coins and medals all had to be drawn and engraved. But it was a fascinating study, for, as Evelyn pointed out to a would-be collector (Pepys), a whole world of history was revealed in numismatics. It was in medals that one saw the heads of the ancient legislators—Lycurgus, Solon, Numa, etc.—and the old bards —Orpheus and Linus. Here one could find the likenesses of Aristides, Themistocles, Epaminondas, Militiades, Pythagoras, Plato, Aristotle, Epicurus, Zeno, and Demosthenes. Through the study of medals one also came to understand weights and measures, the values of money, and when first princes assumed "the radiant crowns", and what the diadem was. And who could fail to be interested in the likenesses of popes, the true effigies of the famous Vespasian, Titus, Augustus, Nero, Seneca, Nerva, Trajan, Antonins, Severus, the great Constantine and his devoted mother Helena? And last, but not least, the beautiful Cleopatra?

The making of a collection, too, was a thrilling pursuit, for one could pick up old coins on the goldsmiths' stalls as one walked the streets.

The time had come, of course, when Evelyn was happy to sit back a little and reflect on the curious changes which time brings and on the absorbing theme of life itself. With regard to politics, he was too old to play with toys, too wise to be taken in. He considered that Parliament needed radical reform, and his dream was of a Parliament which would consist "of brave and worthy patriots, not influenced by faction, or terrified by power, or corrupted by self-interest". But such a Parliament would probably "grow old and dissolve to chaos". Evelyn also strongly disapproved of the method of electing Members of Parliament. The majority of candidates, for instance, could not possibly "fling away a son or daughter's portion to bribe the votes of the multitude". As for professional lawyers—who filled so many seats in Parliament—he thoroughly disapproved of their methods. He had had a mournful experience of litigation which had dragged on for years. In his opinion, too, there should be "a public Register" of land and property, so that owners could be certain of their titles and possessions. This would prevent "an infinity of suits and frauds".

Looking back on his life he realized also that there were many books he had vaguely dreamed of writing which had not materialized. History, for instance, had always fascinated him, and at one time he had possessed some excellent material. He had possessed letters from Queen Elizabeth, Mary Queen of Scots, Charles II, Henry IV of France, Maximilian, Sir Francis Drake, Sir John Hawkins, and many others. He had owned many letters from famous divines, of celebrated women, and of various Italian princes. Unfortunately he had been persuaded to lend part of this valuable collection to Dr. Burnet, the historian, and they had been "lost in the press". Other historical letters and papers he had lent to the Duke of Lauderdale, and these, too, had never been returned. Then when His Grace died and his library was sold, they could not be found. Evelyn's remaining treasures of that nature he had given to Pepys, who at least would value them and treat them with reverence.

The dreams and aspirations of the past, in fact, were both pleasant and amusing to look back on. He had at one time, some thirty years ago, conceived the idea of building, by subscription, a sort of college for men of a scientific bent, probably nine in number. It would be organized rather on the lines of a monastery, and the plan had been to purchase 30 or 40 acres of land in some healthy place fairly close to London. He remembered that he had actually proposed this plan to Mr. Robert Boyle, the celebrated chemist and philosopher, and had even planned the accommodation. There would be a handsome pavilion, a refectory, a library with drawing-room, and a gallery, all "nobly furnished". There would, of course, be bedchambers, a pretty chapel, a laboratory, and a garden with bowling green. There would be a dove-house, an aviary, a physic garden, a kitchen garden and orchard, a conservatory, and stables for two or three horses. He had estimated the cost to be about £1600, and he himself had offered to furnish the place. The orders would necessarily have been rather strict—to rise at 6 a.m., to bed at 9 p.m., a weekly fast, communion once a fortnight, music meetings, etc.

The conception, of course, had remained a dream, and would probably have proved unworkable, for Mary was to be included in this menage, and would not one young woman amongst so many men have created various problems? He had probably, when the idea had formed itself in his mind, been swayed by the desire to withdraw from the world and its complicated problems, to cut himself off from the deplorable spectacle of men constantly striving for power and wealth. A quiet hermitage devoted to the study of science, philosophy, natural history, and literature had seemed a delightful prospect. But it was all so long ago, and his life, eventually, had run in a very different path.

Meanwhile, the exiled King James had solved various thorny problems by making a quiet exit from the political scene; he had died on the 16th of September, 1701, and the news had been received in England with unfeigned relief. No longer could the Jacobites hatch their devilish plots on his behalf. There remained, of course, his son, and his many fanatical followers, who, according to rumour, were still determined to place him on the English throne. The very strictest precautions against William's assassination, therefore, were still necessary. One could not trust the fanatical Jacobites.

Evelyn summed up the deceased King James as follows: "He was an unhappy Prince, who had indiscreetly attempted to bring in Popery and make himself absolute . . . hurried on by the impatience of the Jesuits, which the nation would not endure."

As for King William, it was a sad fact that he was rapidly failing in health. He suffered from asthma, agues, headaches, and dropsy, and had a distressing cough. Apparently he had consulted the most eminent physicians in Europe—though without divulging his identity—but they had given him little hope. His own physician, Dr. Ratcliffe, had said, with brutal frankness, "I would not have your two legs for your two kingdoms".* King William still rode, and even hunted occasionally, but both mentally and physically he was a broken man. How indescribably isolated were the majority of kings. How unenvious was their lot.

The news of William's death, on the 8th of March, 1702, therefore, surprised no one, and from friends who had been in the King's ante-chamber when he died, Evelyn learnt the sad details. On the 20th of February William was riding in the park at Hampton Court when he was thrown from his horse and broke his collar bone. The bone was set and he returned to Kensington in his coach. But later the shoulder had to be re-set, and he had become very ill, probably from shock and incessant pain. Nevertheless, his duty to his country was ever before him, and he had decided that he must perform at least one more task; he had always wished to see a Union accomplished between England and Scotland, believing that nothing could conduce more to the happiness

* William's legs were swollen with dropsy.

188

of both. So he had sent a message to the Commons suggesting that some happy expedient should be devised for making the two kingdoms one, and he had earnestly recommended this question for the consideration of both Houses.

On the 1st of March the King's condition had deteriorated, and by the 6th he was too ill even to sign the Abjuration Bill, so a stamp was prepared which could be used instead of his signature. But the King was already sinking. "I am fast drawing to my end", he had said calmly, and had thanked the doctors for their assistance. He then took leave of his friends, and the bishops knelt down and read the prayers. When they had finished, the King had breathed his last. He was fifty-one years of age. When he was laid out, it was found that he wore next his skin a black riband which contained a gold ring and a lock of his Queen's hair. This he had worn ever since her death.

But the passing of this splendid courageous King did not really move Evelyn. He had never fully accepted William; that military spirit had failed to touch any chord in his heart. Perhaps Evelyn had been too old to change when the Revolution had taken place. There had been so many changes, so many conflicting loyalties. And when he considered all the vicissitudes through which he had lived, is it surprising that at his age he had become, as it were, detached from life. The Commonwealth had ended, as all such democracies must end, sooner or later, in a military dictatorship. Then there had been the Restoration and a perfect fever of affection for the restored Sovereign. This had been followed by the slow but sure reaction of democracy and a disgust with royalty. The conflicting passions of the revolution of 1688 had produced new conflicts, and, finally, had come the triumph of an oligarchy followed by the contests between selfish parties and rival interests. How was faith to be maintained, except in God? And where did loyalty begin and end? It was all very perplexing.

Now William was dead, and a new reign was to begin. The Marlboroughs would take charge; of that there was little doubt.

On the 11th of March the new Queen went in solemn state to the House of Lords. She wore a star on her breast and her royal robes. She was heavy and corpulent, but this was forgotten when that sweet voice spoke. As for the ambitious Marlboroughs, within a week of the King's death he had been created a Knight of the Garter, and a few days later

Evelyn was told that Marlborough had asked for £5000 a year to be settled on him by Parliament out of the Post Office. "This", wrote Evelyn, "was a bold and unadvised request, as he had, besides his own considerable estate, above £30,000 a year in places and employments, with £50,000 at interest."

Meanwhile, Lady Marlborough quickly disposed of all the Court places—a very lucrative transaction—and all the Court officials whom she disliked were dismissed and replaced by her relatives. Was not this typical of times past? The thrusters were successful, as always.

William's funeral, on the 12th of April, was, according to Bishop Burnet, "scarce decent", and he was privately buried at midnight. The splendid coronation took place twelve days later. Anne had already moved to Kensington Palace, and had started almost immediately to build a Banqueting House. Evelyn was in London until the 27th of June, and attended many Court balls and concerts. There were delightful illuminated galas on spring evenings. Anne's was a most popular Court, but, unlike her predecessors, she ate in private and never attended theatres; a few plays were performed at Court. She repeatedly issued Proclamations against immoral plays.

At Wotton, where Evelyn spent the rest of the summer, his daughter Susanna and her family were guests, as they were rebuilding their house at Addiscombe. The house party numbered thirty. A merry crowd. But in October, when Evelyn reached his eighty-second birthday, he reviewed, as was his custom, the past year, and gave "solemn thanks to the Lord for His many blessings". He still found much to enjoy in life. He had repaired the old house and some of the tenants' cottages, and the duties of a country squire had become an absorbing hobby. He was back in the home of his childhood, yet when he closed his eyes he saw again what had so impressed him in his youth—the ruins and antiquities of his travels in Italy. His fellow traveller, Henshaw, was still alive, and he had recalled to him, in a letter, how together they had "admired the superb buildings, visited the cabinets and curiosities of the virtuosi, the sweet walks by the banks of the Tiber, the Via Flaminia, the gardens and villas of that glorious city. I call back the time, and methinks growing young again, the opera we saw at Venice comes into my mind, and I am ready to sing. . . . You remember, sir, the rest, and we are both near the conclusion. . . ."

190

It was written in the Bible, "Your old men shall dream dreams", but they were chiefly dreams of the past. Was this not inevitable?

It was in the spring of the following year that Evelyn visited the Archbishop of Canterbury at Lambeth and then drove out to Clapham to see his old friend Samuel Pepys, who was seriously ill with smallpox. Twelve days later Pepys was dead. In his will he asked that Evelyn should be one of the pall bearers, but Evelyn was indisposed at the time and not able to do so. He had injured his leg and, as a result, had been confined to the house. Yet Evelyn deeply regretted this excellent man, who was "universally beloved, hospitable, generous, learned in many things, skilled in music, a very great cherisher of learned men, of whom he had the conversation". He and Evelyn had been friends for nearly forty years. Few men had possessed a sounder knowledge of naval affairs than Pepys, but when King James had fled the country, Pepys had "laid down his office, and would serve no more, but withdrawing himself from all public affairs, he lived at Clapham with his partner, formerly his clerk, in a very noble house and sweet place, where he enjoyed the fruits of his labours in great prosperity".* Pepys had performed excellent service to the Government as Clerk to the Acts and as Secretary to the Admiralty.

Evelyn now felt that he must make the most of his time, and he wrote in a letter to a friend: "A great part of the year past my health has much declined, nor do I murmur, considering that I have hardly had occasion to keep my bed in sixty years." He was *really* growing old, and he tired easily. Nevertheless, he made a long journey to Addiscombe in his coach to see the new house which had been built by his son-in-law, and returned to Wotton the same evening, "weary", yet delighted with all he had seen. He considered the house to be extremely well built.

On Sunday, the 21st of November, the weather was too wet for Evelyn to walk to church, so his chaplain officiated instead in his own chapel. "He made an excellent discourse", said Evelyn, "on the vanity of this world and the uncertainty of life . . . with pertinent inferences to prepare for death and a future state. I gave him thanks, and told him that I took it kindly as my funeral sermon."

Indeed, Evelyn was not afraid of death. He hoped, as his friend Jeremy Taylor had said, that he would end his days "like a ripe and pleasant fruit falling from a fair tree, and gathered into baskets for the Planter's use".

* *Evelyn's Diary*, 26 May 1703.

191

Besides, there was the blessed thought of heaven, where one would meet one's Maker. It was a glorious vision. He was anxious, however, that Wotton, with all its quiet beauty, should not go to strangers. John, his grandson, would live there, if he was spared, and raise a family. He had high hopes for this boy. His grandchildren were extremely dear to him. Surely he was fortunate to have even so few.

It was on the 26th of November of this year that a terrific hurricane swept over England, with violent thunder, rain, and lightning; many houses were demolished, and numbers of people killed. "It was not to be paralleled with anything happening in our age", recorded Evelyn, "and I am not able to describe it." At Wotton many mighty trees came crashing to the ground, and "tragical" damage was caused to the mansion, especially the beautiful banqueting house. Many of the farms and out-houses also suffered severely. The storm continued all night, and the leads on church roofs were rolled up like scrolls of paper, the Thames at London Bridge was choked with boats and barges dashed together, and sixteen of the largest ships of the Navy were lost with all hands. The Eddystone lighthouse was also swept into the sea and lost. In addition, many families were crushed under their own roofs, and hundreds of people were injured by falling chimneys.

While repairs to Wotton were put in hand, Evelyn and his household moved to their house in Dover Street, London, for the winter. But they were all back again at Wotton when the warm weather returned the following year, and in June 1705 Evelyn visited the new Greenwich Hospital, the child of his dreams. It was not quite complete, but was "beginning to take in wounded and worn-out seamen, who are exceedingly well provided for". He decided that the buildings in progress were "quite magnificent", and he was delighted with the work.

Four months later, on his birthday, he recorded: "I am this day arrived at the eighty-fifth year of my age. Lord, teach me to number my days to come that I may apply them to wisdom." The "bright day was done", and it was the dying refrain of a completed song. But he had had, on the whole, a wonderful life, teeming with interest. He hoped and believed that he had been of some small service to his King and country, and certainly his public work had been, by and large, enjoyable and rewarding. He had been disappointed, in the year 1681, that he had not been given a seat on the Navy Board. He had been disappointed, too, that he had not been asked, in the year 1690, to inspect the timber trees in His Majesty's forests and supervise their culture and improvement. It was a task for which he was eminently fitted. But this appointment had been given to another who knew little of trees. Such disappointments were inevitable in any lifetime. And he had never been "a thruster".

Evelyn made no further entries in his diary until the following year, the 1st of January, 1706, when he recorded that he had made up his accounts, paid bills, wages, and New Year gifts, according to custom, and, although indisposed, had been to chapel (in London) to give God public thanks, "beseeching Almighty God to assist me and my family the ensuing year, if he should yet continue my pilgrimage here, and bring me at last to a better life with Him in his heavenly kingdom. Divers of our friends and relations dined with us this day."

On the 27th of January he entered: "My indisposition increasing, I was exceedingly ill this whole week." He died a month later, on the 17th of February. He had expressed a wish to be buried in the garden at Wotton, but this was not done; he was buried in the chancel of Wotton Church. Mary survived him three years, and in her will she desired to be buried in a stone coffin "near that of my dear husband, whose love and friendship I was happy in fifty-eight years, nine months. . . . His care of my education was such as might become a father, a lover, a friend and husband, for instruction, tenderness, affection and fidelity to the last moment of his life, which obligation I mention with a gratitude to his memory, ever dear to me; and I must not omit to own the sense I have of my parents' care and goodness in placing me in such worthy hands."

BIBLIOGRAPHY

Diary and Correspondence of John Evelyn, F.R.S.
The Diary of Samuel Pepys.
The History of England, by THOMAS BABINGTON MACAULAY.
The History of England, by OLIVER GOLDSMITH.
Memoirs of the Verney Family During the Civil War.
History of the Coronation of James II, by SANDFORD.
Lives of the Queens of England, by AGNES STRICKLAND.
Letters of the Kings of England, edited by J. O. HALLIWELL.
Original Letters, Illustrative of English History, edited by HENRY ELLIS.
The Life of Mrs. Godolphin, by JOHN EVELYN.
Historical Memorials of Westminster Abbey, by DEAN STANLEY.
London, Old and New, by WALTER THORNBURY.
Memoirs of the Court of England under the Stuarts, by J. HENEAGE JESSE.
Brief Lives, by JOHN AUBREY.
History of his own Times, by GILBERT BURNET.

INDEX